Always A *Loveolution*
JOURNEY OF SPIRITUAL EVOLUTION

*Fran~
With Love and Faith*

Holly Peckskamp

HOLLY PECKSKAMP

BALBOA
PRESS
A DIVISION OF HAY HOUSE

Copyright © 2014 Holly Peckskamp.

All rights reserved. No part of this book may be used or reproduced by any means, graphic, electronic, or mechanical, including photocopying, recording, taping or by any information storage retrieval system without the written permission of the publisher except in the case of brief quotations embodied in critical articles and reviews.

Balboa Press books may be ordered through booksellers or by contacting:

Balboa Press
A Division of Hay House
1663 Liberty Drive
Bloomington, IN 47403
www.balboapress.com
1 (877) 407-4847

Because of the dynamic nature of the Internet, any web addresses or links contained in this book may have changed since publication and may no longer be valid. The views expressed in this work are solely those of the author and do not necessarily reflect the views of the publisher, and the publisher hereby disclaims any responsibility for them.

The author of this book does not dispense medical advice or prescribe the use of any technique as a form of treatment for physical, emotional, or medical problems without the advice of a physician, either directly or indirectly. The intent of the author is only to offer information of a general nature to help you in your quest for emotional and spiritual well-being. In the event you use any of the information in this book for yourself, which is your constitutional right, the author and the publisher assume no responsibility for your actions.

Any people depicted in stock imagery provided by Thinkstock are models, and such images are being used for illustrative purposes only.
Certain stock imagery © Thinkstock.

Printed in the United States of America.

ISBN: 978-1-4525-8904-6 (sc)
ISBN: 978-1-4525-8905-3 (hc)
ISBN: 978-1-4525-8906-0 (e)

Library of Congress Control Number: 2013923373

Balboa Press rev. date: 1/17/2014

To my brother, Shad. We share family history and cells, and we connectedly share the future. This was the greatest gift of all: unwavering love. Thank you for my second chance. *I love you!*

Writing is perhaps the greatest of human inventions, binding together people, citizens of distant epochs, who never knew one another. Books break the shackles of time, proof that humans can work magic.
—Carl Sagan

CONTENTS

Foreword xi
Acknowledgments xiii
Introduction xv

CHAPTER 1—Shocking News! 1
CHAPTER 2—Unraveling Fear 9
CHAPTER 3—The First Word 13
CHAPTER 4—Welcome Home 25
CHAPTER 5—A Wild Ride 29
CHAPTER 6—Interval Training 37
CHAPTER 7—Allopathic Triumph 43
CHAPTER 8—Divine Oneness 53
CHAPTER 9—A Waiting Game 69
CHAPTER 10—Expectations of the Heart 77
CHAPTER 11—Choices 81
CHAPTER 12—Simple Math 89
CHAPTER 13—Aftershock 95
CHAPTER 14—A Day of Thanks 103
CHAPTER 15—Thankfully Giving 107
CHAPTER 16—A Gift and a Pose 115
CHAPTER 17—Trust and Divinity 119
CHAPTER 18—Fearless Faith 125
CHAPTER 19—The Power of Prayer 131
CHAPTER 20—In Progress 139
CHAPTER 21—Happy Birthday to Me! 143
CHAPTER 22—Tough Love 145

CHAPTER 23—Home Is the Heart 171
CHAPTER 24—The Moment of the Present 175
CHAPTER 25—Mirror Reflections... 177
CHAPTER 26—Balance 183
CHAPTER 27—Magic Ride 187
CHAPTER 28—The Tidal Wave 191
CHAPTER 29—Samsara, The Ever-Changing Year Wheel 199
CHAPTER 30—Peace 205
CHAPTER 31—Mountain Climber... 211
CHAPTER 32—A Sunset of History 217
CHAPTER 33—The Storm 221
CHAPTER 34—The New, New Year 227
CHAPTER 35—Beautiful Mistake 233
CHAPTER 36—River Watcher 237
CHAPTER 37—Breath of Change 239
CHAPTER 38—Surviving Survivorship 243
CHAPTER 39—Off the Mat 251
CHAPTER 40—Body as a Temple 257
CHAPTER 41—Sharing Your Loveolution 261
CHAPTER 42—The Miracle 265

Resources and Tools... 273
About the Author...283

FOREWORD

To be given love by a friend is one the most amazing gifts in life. For this love to come from the most kindhearted and selfless person makes it that much more special. From the day I met Holly she showed me love. She let me know, no matter what I feel or am experiencing, everything is going to be okay.

We both moved to Chicago and got to experience an insane part of navy life at the same time. In that moment I had met my soul sister. I didn't know it at the time, but once we were both blessed with our beautiful children, we were sent on a journey from God. Holly taught me to love and to open my heart. She taught me to look beyond what society thinks is right and to listen to God and my heart. Love has guided Holly from the minute I met her. Why wouldn't the Loveolution continue to guide her and take her to the amazing spiritual place she has come to?

I remember the phone call I made, driving in Japan, when Holly said they suspected the what would be the worst, Leukemia. We got off the phone and my heart literally died. I continually asked God *why?* After that I watched from another country as my sister went through this journey. We got to talk occasionally, I read her blogs, and we e-mailed or texted when we could. Ultimately I felt like I was leaving my sister to face this alone. I couldn't drive to her house to hug her, I couldn't make food for her and her family, and I couldn't offer words of comfort. I could not do anything. Then I realized the only thing I could do was love her, love the situation, and love her spirit sent from God.

Holly is the embodiment of love. You can see love radiate from her and her family. God brought Holly and me together. She has loved me through so many obstacles in life: pregnancy, the navy, death, and of course Japanese nuclear disasters. One of the most important things Holly has taught me through our friendship has been how to love unconditionally. We should all live our lives showing more love to others than we think we possess or think they deserve. That is how it is done in "Holly's world." I love you, Holly!

—Elise Maudsley

ACKNOWLEDGMENTS

When I sat down to write the acknowledgments, I immediately thought, *There is not enough room to write down and honor all those who have supported me on this continuous journey.* The list seems to grow longer as I move forward, and for this I will be forever grateful. This journey has run long and deep, filled with great challenges, great lessons, and ultimate wisdom. I am so grateful to have had so many amazing people in my boat when I could no longer row.

To my amazing husband, Tad, and son, Sawyer,
you have been my heart and soul.

To my mom and Dave, without you we would have been lost.

To Elise, Colleen, Hannah, and Wendy, you are
the truest friends of all, sisters of the soul.

To my friends who loved me to health in ways that were
divine—including, Marc, Pat, Lynn, Anna, Dr. Birbara and
the many amazing doctors and nurses from Dana Farber who
supported me with the greatest gift of love and light.

Most importantly, to all my family, especially UJ,
who prayed and loved me in many ways.

I am honored to have such a long list of supporters, and in truth, you all know who you are: thank you from the deepest part of my spirit!

In creation of the Loveolution Project:
Tad, thank you for supporting me through hundreds of hours writing.
Elise and Cindy, thank you for your love in editing and guidance!
Jack and Jill, the most sincere thank you for embracing
my son and being a continuum of our family.
Chase Yutzey, thank you for your patience and going the
extra mile while developing www.luvlution.com
Margo, for your heart filled with a vision and for
never giving up on this Project Loveolution.

INTRODUCTION

How did it come to be called "the Loveolution"? An unexplained urge when I woke one morning, a feeling that defied all logic, a moment in time that stood on one single drop of blood. It came down to one simple question: Did I really have leukemia?

In the beginning there was so much confusion, so many decisions to be made on a moment's notice. Within each breath I wondered if all my dreams and desires would be lost or if the strength of my soul would intervene. These were the questions I begged to have answered but would realize soon enough that I had to let go. I had to embrace a trust in my heart to find the courage and strength that would introduce me to my soul. This was the beginning of a great journey that would forever change my life.

As a yoga teacher I was blessed with amazing faith and spiritual wisdom, tools that would help me walk the path of such an unexpected journey. After I gained more insight to the situation and became more grounded, I knew I needed to erase the word *cancer* from my vocabulary. It was one thought that sparked a great decision to love my way through this experience and from that moment a Loveolution was born.

I quickly sent out an e-mail to everyone I knew and shared the previous week's experience. I asked them to envision me surrounded by love and pure health. In addition, I told them I would not be bullied by a word that has taken on such a false force and asked them to refer to my diagnosis as the Loveolution.

It is amazing to think that the Loveolution started simply as a word replacement, taking over the likes of a word that embodies unbearable fear, greater than the image of any monster. Just the simplest whisper of the word *cancer* would be enough to bring most people to their knees. However, what started as a nightmare would soon turn into the greatest gift—the gift of spiritual evolution.

It seemed that this would be the greatest challenge that life ever presented, and with this came a great responsibility. This would be my opportunity to face an adventure and share it with all those who were as ready as I. A journey that would divinely open many hearts and souls to the wisdom that comes from a spiritual evolution. An emotional journey that proved to have many highs and lows. It was a complete mix of doubts and fears, accompanied by a connection to my soul that defined a truth so real that I can't believe I ever questioned my health. It was in this deep space in my soul that I knew I was a pure reflection of God, and this could have no error.

It was shortly after my first e-mail requesting support that I started a blog, hollysloveolution@wordpress.com. This would be my weekly "yoga class," where I would share all my experiences, my deepest truth, and my greatest fears. I would share my vision of this experience and ask that each person envision my health. I have no doubt that this played a large role in my health experience.

Throughout my journey my supporters never wavered or judged me. Even when I didn't make sense or when they couldn't understand what I was feeling, they just listened and supported me until I got to a clearer path. This allowed me to move past a state of *surviving* and into a space of *living*. However, within this space my world around me changed drastically. As I met my soul and created a new normal, I also said good-bye to many close friends; it was the unexpected within the unexpected.

Today I have come to realize this book is the map of my truest heart and soul. Written to share the love that unites us as one, the love that allows us to forgive and fulfill our wildest dreams. However, it has also been the greatest answer, understanding we are all on our own journey to awaken to a divine existence, which can spread our soul like wildfire. We are each on our own personal journey of spiritual evolution, a path to oneness.

This is an open invitation to walk with me through an experience that forever changed my life. It is offered as a gift as it was to me—great wisdom from the divine. It doesn't always have to make sense, and it will be there when you are ready, like the greatest support you have ever known. There are no rules, no judgment—just your choice to meet your soul. A choice to step forward and empower yourself and then those in your circle to awaken to your truth, leaving any suffering or pain in the past, a memory that solidifies an awakening. It begins with the greatest wisdom; love will become the awareness that we do not have to judge or find an answer, but simply listen from the depths of our soul.

It is my prayer and hope that this story will offer some wisdom to awaken your spirit to divine oneness.

CHAPTER 1
SHOCKING NEWS!

OCTOBER 6, 2011

One night I layed in bed watching a full moon dance with the clouds. As it was like watching a slide show, each wave of clouds that went by displayed a different reflection of imagination. Each image touched my heart through my life experiences and in the midst of the night I smiled; I could finally explain the Loveolution. The moon being our soul we are the dance of clouds that reflect imaginative thoughts, more specifically our reality. Then I remembered the start of the Loveolution that began with a single phone call, a simple cell, and a life changed forever. So my story begins:

The phone fell to the floor, slipping out of my numb hands. I felt my knees weaken, and while I made every effort to remain standing, I melted down to the tile floor in the bathroom in slow motion. The dreamlike state was one that I had never experienced thus far in life. I remember hugging the toilet; the coldness against my skin was the only indication that I was still part of this world.

I looked back at the phone after hanging up on the doctor and just shook my head, thinking, *No way; this must be a dream.* There were so many moments that led to a loss for words, emotions with no explanation that seemed beyond comprehension.

They must have it wrong; there must be a mistake or some other explanation. Maybe another patient—but it wasn't. My scattered thoughts arrogantly took me to places that made this diagnosis impossible. It was impossible because it couldn't happen to me. It couldn't happen to me because I was a naturopath, a yoga teacher, and a doula (a nonmedical person who assists a woman before, during, or after childbirth); how could I possibly have leukemia?

In a very antagonistic way, my mind continued to take me on a trail of shock and awe. How did this happen? How could this happen? In the infancy of the first moments, I just wanted a few answers to help me wrap my brain around what was happening. How did I get leukemia? What went wrong? This was a question I asked often, and still it remains a silent answer, an answer that I have learned to look past, trusting that it was to play a role in my spiritual evolution.

When I got some form of composure, I called my mom and uttered the news through screams and tears. She was in complete shock and didn't believe me at first. I mean, how do you even react to such news? Is there a memo I am unaware of? How could my mom even digest something like this? I am a mother, and I couldn't even begin to bear such a thought. I was falling deeper and deeper by the moment, noticing the similarities unraveling like a scary movie. What was lurking around the next corner? As I stood alone, would there be anyone to catch me when I fell?

My mom got off the phone with me and called Dr. Birbara, with whom she has worked for more than twenty years. He has always been the person I turned to for any medical opinions, and more importantly he felt like an extension of our family. Surely he would be able to straighten this out and fix it, which expresses the level of denial I felt in those first minutes. I just wanted to rewind and make it go away.

I believe that is probably a normal reaction when you get similar news; you just want someone to take it away. That is really what I was thinking, and just knowing he was on my side did make me feel a little better, even though deep down I knew it was a false sense of security. I just needed to get through these first hours. Even on a subconscious level I knew I was in denial, but my head was spinning so fast, I couldn't keep images of a funeral far enough away from watching my son graduate high school. Scary moments often leave a mark, but this was going to be a life-changing experience. I would never be the same, in the most unexpected way. It was my moment to look the greatest fear in the world right in the face, lock eyes, and fiercely say, *I will win with love.*

The doctor's office called again, because the first time, after they told me the news, I fumbled the phone and hung up as they were asking me to come into the office to discuss details. I was shocked that they expected me not only to have enough composure to drive but then to wake my sleeping two-year-old and drag him into the office with me. All the while, I was swerving, with thoughts like a lunatic, and couldn't even see through my tears. Even under such extreme shock, I still knew asking me to come in was a ridiculous request.

Finally, as I calmed, for a brief moment I looked at my hands and skin; it was almost as if they weren't really there. Am I fading away, or did my brain go into extreme fight-or-flight mode? Has my brain gone so far over the edge that I am having an acid-like affect, or have I shifted dimensions, *The Matrix*–style? What do I even do? I felt like my feet were stuck in the mud and my body was in total shock.

Then, as if someone were leading me through the darkest of days, I remembered I needed to call my husband, Tad. That was the most difficult phone call and one that still pulls at my heartstrings today. The words were so simple, but the meaning behind them meant all our dreams, all our hopes, could be erased.

I called him and let the words slide off my tongue, as I still didn't know what to make of it all. As I heard my words, something shifted inside me. Again I was in lunatic mode, thrashing on the floor and crying through my screams. Or was I screaming through my cries? Not sure.

Either way, Tad said, "Holly, it's going to be okay. I'm leaving right now and will be home in three hours. Can you call Colleen or Wendy to see if they can come be with you?"

I called Colleen, who works in a chiropractic office, and it wasn't even a few seconds before she was out the door, heading over to my house. I didn't even have a chance to tell her what was happening; as soon as she heard the words, "I have leukemia," her maternal friendship kicked into high gear.

Colleen and I have a very special friendship. There was a time when we almost "broke up," but the universe works in funny ways, and through gentle conversations and honesty, things returned to "normal" (whatever normal is). It was like we didn't skip a beat.

She came through the door with her hair flowing all over, similar to the Celtic goddess Brigid, and as she came closer, she seemed to glow. Then I realized again that I was in some kind of false reality. My spirit was forcing me to embrace with love, but my brain wanted me to run and just keep running, with nowhere to go.

She ran over to me and just hugged me as I sobbed on her chest. I felt tears trickle down my face, dropping onto her chest, but she just held me tighter while offering every intention of healing. However, my mind was doing everything to divert my new reality, bringing me back to my scary movie. Inside my heart, I remember hoping that maybe she would take this from me, and as you will read in the pages to come, she did in many ways.

Shortly after she came over, I heard Sawyer, my two-year-old son, upstairs in his bed, beginning to awaken. I had to get myself together, as he is very in-sync with me and would know something was wrong. So I splashed some water on my face, brushed my long, blonde hair, and cried again, knowing that my hair would soon be a distant memory.

"Mommy, why are you crying?"

"Mommy is just a bit sad right now, but I'm going to be fine." Like a changing wind, I asked, "Want to go for a walk to the lake?"

We all made our way down to Highland Lake, a spot that was filled with such beauty and serenity. It was amazing the amount of fun and love that has been shared in this space. We have had parties and made many swims out to the raft centered in this beautiful, natural spring lake. The old wooden raft has an attached diving board that Sawyer was jumping off before his first birthday. This raft reminded me how similar Tad and Sawyer are; I could see them jumping off the dock, holding hands like it was yesterday!

We lived in a house about one hundred steps from the lake, so the walk was short, which was good, because my legs still felt like rubber stilts. As we rounded the fence, I saw the beautiful lake, and it quickly reminded me of the many nights I stared out our bathroom window, watching a full moon glisten on the water. Maybe if I stuck my feet in now, it would renew space and time, going back before the phone call. Just as I was seriously entertaining time travel, my DeLorean within reach, the phone rang again. It was the doctor, and she wanted to discuss details regarding an appointment that she had already made for me, since I was unable to come to the office. I just wanted her to leave me alone, because before this "blood test" I was Holly, the yoga teacher, doula, and naturopath. She took this away from me in one single sentence.

"Holly, you have acute lymphoblastic leukemia." She spoke with a stern voice, as she too sounded a bit confused by the news. "I realize this is difficult as your blood work was all normal; however, upon further testing they found a form of leukemia."

I am sure this is difficult news to deliver over the phone, but I immediately got angry as I felt there was such a lack of compassion. However, I am sure a great majority of this was coming from anger and frustration, feeling lost with no sign of light to guide me. It felt like a tsunami hit me; I was in no place to understand or respect the difficulties that she faced as a doctor.

She began talking again in such a monotone voice that I thought for sure she was not serious and had it all wrong. "Holly, I have made an appointment for you tomorrow up in Wisconsin."

As I had yet another moment of irrational behavior, my ego was running further away from me. I realized I disliked the conversation more and more and was at a significant loss for a response. In my unstable mind I didn't think there was a doctor in the state of Wisconsin who had a title long enough to help me. Wisconsin is known for cheese, and cheese-heads. How was this going to help? I felt like giving her the finger through the phone because I didn't understand why she was sending me to Wisconsin. I was wrapped in a ball of emotions that took with it any rational awareness, a feeling of going farther away from my destination. I know she was trying to help, but in moments like these we don't know how we would ever react. It may not be butterflies and roses with an Emily Post–like etiquette response. I felt more lost by the moment and knew someone was stealing my popcorn trail and I might never find my way back. I didn't even know how to feel and really, in this moment, there wasn't any medical institution that would have been good enough for me, and this was coming straight from the mouth of fear.

After I got off the phone, getting organized with all the information she gave me for my appointment, I looked down toward the lake where Sawyer and Colleen were playing. I just watched for a few moments, taking in the sweet smells of fall, and I could not help notice the undeniable innocence that always surrounded Sawyer.

Soon after, we made our way back to the house, and I still felt like I was in a dream. Tad pulled into the driveway, and when he came into the house we all just hung on to each other. One at a time the tears began making their way down our cheeks like the moisture of the morning dew on grass. We all knew it was going to be a long road, and right now we didn't really have any answers. Colleen stayed to help out with Sawyer, as she could tell I was still in slow motion, my new dreamlike pace.

Once we got it together, Colleen went home to rearrange her schedule so she could watch Sawyer the next day. Tad and I spent the next hours crying and packing an overnight bag because there was a possibility I would need to be admitted, depending on their findings. There were so many unknowns at this point so much that was unexpected, it forced me to live in the present. I just wanted to go home and be with my mom, as I was still skeptical and needed her assurance and motherly love. Not to mention I wasn't making any sense in my own head, so maybe there would be some normalcy in hers. It is amazing how much the nurturing love of a mother can become your world in one swift moment.

My mind was still whirling; there really were no words to explain those first few days. I was being torn apart in my body, mind, and soul. All my beliefs were being tested at the highest level, and I had choices to make.

That night, Tad and I sat in silence, and when I felt a moment of strength I would call another friend to share the news and ask for prayers. I asked my best friend, Emily, to come to Chicago to be with us, and she said she couldn't because she had so much to do with her two kids. I understood but knew by her voice what was to come, and it was only a matter of time.

After several shocking phone calls, Tad turned on the television to watch our favorite show, probably to distract me for a solid moment, and I immediately paused it. I began another spell of waterworks, and through my tears I asked him if I was going to die. He shared his emotions with me, explaining that on the way home he cried as he felt the fear that was holding his thoughts captive. However, even with strength and determination he could not shake it until he got home and hugged me. He felt my truth of love and peace, and right then and there he committed to himself that he would never allow those types of thoughts to enter his mind ever again. Even if he had to fight it every day, it was never welcomed. Surprisingly enough, after that moment in time, he never feared death; he was just sad for what he knew I would be going through in the upcoming months.

That is love: he gave me strength and courage when I was lacking it because of shock and fear. That moment before I pressed play to start the program I asked him again if I was going to die, and as he mimicked his military training he postured himself, affirming that we could not allow our minds to be hijacked by such thoughts. We were going to direct and write this journey and he wasn't messing around; This gave me great confidence.

While watching our show I was in a daze, flashing back to the events of the afternoon, my first reaction to the news; I was still in a dream. My mind again was all over the place. I went upstairs to envision what the following days would bring. I sat on my bed next to a sleeping Sawyer, as there is really nothing quite as comforting as a sleeping baby.

As I watched Sawyer, the reality of our future again became overwhelming and I needed to take a few breaths. With a clearer head I felt gratitude as I did have quite a bit of support and I needed to keep them all in the loop. It all came flashing in on one soft inhalation. *I am going to take the advice of Deepak Chopra and love my way through this journey. I am going to replace fear or anything that scares me with a positive label or no label at all.*

I would not fight unless it was by accident, and I would love my way through each step, each minute, although it actually came down to each second. That night it was like a windstorm. I felt my mind being blown into false territory, and during this storm I stayed true to my heart, knowing I was healed.

CHAPTER 2
UNRAVELING FEAR

OCTOBER 7, 2011

Sleeping was surreal, and for the first few nights after hearing the word leukemia, I couldn't even find a space of rest, never mind sleep. I found myself leaving my side of the bed to fold into Tad's arms. He held me tight, allowing a sense of security and a knowing that all would be as it should.

The next morning the phone rang off the hook; the news slowly leaked to my circle of friends and loved ones.

When you hear shocking news like this, you can't help but apply it to your life. Some do it to try to understand what a family is going through, others are in a state of fear due to the notorious "what if it were me?" question, and others because they can't help it. It is an instant reminder of our own mortality and that we are not invincible. It is the greatest unknown, which is why living in the present moment is so important. Living in the future only provides an opportunity for fear.

We have all put ourselves in someone else's challenge at one time or another, but until you walk in that person's shoes, it is very difficult to truly understand. However, as they say, we all have something to learn from another's experience, and only the fool rejects this chance. Life is one big classroom, and we move forward evolving with life's wisdom, unless we allow fear to block our path of learning and living.

After sharing all the information from one conversation to another, I began to feel an internal fire of fear building up inside me (maybe a little more than some). It was at this time I realized I needed an outlet, not only to share my experience while updating all those whom I love, but also so I could begin some sort of personal therapy. Writing things down immediately organizes your thoughts so you gain simple perspective. Blogging would be an opportunity to do both at the same time, my personal private yoga studio.

I looked at it like a daily yoga class, which would be freeing and informative all in one. However, before getting too far ahead of myself, I needed to stay with each breath, as I had my appointment up in Wisconsin. I realized I needed to let God guide me to the doctors who were going to be part of my healing and spiritual awakening.

This was the first grounding moment I'd had since the first day, slowly stepping back into my body. I laughed at my previous thought process, as I know Wisconsin is a beautiful place and I have met many amazing people to prove this. But it was my ego that took me on quite a trip, deciding I needed to be in the best institution to get the best care. But what is the "best care"? What I learned over the next few days was an extremely important part of this journey because it wasn't about getting the best health care, it was, more importantly, listening to God's guidance. The outcome would be the same wherever or not I chose to receive treatment. Letting God guide me through a spiritual and physical challenge was fully putting my heart to trust. This was an amazing experience and the first time I honestly felt such trust in something that was not tangible.

It was Friday morning; Tad and I got dressed and prepared Sawyer to spend the whole day with Colleen. We were heading north to meet with Dr. Hayden to get more information through several tests and decide on a treatment plan.

Colleen walked in, and there was sadness in her eyes that I was beginning to understand. When you love someone, the fear of losing him or her is difficult in and of itself. This was a journey for both of us.

While Tad put Sawyer's car seat in her car, I felt a knot growing in my stomach. I wasn't sure if there was something to worry about or if it was just the day that lay ahead of us creating havoc.

Out the driveway they went as I watched from the front windows, tears streaming down my face. Then Tad reminded me that we had to get our bags packed as they told me to prepare to be admitted. Again, we had no idea what was going to happen, and being "prepared" didn't make me feel any better.

Just as fast as they left, I heard my cell phone ringing, and I just knew what had happened even before Tad answered the phone. It was Colleen. Someone had rear-ended them at the stoplight down the street. I don't think Tad and I have ever moved so fast. As we pulled into the gas station, I saw Colleen, and this time her face was extremely pale and defeated. I felt bad because of such a terrible situation and awful timing.

I ran to the car. Sawyer was sitting in his car seat, still kicking away at the back of the seat with a big old grin, wondering what was happening. The ambulance pulled in right behind us and immediately got Sawyer out of his seat. He was so excited to be checked out inside the ambulance that this seemed like the best day ever, as Colleen and I looked on in silence.

Funny thing was, Colleen's husband, Mike, is a fireman, so I believe we both sought comfort in that. Mike pulled in to make sure everyone was okay, even though he wasn't on duty yet. It was the first time he saw me and didn't quite know what to do except give me a big hug and say, "Everything is going to be okay, kiddo." Mike is a great guy, and I knew he would be a huge support for Colleen and our family. He is like one big teddy bear that would do anything for anyone.

Once again, Tad made the call that we had to go. Sawyer was fine, so he got back into his car seat and kissed me good-bye. I told him, "I love you to the moon and back, always." He smiled, not having a clue what would be coming our way over the next few weeks.

CHAPTER 3
THE FIRST WORD

OCTOBER 10, 2011

My body felt like it was neither coming nor going—that dimensional feeling kept coming to my mind—as there was no other way to explain it. We entered Dr. Hayden's office, where the plan was to undergo a series of tests that would broaden the picture of details. As I gave the receptionist my insurance card, she looked at me with such love, wanting to fix this for me too.

She had us go right back, and the nurse immediately came into the room. I don't know what happened, but I just started crying, extremely hard, asking her if I was going to die. Looking back, it was the weirdest order of thoughts. I mean, who asks someone she doesn't know if she is going to die? The funniest part being she told me *no*, as if she had some direct connection to God to answer such a question. From that point the lines blurred and I needed something more. My next words were, "Do you have anything that can help me calm down? Because I feel like I'm teetering on the edge of the rabbit hole."

She came over and held my hand as two other nurses came in to help calm me down. They gave me something that made me feel like I'd just melted into a puddle. I was crying and felt my tears jumping over each other as they ran down my face. My mouth was dry, my nose was running, and I talk/cried, explaining to them—how I had a two-year-old and an amazing husband and family, so I couldn't die. I didn't have time to die.

Then the doctor came in and got stern with me, which I totally needed, a good slap in the face. But as soon as I was calm I asked him if I was going to die. I think I would have asked the guy at the coffee shop if they hadn't drugged me.

Dr. Hayden was amazing, and as I said, God would guide me exactly to the person who would be part of this journey. He told me I would be going through a series of tests to identify what was happening in my body, as he wasn't convinced it was A.L.L. (acute lymphoblastic leukemia) due to my nonsymptomatic nature. The reason was that when someone has A.L.L., he or she presents as "really sickly," and I didn't even have a swollen lymph node. It was all just so bizarre and fit inside a can of crazy.

I had a CT scan and a few other tests. They were all normal, until he did a bone marrow biopsy. Dr. Hayden was a little on the shorter side, so as he was trying to dig into my bone to get to the marrow, he realized that he would need a step stool.

"Holly, your bones are so strong, I don't know if I'm going to make it through," he joked, but was partially serious. I felt him grinding and working so hard, when I turned around I saw a bead of sweat drip off his forehead, which made us all laugh. He was a very direct man and said he would tell me exactly what he found in the blood smear. Although it takes a little more than a week to get the full genetic profile, the one thing they can see when they smear blood on a slide is whether there are blasts (which means the cells are rapidly multiplying at an abnormal rate). I do not want to get too detailed with the components of A.L.L. because it doesn't matter. All that matters is that I had an illness that was going to be the biggest challenge of my life, and Dr. Hayden had just confirmed it.

He then sent me to another doctor the next day because he didn't want to admit me to the hospital. He shared that the nurses at his facility did not see enough of these cases to adequately care for me. I appreciated his honesty and welcomed another opinion to make a little more sense.

The next day we went to Dr. Shiley, and she was less assuring. When I asked her if I was going to die, she said she didn't know. Wait a minute! Everyone else was saying I was going to be fine, so why was she saying she didn't know?

She explained the seriousness and all this other mumbo jumbo. I asked her to stop and told her that physical suggestion is a very powerful thing, so I didn't want to know details, just options. In addition, I could feel the anger well inside me because I felt she was bursting the bubble I was creating around me that was protecting me from the fear that continually tried to break through. In reality she was trying to help me, but I was in no condition to see it this way. At this point she shared that I should go see Dr. Steck down in Chicago. There are only around fifty thousand cases of A.L.L. a year and Dr. Steck was the clinician in charge.

Down we went the next day to see a doctor who usually can't get patients in for weeks, but the nurse squeezed me in, as it was part of the divine plan.

I met Dr. Steck the next morning, and she was a breath of fresh air. Even as I write this it stirs so many emotions. When I began crying while she told me about my genetics, I of course asked her if I was going to die.

She immediately said, "You are not going to die." And then she did something that no one had done thus far—she began listing all the reasons I was going to make it. I was young, I didn't have the "Philadelphia chromosome" (whatever that meant), I was strong and healthy, and they caught it beyond early. I felt Tad squeeze my hand as she listed away, and for the first time I felt like maybe things were going to be okay. Still, "why?" kept filling my head at different times, as much as I tried to push it out.

She talked about admitting me right then and there until she asked one more question: "Do you have any biological siblings?"

"Yes."

"Where does he or she live?"

I knew where this was going. I told her that Shad, my brother, lived in Massachusetts with his wife and three daughters. She said she was sending me to Dana-Farber Cancer Institute to see a doctor she worked closely with on a regular basis. She said they would take great care of me, and since they work from the same protocol (a pediatric protocol), it didn't matter if I was treated here or there. However, what did matter was that Shad could be a possible match for a bone-marrow transplant. Transplant. This was the first I'd heard of this. The only knowledge I had of a transplant were a mental image of two people holding hands as they were being wheeled into the OR. She explained the process a bit more, and once again I stopped her as I didn't want any physical suggestion to be in my way.

Tad and I got in the car, both of us feeling much more hopeful, knowing this was going to be a journey in our lives that was going to expand our expression of love and our understanding of forgiveness. On the way home, I called my dad, who had flown in the night before to help out with Sawyer, and immediately upon the news of my going home, he began searching for flights.

That night Colleen and Wendy came over to help us pack up our essentials and motivate me for the journey. They were so helpful and kept my mind occupied with laughter and love. In addition to packing and organizing, they helped me create several "vision boards" to put up in my room at Dana-Farber. Many of you have probably heard of the book *The Secret*, which is now also a movie. It explains how, by way of pure physics, every word you release becomes a vibration attracting that which you are asking for, and for obvious reasons this is called the law of attraction.

As there are many ways to set up your vision, a vision board is just one way to stay focused and connected to the ultimate goal. It is not all that much different from a company's mission statement or personal goals that one may write in a journal. The only two differences is that a goal is something you plan to create in your future, while a vision is something you believe in *in the now*, as if you already have it. My vision boards had pictures and writing, so this way I was covering visual goals as well.

They were beautiful boards that helped me stay focused on the healing, keeping out fear or physical suggestion that was negative. I was grateful to have such a positive start as I was still in the fog of fear regarding a scary diagnosis.

While we were finishing up the boards, the doorbell rang; it was Paul, Anna's husband, dropping off food for the night. Anna had set up a whole month of food drop-offs so Tad was set for the rest of the week, until they left to head back to Massachusetts. Anna was also amazing right from the start and another reason that I have gotten through this journey the way I have.

That night as the house became a whisper, I sat at my computer with a blank stare, unsure how to share the information we had discovered over the past few days. It was in this moment that I wrote the following, in an e-mail, to share the news with all my loved ones:

From the Heart

*

To my dear friends and family,
It has been a day of shocking news and a great opportunity to put into motion all of my truths in life. Today I was told I have leukemia. Tad and I have decided to change the name to

Loveolution (this is an inside thing) to make it seem much more loving and less fearful. Truly I get to decide what I will give power to and what will take control. We have been designed and brainwashed to fear cancer instead of looking at it as an opportunity to see the amazing work our physical vessel is capable of.

My spirit is divinely perfect, as it is created and made in the image and likeness of God. Therefore I am well, whole, and complete. I need you all to hold that thought for me as well.

I will be starting chemotherapy in the upcoming days and I WILL love my way through this journey. I have decided that fighting is just not my style, but loving my way through is a much better option to embrace this gift. With any disease, it will linger and recur when it's nurtured by apprehension, until embraced as a great teacher and gift. Already in a day the internal shift that I have felt is beyond words. The amount of love I feel doesn't translate to anything I have ever known. I have moments of fear, but those moments are the moments that I attach to false outcomes. I can easily see my ego trying to keep me separate from my God. However, with that being said I have taken the time to be scared, grieve, and make peace with this so I can move forward. Looking into the eye of the tiger was a very scary moment. That moment proved to go so far beyond fear that it brought me back to truth. I have decided this is going to be the most amazing experience of my life. I will align and apply all of my spiritual tools and beliefs to this point in life; I have been blessed with the opportunity to do this in a very short frame of reference.

During this time I have been so thankful for the quick outpouring of love and support. You are never bothering me. You have no idea how good it feels to read strong words of encouragement and love. I have a couple of requests. First, I ask that you take your moment of fear/sadness face that and then embrace the beauty in this. I ask that you envision once a day (or more) me telling you how easy this is and how I am already free of the Loveolution. Envision the trillions of cells in my body working together in light and love. Envision me telling you *I am well!* Secondly, any prayers or prayer chains to help keep the loving energy coming my way would be such an appreciation. I feel all the love and am welcoming it already.

I will probably be an inpatient for a month, but at this time I am not sure where I will receive treatment. I cut all my hair off and donated it to locks of love. (Thank you, Colleen and Becky.) Tad has reminded me that I do not have to plan to get sick from chemo, so I am working to create an amazing manifestation of health and wellness during this treatment.

The good news is that there is no conflict in my treatment. My naturopathic friends have assured that this particular Loveolution is actually treated very successfully with chemo. After this first part, I will begin my healing and cleaning up my body. At this point and time I have no symptoms, it was by the grace of God that I just went to get a blood test to check my blood. Even so all my blood work was completely normal so the Angel in the path lab just happened to see something he thought needed more testing.

*

The next day Wendy picked me up in her bright-yellow car-truck (A truck that missed its mark as a car) and we made our way down to O'Hare Airport at five that morning. Before we left I gave my little and big guys the biggest kiss possible.

It was a somber drive even though we small-talked the whole time. I knew I would have another sad good-bye, and that was something that would be very difficult. In addition, I knew I was leaving a lot of close friends without a chance to say good-bye. It was really hard, but there was no other option; the clock was ticking.

When we got to the curbside check-in, the tears began to swell. She helped me with my bags, gave me a huge hug, and off I went. I looked back at her and smiled. Wendy and I had so many fun times, and I knew we would have many more. Just looking at her yellow car-truck was a perfect definition of one of them.

Going through the baggage check at O'Hare is always an interesting experience, and this time was no different—except I felt like everyone knew my secret. Isn't that funny how you think people are staring at you when they really couldn't care less? You create this story in your mind and your ego runs with it.

To avoid the radiation of the X-ray machine, I agreed to the pat down. I figured I was probably going to get enough radiation and didn't need to start early, plus everyone likes a little pat-down at the crack of dawn.

I went to my gate, silently drinking my venti chai latte and eating my blueberry muffin, thinking of the long road that awaited me on the other side of this plane ride.

Back in Chicago, morning had begun, and when Sawyer woke, he ran downstairs screaming, "Where is Mommy?" For a two-year-old this is a big deal, even if he does have Papa (his grandfather) and Daddy in tow. Tad's heart sank as his reality began too. He ran downstairs to tell Sawyer that Mommy had to go to Massachusetts and we would be soon behind her.

Tad had ordered the one-way rental trailer to be picked up this morning. It would be packed with all the necessary items we needed to live in my parents' house, and the rest would be packed up and sent to storage. Tad, my dad (Papa), Sawyer, our four cats, and Java Joe, our chocolate lab, would be setting off from Grayslake, Illinois, to make the sixteen-hour trek to Massachusetts. It brought laughter to my heart when I thought of this journey, especially because Papa doesn't like cats or Tad's driving.

While I was boarding the plane in Chicago, it was a typical Monday-morning commuter flight. Everyone was dressed in suits, on their iPhones and iPads, trying to crunch last-minute numbers or have that last important conversation before they went off the grid for an hour or so. Watching this made me think of all the traveling I used to do for work, realizing how much stress was created in the name of business, moving so fast with a sense of urgency that really wasn't there. These emotions surfaced to assure me that after a great deal of doubt, I knew I had made the right choice in leaving the pharmaceutical industry.

I boarded the plane, settled into my seat, and thought about Tad and what an amazing partner he was, how calm he had been with such ferocity on our backs. Our whole life hung in the wind of change, and he just simply stated, "We'll be okay." He is such a positive person, but has a strong bite as to protect his kindness. It is this kind of bit that would deflect any chance of someone taking advantage of his kindness and love. It is an important element for all of us to carry.

I thought back to the day I met Tad. We were both in the wedding party of two close friends, Bob and Stella, who got married in New Hampshire.

He brought a crazy girlfriend, and I brought a soon-to-be-ex-husband (what a match) while no one even knew we were separated. It was going to be a difficult day, but I was going to make the best of it, especially with this new eye candy.

We had caught each other's eye several times before the wedding during the night of the rehearsal dinner and the next morning, before the wedding started. He is a strikingly handsome man with an amazing energy about him that radiated beyond outer limits.

After the wedding was over, we went to the beautiful shore of New Hampshire to take pictures at the rocky cliff. It was so romantic and the perfect backdrop to a perfect day.

As I was done with my portion of the pictures, I began to make my way back to the limo and was struggling because I'd recently had a run-in with my stairs and lost. He saw me having difficulties and swiftly picked me up in his arms. I felt my face change color, which is a rarity for me. I felt his strong arms as I held on for dear life because I wasn't ready for the knight-in-shining-armor routine. However, he had other plans and carried me up to the limo. The driver opened the door with a smile, while Tad gently placed me in the seat and motioned for me to slide over.

"Well, hello to you," I said in a very seductive, silly voice, but half-meaning it. He joined me in the limo, pouring two glasses of champagne. We laughed and got to know each other as if the conversation had been scripted. However, I didn't think much of it as I knew what my fate was, and he had a "crazy legit" girlfriend. This we still laugh about today.

After the wedding we went our separate ways without a thought that we really could be together. It wasn't until about a year later when I invited Stella and Bob to join me at a Red Sox game that something happened. I had third-row seats behind home plate, and I knew they would be the perfect fans for such an event. Stella called me later in the week to ask me if I had or could get another ticket. Surprisingly, I did have an extra ticket and was just about to sell it to a client. So it divinely work out, I would say, to my advantage, and that was just the beginning.

When I got to their house in New Hampshire to pick them up, I honked the horn and looked down to my iPod to pick my favorite play list for our drive into the city. When I looked up I almost slid back down in surprise. The extra ticket was for Tad? I couldn't believe it. Inside I was a monster ball of excitement, fear, and courage. He was certainly as striking as I had remembered, so it was going to be nothing less than a fun night.

We laughed the whole way down to the city and continued while we got settled at the Colonnade Hotel. This was going to be an interesting night, to say the least. Almost immediately, Tad and I were back to where we left off at the wedding. I think I forgot to mention that after several glasses of wine, at the wedding, I was spanking Tad on the floor in a rousing eighties-style dance.

We talked all night, gazing—yes, gazing—into each other's eyes, and holding a bag of peanuts between our knees. It was magical, and I didn't want the night to end. I was so excited, and then I remembered that he was still in the military. As the night drew on I carefully brought up questions about his career, such as where he was stationed, and here came the words I'd dreaded from the beginning of the night. He was on leave until he left Friday night for Italy. *Italy!* I meet the man of my dreams and he was going to Italy. I could hear the song "Another One Bites the Dust" playing in my head. What a major bummer.

The next morning I dropped them back off and told them how much fun I'd had. I wished him well in his next step in the military, and off I went. I never expected what happened next.

About three months later Bob called me to ask how I was doing, small talk for the most part. He then slipped in, "Hey, you should e-mail Tad."

Really? I mean, he was in Italy. What were we going to be, pen pals? Then I thought, *Well, maybe I can go visit a man I barely know in a country I have never been to—sounds like a perfect plan.*

That night I spent an hour writing a two-paragraph e-mail, closed my eyes, and hit send. He responded in a couple of days, maybe playing it cool, or the time difference may have played a factor. We began e-mailing daily and then talking on the phone.

Then it happened. He was going to come home for Stella's surprise thirtieth birthday party. I didn't expect that he would be able to do this but was so excited I thought I would jump through the phone.

Together, Tad and I concocted all the necessary arrangements for an epic surprise. I picked Tad up at the airport after a long drive from Maine to Virginia, and at 11:00 p.m. we were knocking on Bob's door with wine in hand and a big surprise. We spent the night laughing and drinking. It truly was a special night as Tad told me he loved me, and I knew in my heart that

I loved him from the night we'd first met. As cliché as that sounds—and I would never have believed it—it was true; I was in love.

I cried as I left to head home and he headed to the airport to fly back to Italy. We had decided we were going to try a long-distance relationship, but I still felt sad. I wanted to be with him every minute, and now he was flying halfway across the world. The good news was that I would be booking my flight to Italy as soon as I got home.

When I got home that night I set up the perfect arrangement as my fingers rolled together one after the other. I was going to tell my parents that I was going to Italy with my great friend Maxine. We were going to explore the country of Italy, so they had no worries. As I stood in front of the Basilica of St. Peters I called my mom and told her how much fun "Maxine and I" were having. She would have a cardiac arrest if she knew my real plan. When I got off the phone I thought, *Wow, even at the age of thirty I have to be gentle with Penny* (my beloved mother).

For months we racked up humungous phone bills and traveled back and forth, using and creating many sky miles. Through those miles we fell deeper and deeper in love. Each trip we traveled to a different part of Italy; having the opportunity to visit so many places, it was amazing. Finally, my parents met Tad and loved him as much as I did (maybe not as much). It was then that I told them of my previous cynical plans to meet a man I didn't know and stay at his home in Italy.

It was a big pile of romance, and learning about the Italian culture was an opportunity I never took for granted. It was such an amazing start to a great relationship.

We were on one of our visits and decided to fly transatlantic from the United States directly to Munich, Germany. We stayed in a military resort in Garmisch-Partenkirchen, which was around an hour or two south of Munich. We planned to visit the many caves in Zugspitze, and then travel to Austria and make our way up to Munich before heading back to Italy.

It was a beautiful snowy night as we made our way through the caves with our torches in hand. It was an amazing climb to the top where we enjoyed some hot apple cider that was spiked. I thought this was not the best-laid plan, as we still had to make our way back down the mountain.

We slowly began our decent down, realizing there were many steep declines and icy edges that shimmered off the reflection of our torches. Each step was carefully calculated.

Tad yelled my name, and when I looked back, he was kneeling on the ground. My heart jumped out of my chest as I realized what was happening around me. He was on one knee with an audience of tourists looking on with passionate eyes of love.

"Are you okay?" I yelled.

"Will you marry me?" he yelled back.

Oh my God, I was so surprised and still wasn't sure if he had fallen. I dropped into his arms as he held me so tight, and he opened a small box with a beautiful light-blue stone that spiraled with sparkling diamonds all over. It was one of the best nights of my life. There were a few other surprises that night, but I will keep that to myself.

When I got home, I told my parents that I was engaged. They were cautious; although they liked Tad right from the first moment they met him, they had concerns that we were moving too quickly. However, no one really knew how long I had been alone as I was separated for a very long time before I told anyone. It was at this time that I realized I needed to live life for me because following the "path of happiness" designed by what we are "supposed" to do didn't work. In fact, the truth is that it usually doesn't work for anyone. It is when we follow our heart instead of society's timeline and embrace God's guidance for our journey that we find amazing connections and happiness.

About three weeks later we were all up to our elbows in wedding plans for a small, intimate wedding with so much love. Once again I received some more unexpected news: I was pregnant. This news really sent my Catholic mom over the edge, but in her heart, she too saw the natural connection of love and was happy about the gift.

Soon after the shock she was onboard and extremely excited to invite Tad into our family. In a Catholic family you can't help but worry what other family members will think, but soon enough everyone would see the love we shared. When you saw us together, it was a beautiful love to understood, two souls drawn together, love on its most natural journey.

Unfortunately, the pregnancy resulted in a loss, and I had emergency surgery to eradicate an ectopic pregnancy.

Tad and I went through a lot to bring Sawyer into this world, and we have been through a lot as a couple. We have had our ups and downs. However, our hearts are so strong and filled with love for each other that I will be forever blessed that he was my partner while going through such a difficult life challenge.

I will not act like it was not difficult and it was all butterflies and rainbows. It was a tough year, but we are moving through this just as we thought. We are getting back to solid grounds and building our home with an even stronger foundation than before! We are starting a new relationship with the experience of this wisdom as our base. We trust more now than ever and hope to grow our family strong.

CHAPTER 4
WELCOME HOME

> Nothing ever goes away until it has taught us what we need to know.
> ~Pema Chodrone

OCTOBER 13, 2011

I realized I had fallen asleep when the wheels touched down in Boston. I got off the plane to find my mom and Uncle Jim waiting for me. My heart felt full when I saw my family because I knew no matter what, they had my back. It was a sigh of relief to put my feet on the ground where I'd spent the majority of my life. Again, I had the feeling that this was part of the journey, and I was taking each step in its proper divine order.

We all went out to get some lunch as we didn't know what would happen when we got to Dana-Farber for my two o'clock appointment. Would I be admitted? Would I be sent home? The list of questions just went on forever in my mind.

We caught up over lunch, but my mind couldn't have been any further away from the conversation as I was more worried about what was happening back in Chicago with Sawyer and Tad. After lunch we ran back to the car while the rain poured gently onto our heads, almost as if the angels were sending healing waters to restore courage and strength. In the current moment all I felt was fear and anticipation. Then began an interesting drive over to Dana-Farber. Driving with the Keddy family is quite an experience. The Keddy family, my mom's side of the tree, is a very large Catholic family who has always supported each other to some degree. Being such a large family some of that closeness gets lost, but it makes it way back in the times of hardship and celebration. Knowing that while driving in Boston we would be relying on memory of old trips into the city, I just sat in the backseat watching us go in circles, barely missing one-way streets or heading away from the hospital. It was just the humor I needed, as I really didn't know how to feel in this moment. Grateful that I had family to pick me up and take those first steps into Dana Farber.

Once we got to Dana-Farber I paused as we walked through the door. I took a deep breath and realized this place was far too familiar. For several years, I worked as a hospital representative, contracting products with the pharmacy. I spent many hours at Dana-Farber and not once did I think I would ever become a patient here.

We were directed to the insurance desk first. My heart dropped because days before I was alerted that my insurance had ended, and I was in a period of COBRA coverage. This meant that although I still had coverage, all my information was in a state of transition. It would go retroactive to the beginning of the month, but each institution wanted direct proof that this was accurate and they would get paid.

What a moment! Was it a sign I didn't need treatment? Was it just a challenge within a challenge, a test? Either way it didn't matter as I worked out every detail with the utmost patience (most of the time). The only problem was still providing proof of insurance; I had to explain the situation to each office manager, receptionist, and billing agent, and it seemed like even the janitor wanted proof of insurance. It was exhausting, and as I understand it, it's one of their top priorities, although certainly not mine.

It was getting late and we needed to go upstairs to meet with Dr. Woods. She was supposed to be one of the best, and Dr. Steck had referred her, so I already had a sense of trust.

When we met, I immediately felt that fear, as she was not prepared to answer my staple question. I began crying through my words and questions; we definitely didn't get off on the right foot. I needed some coddling and loving because I was scared. She was a bit hard and ready to just give it to me straight—not to mention she was the doctor who was going to save my life. However, moving forward, for each moment we spent together with each visit, the more we grew to respect each other, solidifying a great doctor/patient relationship.

From this appointment, it began. I was sent to procedures to have my third bone-marrow biopsy because Dana-Farber wanted their own test results for a clinical trial I was going to be enrolled in. It was disappointing that they could not use the previous data, but on the bright side there was already a spot, a brilliant hole waiting to guide them to their bone-marrow sample, a blood sample that would become a representation of healing at its finest.

As soon as we got to the procedure room, I knew what to expect, so I felt myself let go for just a moment. I knew it was not going to be the most pleasant experience, as I had been through it two times before, but I was tired and just wanted to get it over with. Shortly after what felt like a flashback, we walked over the connecting bridge from Dana-Farber to Brigham and Women's Hospital, where I would be admitted and would take up residence for the next month. This would be a space that I would make work for the purpose of healing, allowing my physical body to catch up with the reality of my soul—the reality that I knew I was well.

As I entered the room, I realized this small space would be filled with faith and hope, working in every direction, mentally and physically, to believe the truth about my survivorship. I immediately hung up the vision boards that Colleen and Wendy helped me make before I left for Boston. This was an important night as the room was bleak, and I needed to bring it to life to support my healing. However, I reminded myself that this was a temporary space and that home was already in my heart, the seat to my soul and connection to my God source.

So it began. Already a Loveolution began fulfilling its purpose as a journey that would evolve my spirit in so many ways. I was prepared to share every experience, as I wanted those who were supporting me to have a clear picture to envision my health. As a yoga teacher, I saw that each day offered a lesson of wisdom fit to share with any journey.

As I saw that their would be many gifts and lessons throughout this journey, I knew in my heart it was time to start a platform that I could easily update all those that were supporting me. I would start a blog at word press called Holly's Loveolution. The intention would be creating a space for healing, updating friends and family, and finally a safe place to share my journey. My intention was that each post would roll from my soul to the pages with a directive from higher power. Each word cleansing my soul and taking with it fear or anger that my ego would try to insert with the hopes of control.

I believed this would be the perfect venue to share my truest heart, without fear of rejection or judgment, an opportunity for more healing. hollysloveolution@wordpress would be my little safe space to be honest in my learning, while spreading wisdom and love. This journey and the lessons that came from it would make perfect sense to some and others would just meet it where they were. As the saying goes:

"We don't see things as they are, we see them as we are."
~Anais Nin

CHAPTER 5
A WILD RIDE

OCTOBER 22, 2011

The first day Tad and Sawyer got to Boston after their long trip from Illinois, there was not a whole lot of laughter. However, I have to say it would have been hilarious to be a fly on the wheel during their twenty-hour drive back to Massachusetts. As I thought about their trip, I immediately thought of sending them light; Jesus take the wheel. Tad drove with my dad (who was always very nervous to be a passenger), our seventy-pound chocolate lab, four cats, and Sawyer, our two-year-old son, in an expedition with a trailer; it just sounds too funny. Road trip, anyone?

Back at "The Brigham," I was practically a shell of thought and I was back to simple steps, moving forward minute to minute, trying to hold a loving space. Most of the patients on this floor were much older, so I was marching around like I didn't have a care in the world, but trust me; underneath it all I was a mess. So I distracted myself with the funny mix of personalities, experiences, and just pure joy that would happen on floor 4C. In addition to movies, some of the e-mails people sent were hilarious, and of course there are a few monumental things that I must share.

The next morning after being admitted, Dr. Woods gave me great news. She was offering a day pass to go out and explore the city because treatment would not start until Monday. I was still not showing any signs or symptoms of the Loveolution, which made such a diagnosis very difficult to embrace. The four doctors I had seen so far were quite surprised how healthy I appeared, although my blood told a different story. Dr. Hayden didn't even believe the first test results, as my physical body didn't show any of these signs. Most people who have A.L.L present with numerous symptoms and not feeling well. This made it even more difficult to really understand and moving forward with treatment even harder.

"Enjoy the weekend," Dr. Woods said with a genuine smile. Then came the most unfortunate of words: "Just check in by 9:00 p.m. and you must wear a mask and gloves everywhere you go, all day."

Wow! This was really all I had in the moment as I heard the words roll off her tongue. However, I wouldn't be the only one wearing a mask as it was Halloween and the city was full of life. It seemed like everyone was dressed to impress, expressing a part of his or her imagination with amazing costumes. I just knew this would be such an exciting weekend for Sawyer, and I couldn't wait until they got to the hospital.

It was their first day back to Massachusetts, without even a moment to settle into my parents' home. Tad and Sawyer raced up to the hospital to pick up my mom and me. We were all so excited to begin our day tour of the city, hoping to escape the reality that was knocking down the door. We drove down town to Quincy Market to be outdoors and enjoy the hustle and bustle.

Really, anywhere in Boston you are guaranteed some kind of laugh, but without question Halloween brings out all the shining spirits. It was an amazing day, and I was grateful because I wasn't sure exactly how I would feel. It was certainly interesting to question whether you are having fun or just pretending because the journey of your life hangs in the balance of the winds. I will never for sure know, and I was still feeling surreal, so the combination made it near impossible to figure out. Therefore, I let it be, which was my mantra for the weekend: "Surrender."

I definitely had some difficult moments, such as watching Sawyer and Tad play as if there wasn't a care in the world. That was just their kindred relationship. They just connected on so many levels with a natural synchronicity, and I knew that no matter what happened to me, all would be fine.

They were chasing each other all over the park, and a couple stopped as I was taking a few pictures. The very kind woman assured me that her photos some twenty years earlier made for some beautiful memories. I considered this a sign, one of many to come.

Signs are an interesting concept. Again we can wonder if they are real or just perception trying to disguise fear within our need for hope. However, it never seems to stop. When I ask for a sign there is always a bright beacon of hope that I am on the right path. I've asked for many of them, and God never disappointed.

I have learned a great deal about signs from many people. These people from all differing walks of life have gifted me the very subtle alliance that signs bless on a soul. Signs may be seen as angels (God's helpers) giving you direction in a time of need or given directly from God or Source. As we are one with this source, it is when we slow down our breath and specifically ask that we receive. It is such a beautiful awareness as we feel it tingle the very essence of the physical body right down to the very tip of our soul.

After I took my last photo opportunity, my mom and I ventured over to "Tia's on the water" which is a hotspot in the Boston summer. We watched all the boats gently move through the bay, enjoying the feel of the fresh, salty air press against our faces. We embraced the beautiful scenery that the bay harvests to nourish your thoughts.

After a few moments we noticed a man going barrel-to-barrel looking for food, and in my current state I wanted to make everyone's life better. So I made my mom do the dirty work. She began to make her way over to the man carrying a twenty-dollar bill in the hopes of providing him dinner. When she tapped him on the shoulder, he slightly jumped. He then proceeded to rip up the twenty dollars and call her a fat, ugly hag. I think he threw a "whore" in there too, but I can't remember, as I was laughing so hard it was a challenge to stay focused. He was not well, and clearly my offer was not either.

My mom and I almost peed our pants, especially when we tried to recoup the twenty dollars he had thrown back into the trash without being exposed to "germs." I was the likely choice because I was already equipped with a mask and gloves. I believe twenty dollars is a lot of money, but this was more of a task, as I felt we needed to have a triumph after such a disgrace.

Shortly after, we heard Sawyer and Tad yell over to us that they had to go use the restroom. While still laughing at the very thought of our recent experience, we made our way over to the Long-Wharf Marriot to meet them. Sawyer joyfully skipped toward the restrooms while Tad barely got to him before he entered the women's room. It is amazing how a journey to the restroom can be extremely exciting for a child. So many things to touch, so many sounds to observe all in one space—how could it not be exciting? This is yet another example of how as adults we have lost the fun in so many little things such as what can happen in a public restroom.

Tad and Sawyer ran out of the bathroom laughing uncontrollably, both trying to tell their version of the story first. When they finally calmed down, we sat in the lobby with eager ears to hear what was so funny.

Tad began, "I finally got Sawyer set so that he wasn't touching anything and it began like it was all on cue." A few stalls down, a young man was having a very rough go at it. As he proceeded to grunt and groan, he released what in Boston they call " A wicked loud fahht" For all of you who know my son, there would be the perfect response to the perfect storm.

Sawyer quickly responded, "I heard that." Sawyer then began to have a conversation between stalls, probably taking this man deeper into his state of embarrassment.

It was these two events, within moments of each other that were filled with so much laughter, which allowed me to find comfort in the journey that lay ahead. There were tears, laughter, motivation, support, and all coming from the most divine person when least expected. This all happened when I just let go and let God.

I officially surrendered, and it felt so freeing. I knew I would be eternally grateful for this moment, as it set the stage for healing and many lessons in truth. In addition to this gratitude, I found it convenient that it was Halloween night. There were not too many stares at the mask and gloves because I looked like I was dressed as a surgeon. This created such ease, which flowed in the direction of divinity to making this experience as bearable as possible. I could learn and discover all the lessons without too many scars. It was quite spectacular when I put it all together.

Driving back to the hotel—I mean hospital—was surreal. I had walked these halls so many times as a hospital representative, and now I was a patient spending Halloween, where fear aluminates the halls, instead of dressing up in a host of creativity and imagination.

Halloween night has been a different force of energy through the ages. For a child, it is simply a night where you visit your neighbors and receive a few pieces of candy in exchange for wearing your costume. For teenagers, it becomes a night of inflicted fright to see who can find the spider gates, which is the mythical legend that takes you past eight gates each posing a different dimension of fantasy. If you didn't know about the gates you would find the closest haunted house or rundown farm to tell a legend of your own. For adults, it can be a complete mix of childhood memories, joy as you watch your children create new memories, or a night of spiritual embrace.

Many believe this special night shares the whispers and secrets of the universe. It is said the veil between heaven and earth is the thinnest on this day, making it easy to manifest dreams and connect to God's will in a renewed way.

You can surrender to the most Divine power and listen, making the most beautiful changes in your life, to live with happiness, to love with reckless abandon, and to forgive peacefully. I couldn't think of a better time to pray and have my wishes of health be heard aloud.

This thought alone made my tiny room grow with confidence and love as I got a little more comfortable with the process I would face on Monday morning. I began to soften and allow reality to embrace my heart. I began to write. It was so healing, and just the thought alone that I would share this gift with others melted my heart into a million pieces. I welcomed each moment, as it seemed I couldn't keep up fast enough with the lessons. As soon as I opened the door, they all came rushing in, so I wrote. We can all learn from each other, and many of the writings were my gifts to share with others who needed similar guidance or even just a sign that all was well.

That night from my twin bed at Brigham and Women's Hospital, I started to blog. Other than a few official e-mails, I had never blogged or knew much about it. I had been planning to write privately, but after my first e-mail it sort of took on a life of its own. My husband started a "caring bridge" site, which was an important way to connect with my loved ones. However, I knew I wanted to create a space that was connected to my heart and would help me uncover the many mysteries that would awaken within this experience.

Svadhyaya means "the study of oneself." It goes far beyond self-education and in essence becomes much more than a way to achieve or understand an external process. It becomes the mirror in which we can learn to truly see ourselves on a much deeper level. For each of us, this comes at a time in our life when we are fully willing to look at our internal behaviors and motivations we habitually use to maintain our self-image. By letting go of this need to uphold an image, we practice Svadhyaya to pierce through the veil of ego, allowing our spirit to shine bright.

After I sent out the initial e-mail sharing the news with as many loved ones as I could, I christened hollysloveolution@wordpress.com and wrote:

FEAR = False Evidence Appearing Real

*

I cannot really explain what it felt like the first few days after hearing news of the blood results. Each morning was like reliving it all over again; all the emotions flooded in, trying to knock me off course from what I had decided and worked through the day/night before. It was simply fear: false evidence trying to appear as real as could be.

Fear is such an amazing element of life. We can fear all kinds of things, like flying or heights, but those are just boundary testers because just as we know this is a fear, we can work slowly toward overcoming or staying as far away as we would like. There are many complex levels of fear that go in many directions. However, the bottom line is that *fear* creates a boundary, which simply takes away the very freedom that keeps us alive and connected to God. It slowly breaks us down when we embrace the physical evidence to be true, even when we know on many levels it is not.

I have taught many yoga classes on fear: how to minimize fear in one's life, how to embrace the challenge to learn, how to create more freedom—the list goes on. However, after reflecting upon fear and doubt, I have come to the realization that it all boils down to two ultimate fears: death and the unknown. I believe it is this ultimate ideal from which all other fears stem. It took one phone call to bring me eye level to this ultimate fear. In truth, I believe there really is no such thing as death. Our physical vessel in the material world feels very real to us all, but it is the spirit inside that really radiates light.

This spirit (energy) cannot die, so if we come full circle, there is no such thing as death. Historically, this is why so many cultures celebrate this experience. However, this news definitely tested this idea to a whole new level. It is one thing to ponder or be a risk taker, it is altogether different when it is put on your plate and you have no choice but to embrace it as a gift and challenge, to look it straight in the eye and let go (truly let go) of false evidence and outcomes and just live in the truth.

The truth is that I am a child of God. I believe I have written a journey earth side to learn and evolve spiritually. Each challenge in your life is an opportunity to live fearlessly with faith, to set yourself free from fleeting illusions and let love and God navigate you through. A very good friend told me that, and I couldn't find a better way to share such wisdom.

There have been several days that I have failed to adapt to this truth, letting false evidence create fear of death, leaving my family behind, etc. But I know this is not real. Most days I move forward with God's guidance, embracing the new lessons that are shifting inside me faster than ever before. The realization that love and forgiveness is the bottom line, and applying these truly within each breath is a lesson of the moment. When we choose to live within each moment, we truly begin to live.

This experience has forever changed me, and I believe it will bring forward much understanding in our connection to one another.

The words and encouragement that have assisted and lifted me up have been overwhelming. We are all one, and it is amazing to share and learn from one another!

Remember: "Life ain't always beautiful, but it is a beautiful ride" (Gary Allan). This is going to be my beautiful ride!

CHAPTER 6
INTERVAL TRAINING

OCTOBER 29, 2011

After it became a reality that I was going to be spending the next month at Brigham and Women's Hospital, I had to get "my head on straight". Brigham and Women's Hospital, popular in its own right, also supports Dana-Farber with all the patients who need inpatient care. There is a bridge connecting these two popular and highly respected institutions, giving them a force of one.

After crossing the bridge from Dana-Farber and seeing my new room at The Brigham, I knew there was no way I would be comfortable confined to an extremely small room with a bathroom that had a slight tilt and horrible tiling. Do you remember the tiling that mocked every girls' and boys' high school locker room in the 1980s? I didn't need or expect five-star décor, but I knew I would have to make some adjustments to enlighten this space to enhance the healing process.

I was certainly grateful in many ways, as once upon a time these rooms, as tiny as they were, housed two patients. I laughed out loud when I thought of how crazy that must have been. They may as well just put in a king-sized bed and ask the patients to share. Once again, this was a reminder of how lucky we are today to have the privacy and space for healing and reflection.

When I enquired about the past life of the room, I was told some extremely interesting stories as each room had its own experience. You could feel the blended energy of love, fear, grief, and pain rolled into a space of joy. There have been many good-byes and many days of welcome, but overall it is difficult to find the right words to describe a hospital room, a place of transformation to find peace, transcendence, and comfort.

I began to meet some of the nurses who worked on the floor, and they were all extremely nice. However, a month is a long time, so I was sure I would get to know them on a much more intimate level. The funniest one was Mel. She too had a health challenge that she had just healed from, and her way of doing so was through constant comedy. She definitely slapped me out of my personal "pity party" on several occasions but in the same breath wrapped me with support and the utmost love and empathy. She was very honest, which made some sense of how I would get through the next month.

The entire staff was extremely skilled and filled with empathy. They made the journey very personal for me, as I did not feel like just another patient. They acknowledged the days that were difficult and shared joy in the days that brought success. Many of them definitely toed the line, which was great because there were a lot of restrictions. However, they did everything within their power to make the experience count toward wellness.

One of the first things Mel showed me was the walking track that they encouraged patients to use for exercise. She went on to explain that I was welcome to walk the floor outside my door (wearing a mask and gloves, which was just the beginning). This "floor" was the circular walkway outside each room, but the "track" was the circular floor outside each unit. Twenty-two times around this small circle was a mile, but hey, you have to make lemonade right?

I made my way onto the track every day, with my mask and gloves, sometimes twice a day. It was my interval training, forty-five minutes on the stationary bike in my room, which they brought the very first day. After breaking a strong sweat, I made my way to the twenty-two laps on the track that equaled one mile. I do not think it was ever mapped out, a guesstimate at best, but it at least gave you something to work for each time you felt like you were ready to tip over with dizziness from walking in such a small circular space.

I had many visitors venture on what became known as "my" track with me, my mother being the most constant in attendance. We would talk about all kinds of fun things, and at least once a run I would ask, "Do you think I am going to make it?" She assuredly said yes every time. Honestly, what else was she going to say? But I know my mom. She has a deep, intuitive sense that she keeps very close to herself. Always in the right moment she would assure me that this was for a greater good, and I never questioned her.

There were other patients I met walking the track, trying to make the same sense I was trying to make as you look to the deepest space of your soul without a question but still feel an answer.

Wendy and Colleen both got an opportunity to walk the track with me. Colleen got a migraine about five minutes into our walk because she got so dizzy walking in such a small circle, and Wendy spent a good fifteen minutes in the bathroom. I believe she was trying to avoid at least half a mile.

When I wasn't using the track, I made all kinds of use of my time such as writing, watching bad TV, watching really bad TV, making phone calls, or writing e-mails—the list went as far as I could see.

Beyond healing and filling time, I was blessed to have so much support, coming from so many directions. In addition, the hospital also provided a great deal of support.

At least a couple of times a week a "Reiki practitioner" would show up at my door to ask if I wanted a session. The answer was always yes! Reiki is a healing energy and the extreme opposite end of the allopathic spectrum, so you can imagine my surprise when I learned this was an option while in the hospital. Reiki has been around forever. It is believed Jesus taught Reiki techniques in many of his healing sessions. Reiki received most of its notoriety during the late sixties, when Harvard led some of the most astonishing clinical trials on energy healing. The results showed profound effects in reduced heart rate and reduction in blood pressure.

In addition, their science was consistent with stress reduction and included transcendental meditation (TM), which is two-step meditation, created by Dr. Herbert Benson of Harvard Medical School. The transcendental meditation technique allows your mind to settle inward beyond thought to experience the source of thought, pure awareness, also known as transcendental consciousness. This is the most silent and peaceful level of consciousness, your innermost Self. In this state of restful alertness, your brain functions with significantly greater coherence, and your body gains deep rest.

After a number of successful clinical trials, they began to put this practice to use in the hospital. Nurses were the first group encouraged to take the training called "healing hands." It is a program that still exists and is a blessing for many patients.

After researching this information, I was consumed with a renewed faith in the medical establishment. After my first Reiki session, a doctor who was unfamiliar to me popped his head into my room asking me for a moment. He was the director of Dana-Farber's Zakim Center for Integrative Therapies, a holistic healing center filled with physicians trained in all types of naturopathic healing modalities, including nutrition, acupuncture, massage of all types, and yoga. It was amazing that it stood within the confines of a hospital that sets the gold standard of medical care across the country.

One of the many amazing aspects of this journey was that people supported me in their own way, which was divinely what I needed. It was a special experience where in every situation, every moment, the right person seemed to appear or the right e-mail would sing its way into my inbox. It was like as soon as I started to get a bit down, something would appear to lift me up and remind me that I got to decide how this journey went.

In his popular book *A New Earth*, which fosters the relationship we have with the ego, Eckhart Tolle shares, "Life is the dancer, and you are the dance." The ego/I maker is a challenging aspect of the mind, so understanding the ego on a deeper level is how you get past many fears of illness. The ego or mortal mind is something we will cover from all angles with many differing opinions. However, in doing this work it uncovers the veil of self-acceptance and self-awareness to make way for healing and evolution. It may take many lifetimes to peel the ego away, opening the door to the wisdom of oneness. I was ready for the difficult challenges that the ego would present me, hoping to face each set but win the match.

One night I seemed to be on quite a low ride, as I knew the next day would be my first chemo treatment, a lumbar puncture. I was scared and had so many feelings that I do not think I could put them into words, when my phone rang. It was Anna, the owner of the Yoga Effect studio, and a good friend.

Anna actually hired me when I presented her with the concept of a labor training I created called Earth Mother Birth. It is a training that reconnects you with your natural intuition to birth, and at the same time dispels the societal influences that leave us with poor birth outcomes countrywide.

Upon meeting Anna, we had a natural connection, sharing in many personal and spiritual beliefs. Anna is an extraordinary person, and working for her was such a special experience.

From the very beginning, the yoga studio felt like home. It was a space that foraged many great relationships and created a loving environment to build and hone in on my teaching skills. It was difficult to leave without getting to say good-bye to so many of the yogis I met through the studio. However, after a very short time I realized it was not good-bye, it was "until we see each other again."

When I heard Anna on the other end of the phone, I was a bit confused because I had just talked with her earlier that day, but this call had a very special purpose. Anna and Wendy had organized a candlelight prayer group for anyone who wanted to attend with the intention to hold a strong influence of health for me.

They ran the circle group with prayers, intentions, and songs. Many in attendance told me it was such a beautiful night. Each person shared his or her own blessing and love in my honor, and I can't think of any better gift. At the end of the prayer group they decided to call and share their thoughts, with a small need to hear my sweet voice to warm their hearts.

I remember the call very well as my mom and friend Cindy were visiting. I almost decided to call Anna back later but had a feeling it was important. I am so grateful I answered the call that night because I immediately felt all their love streaming through the phone. It was truly amazing, and there are no words that reflect such deep care and support.

We all spoke at once, and I could immediately identify some of the voices. I caught them all up to speed and held back many tears during the call, as most of them did not even get to say good-bye. It was difficult to share all the events thus far but so beautiful to have all the love and support.

When I got off the phone, I couldn't stop the tears flowing down my cheeks. The intentions and thoughts of healing were undoubtedly part of my fast and successful wellness.

When I was diagnosed, the teachers at the studio and Emily (my best friend from home) set up a meal plan and arranged many of the small details so our family could stay focused on the most important thing; healing. In addition, Anna placed a box in the back of the studio for people to pile their intentions and motivational thoughts of healing. These were some of the kindest words spoken on my behalf. The following are just a few of the many amazing notes:

1. Holly, you have so much compassion and warmth as a teacher you have touched so many lives. Your love for others and for life is shown clearly with your radiating energy for others. Be strong and heal fast.
2. Look up, Holly—see the bright sun shine on you and feel its warmth wrap its arms around you. Feel it heal you, feel it smile upon you.
3. Over the next few months, as you heal, may we be the inspiration to you that you have always been to us.—May this Kundilini Prayer offer much love and light:
May the long-time sun shine upon you,
All the love surround you,
And the pure light within you guide your way home.

These were just a few of the many amazingly kind words that were spoken on my behalf. Many shared their love about my teaching and guidance, as I often reflected my gratitude for their wisdom in return. This is the beautiful gift of yoga. When you become a teacher you learn from a different angle. However, the student inside you always comes first.

How blessed I was to have impacted just one life, and the more I learn with each passing day, the more I realize we impact people regularly with just a simple smile. What a simple donation of love so many of us regularly overlook.

It was motivation, kind words, and a great amount of love from family and friends that got me through my four-week stay at La Casa de Brigham and Women's. It was through working low impact in my soul space, setting intentions, meditation, and working with my vision boards. On the opposite side, I would work with intensity, physically keeping myself as strong as I could in mind and body. Don't misunderstand; I had many moments of weakness and fear, but those were the challenges and lessons.

As you will see from the blogs, this gift—leukemia, a.k.a. my "Loveolution Project"—taught me wisdom through the highest power of love. It is love and only love that allows one to see and hear our inner guidance. It allows us to forgive and serve our highest intentions the way we were divinely designed. As free will is part of this journey, it was those first few weeks that I decided yes, I am going to survive.

CHAPTER 7
ALLOPATHIC TRIUMPH

OCTOBER 30, 2011

It was early Sunday morning when I woke to the reality that I would be starting treatment on Monday, and it was surreal. The night prior I was blessed with many loved ones praying for me, and today I was alone in thought. I could feel the idea of fear trying to creep into my heart, trying to take over; I would refer to it on that day as a "faith stealer."

They came in the day before with a schedule for treatment, and it was difficult to digest—not to mention that it went against all my beliefs in living an organic life and the mere fact that it was just plain scary. However, in life we have to make the best decisions we can with the information we have.

My friend Hannah has always reminded me of this ideal for many moons, covering many different situations in my life. I'd tried really hard, but fear was winning. I beat myself up over things I could not control. I could hear her voice, a whisper in my ear, reminding me that I'd made the best decision I could with the information I had. This was always the truth when I made a decision, so why look back?

The day I called Hannah to share the news about the Loveolution was a difficult one. It was her daughter's birthday, but I knew if I did not tell her she would have been upset that I withheld such news.

I'd met Hannah at our first pharmaceutical job, and we became best buds from the start. We lived in two different parts of the country and were partners in crime at every sales meeting.

Culturally we couldn't have been more different. However, our hearts were the same, and we always support each other no matter what. I say that with an emphatic "no matter what" because although we may not always agree, we support each other with love. It is a special relationship that I considered blessed to have in this life.

During treatment we talked as much as we could. I know it was difficult for her since she felt helpless about what she could do to help because of the distance that kept us apart. However, here is the lesson: no matter how much support one gives, love is the ultimate connection. All while I was going through my greatest challenge, she faced hers and still gave everything she had to support me. That sums her up; she would give you the shirt off her back and get your back all in one. Priceless!

After I got home from my first inpatient stay and Brigham and Women's, I knew she could see the hurt and fear in my soul. Without discussion, she was on a plane that next weekend to visit, flying into New York and then driving to Boston.

It was definitely a challenge for her as she was the only one, other then my family, to see me right after treatment. It takes a few days to "get the hospital out of you," but she hugged me harder then she ever had. She told me I was going to be fine because we had enough information to support it.

This led to making the decision for treatment, which was confusing and difficult for many to believe. Even though time seemed to press hard on my mind and soul, I leaned on a number of naturopaths, including the work of Charlotte Gerson, Russel Blaylock, and Dr. Andrew Weil, as well as Patrick Hatwan, an amazing friend. (I will talk about Pat and his wife in detail later) however, for now it is important to know that they were ready to drop all to be with our family. This follows the blessing I discussed in a previous chapter. I had such divine support that I was always covered in love, with the perfect spirit, perfect love, and perfect words.

While I feverishly searched for answers, each naturopath mimicked the same message within close proximity, through research and their personal experience. If you have an acute blood disorder, allopathic treatment is statistically the most successful option. Even with that being said, it was still difficult, as I believe we are sold a bill of goods when it comes to the "cancer industry."

After spending ten years in the pharmaceutical industry and reading a lot about the "cancer industry," this was a difficult decision to make. Sometimes you realize you have to embrace a choice naked. (Not literally sitting naked until you deicide what to do, but peeling off all the layers of judgment, the many lies, correlations, and just listen to the facts and your intuition.) In this case, as each case is different, I believed I was in the right place.

There are hundreds of documented cancers that have been healed with naturopathic medicine. There are many people who will never believe this truth, and there are many who are waking up to this truth. However, the proof is documented and is out there for all who care to see.

My journey of understanding this truth started with my first yoga class. I could feel this power trying to take over me in the poses, to be stronger, push myself harder even as the teacher stated, "Soften in the posture, allow your breath to flow freely." My face was red as a beet as I attempted a new arm balance that I was going to get into regardless of whether my breath was there or not. I had just met my ego for the first time. I didn't know it then and maybe it took months, but it was in a small, heated power studio in Boston that started my awakening fifteen years ago.

I began to hunger for more truth. I was like a child who had found out Santa wasn't real—what else? I couldn't believe so many things were happening right under my nose and I didn't even know it. I felt like a fool because there was no excuse; I should have become an advocate for myself much sooner in life. However, one of the most important ideals is that we can't look back; we can only carry the lesson into the present.

Once I began on the path of truth, I met many people along the way who participated in my awakening. "When the student is ready, the teacher will appear," As the saying goes. This is the truth and I met many teachers. They shared with such love the truths that are hidden in our world on a spiritual and physical level. They didn't withhold information to create internal power; they shared all that had been funneled to them on their journey. It was commanding and took a stronghold of my heart, which had felt extremely deceived.

This is when Pat shared some crucial words of wisdom: "The more we learn, the more we need to forgive and open our hearts to more truth. If we don't, the blood is on our hands." It was this very sentence that propelled me out of a great state of anger to a state of love and understanding. This eventually took a turn to forgiveness, which opened up to moving forward with more learning. I have much gratitude for Pat and his wife, Lynn, who both have been amazing teachers in different ways.

With all the teachers that surrounded me, I still needed to follow my intuition. I continued to research in every direction, searching clinical papers, medical journals, and websites that supported experiences of those who have gone through A.L.L. I researched a variety of conspiracy theories to see if there was any solid truth. Many of these theories were based in pure fact, but it was a little more difficult to shift through to get accurate information.

Have you ever heard of Dr. Morris Fishbean? Dr. Morris Fishbein (1889-1976) originally studied to be a clown. Realizing he could make more money as a doctor, he entered medical school (where he failed anatomy), and then barely graduated. He never treated a patient in his life. However, his big claim to fame was that he became the head of the AMA (and editor of the Journal of the American Medical Association from 1924-1949), he decided which drugs could be sold to the public based only how much advertising money he could extort from drug manufacturers, whom he required to place expensive ads in JAMA. There were no drug-testing agencies, only Fishbein. It was irrelevant if the drugs worked, not too far from bloodletting, eh.

Then there was the most famous of ads that he stood behind, the good doctors that smoked camels. Do you remember the massive campaign the tobacco industry ran using doctors as their main power piece? It is so easy to find as it is all over the Internet, but not so easy to believe we allowed this to be a part of our history. This was the beginning of the first medical journal that was financially backed by industries that were filled with corruption and had millions to dedicate toward advertising. This is where it becomes hard to separate fact from fiction as I saw firsthand, sitting at the helm.

In addition, there are many books that tell this story of truth on a much deeper level, offering solid proof to back it up. Books such as *When Healing Becomes a Crime: The Amazing Story of the Hoxsey Cancer Clinics and the Return of Alternative Therapies* by Kenny Ausubel; *The Curse of Louis Pasteur* by Nancy Appleton; or *Healing the Gerson Way : Defeating Cancer and Other Chronic Diseases* by Charlotte Gerson cover this material. The list is long and travels through many generations, making its way right into the twenty-first century.

An additional fact, that may pique the interest of some are the difficult questions that arise when we begin thinking critically. For example, why are there only two countries that allow pharmaceutical companies to directly market to the consumer via television ads? These commercials on TV cite specific symptoms, which create a need for the company—more importantly, for their product. Then comes the laundry list of side effects. It has become the center of many jokes but still remains to affect the subconscious of many. It serves its purpose as the "pied piper", millions of patients march to the doctor asking for their medications because they believe they have symptoms.

Knowing there are three sides to every story, 2 sides full of messy lies and power, and then a third that somehow over time weeds out the lies, leaving pure truth, I was on a mission to find the great "truth". At this time I continued researching until I had enough information to make a solid choice regarding treatment.

While I sifted through statistics, papers, and clinical trials, my soul took a turn down memory lane. It was one special night that I decided to listen to a learning conference call hosted by Clayton College. Pat, who would be referred to as "Pat in the Hatwan" led the call and from this moment forward he would take me under his wing. He would continue to share the knowledge and wisdom he gained from his previous schooling and life experiences. I would listen.

He often held my emotions in the palm of his hand and gently nurtured me as I argued his points. He let me argue what I thought was truth until my own ego brought me full circle. I have been on the opposing side of that conversation, and it is not always easy to listen to someone argue a point that you have learned the hard way is not the truth. This is where Pat has earned the title of "gentle giant in the school of hard knocks." He is a gentle soul who only cares about helping others toward light, to the truth of their soul, to the essence of life. Without his help and the help of many teachers, this would have been way too difficult a challenge to bear on my own.

During my great search in making the most difficult decision regarding treatment, Pat was a great source of information, as he too was researching what path would be the best for me. However, the truth remains that as one can offer guidance there is a line that no one can cross and there is only one who can make the ultimate decision, in this case it was I. Pat took this quite seriously and has always respected the decisions I have made, even if he didn't agree; this is one of the many great attributes that make him an amazing friend.

Through much guidance and research, Tad and I made decisions that were based on a number of factors. The list was long and wide, citing previous statistics, new clinical trials, research from the most respected institutions, but ultimately the decision was made delicately with trust and intuition. We looked to make a decision that supported solid evidence for physical healing and felt guided by God.

Again, in the midst of confusion, I thought back to an experience I'd had while working for a very popular hospital. I was sitting in front of a well-known physician, who told me, "It doesn't matter if you eat McDonald's every day, as long as you only eat small portions." In that moment I was shell-shocked and couldn't believe what I was hearing. Even now this is still a shocking event, which leads me to a message of guidance. The message is not that doctors are bad in any way; it is that doctors are human and fallible. Many physicians I have met over the years are interested in staying on top of best practices. However, every physician gets to choose how he or she wants to practice and move forward the best way to treat his or her patients. They get to choose if they want to be a part of preventative medicine or treating symptoms.

Physicians go through a significant amount of schooling to attain their goal of becoming a doctor. However, it is important to keep in mind that just like each state has an educational board, medical schools have a board that decides upon and creates a certified curriculum. This curriculum usually finds itself well behind the gold standard of care, forcing physicians to stay up-to-date with clinical information.

It is now becoming mainstream knowledge that the current medical curriculum lacks nutritional training, alternative practices, and is highly organized by the pharmaceutical industry. This just reinforces that you have to thoroughly research your options before making choices for any type of treatment.

There is no question that physicians have many crosses to bear when practicing medicine. With insurance protocols and hospital and pharmacy formularies, this creates a significant disadvantage for the patient and the doctor. This means less time with each patient and less time for a doctor to be a doctor.

On a physical level, we have uncovered many facets about the human body that we have never known before; it is an exciting time in the history of integrative medicine (the combination of practices and methods of alternative medicine with conventional biomedicine. It emphasizes treating the whole person, with a focus on wellness and health rather than on treating disease). However, it has never been a mystery that if you interrupt the process that allows your body to embrace quality nutrition and block the ability of your body to detoxify, then your cells will turn on you.

On a spiritual level you reflect God, and it is believed there is no possibility of error in this reflection, as this would be saying God is flawed. In my heart I believe we all are a perfect reflection of God, so disease has no home here. This is the journey of evolution as we learn how to attain this level of understanding and enlightenment. This we will talk about a great deal in the chapters to come, but for now it holds its space, a moment to ponder where you are in your evolution.

Once you pull away all the layers you begin to learn the truth, and it is quite shocking, but still many remain hypnotized by the hype of the pharmaceutical industry, which gains power through fear and manipulation. This can also go in the opposite direction, as there are many naturopaths who use scare tactics toward those who are just beginning to open up to all the amazing possibilities. Many people have opened their eyes and hearts to hear another side of the story, but still the masses sleep.

After going through a long learning cycle, it took a number of years to shake the anger of being lied to by a number of large organizations. However, as each layer is peeled back from my soul, I realize we all have to go through this awakening in a similar process: first disbelief, then anger supported by fear, and then acceptance moving forward lovingly, knowing when to share, when to listen, and when to walk away.

After what I considered an emotionally long day, I sat down to write a few simple words. I opened my computer to what is now called hollyloveolution@wordpress.com and typed

> "We are shaped by our thoughts; we become what we think.
> When the mind is pure, joy follows like a shadow that never leaves" (Buddha).

*

I felt like the walls were closing in on me as I waited for my first day of treatment. When it finally came I decided I would correlate it to my emotional soul. The medicine was designed to drop my white-cell count to zero, which would put the Loveolution into remission. As my white-cell count dropped, I would compare it to my ego dropping to zero, and as it built back up it would represent my soul and pure love.

I realized I was at a very important impasse, a choice of epic proportion. I could choose my ego or God Source; it was as simple as that. The divided mind is set up into two pathways: one the ego, which sets up the landscape of suffering through fearful thoughts, negative outcomes, false attachments, and sometimes may even try to be the voice of reason. The second is the God mind, which is the most brilliantly lit path that guides through a constant love and truth. So this should be a simple choice. It is a simple choice, but it is the interweaving of the paths that creates the learning lessons of life and free will.

It is now that I want to make a very important statement. I speak of these two minds and how they try to direct your decisions either with fear or love. It goes layers deep, and we can only make the best decisions we can based on where we are in our evolution. My choice of treatment, although many may feel antagonistic to this belief, was a mix of both that supported where I was in my evolution. When it came to a child I let the soul stay on course, however, mortality was the greatest fear I ever faced. I think that if I was faced with this again each time I would make a different choice based on how the experience and challenge moved me forward; there is no room for judgment.

The polarities of the ego mind versus God mind are so deep and intricate that we could and do spend a lifetime sorting through them. Taking notice of the scenery in the ego mind is the contrast to the space that God invites us to live each day, until eventually the ego mind has been passed by through the whisper of wisdom.

There are so many examples of how the divided mind shapes our lives. When hearing stories of the Chilean miners, most of them spoke directly of the ego thoughts that tried to weaken their spirit and their will to survive.

There are countless books that guide us on the journey to

understand and move past blocking points of the ego. This is where we need to build off the discoveries of others, so we can continue to move forward in our own evolution.

In my opinion, *A New Earth* by Eckhart Tolle is one of the greatest books outlining the voice of the ego, detailing the intricacies of the ego and offering a how-to in moving past this voice.

Living in the present moment alone is a challenge; it can seem a daunting task to keep the weeds out of the garden of the mind. However, we take small steps, utilizing tools that can help you connect with your inner spirit.

Some of these tools I have come to use daily and may be familiar to many of you:

1. **Present Living**—Feeling is the language that speaks, feel as though your goal is accomplished, and your prayer is already answered. However, in the midst of this vision, don't forget to be grateful for what surrounds your life in the present. A great tool to help in this process is a vision board, which allows you to see your dreams in the moment of the present. This is a gift.
2. **Like Attracts Like**—Make sure you align yourself with the directives of your God mind/soul, because what you put out will reflect right back to you. This is your chance to identify who you really are, what your core values are. You don't need to send out a memo to all those in your circle, you just need to start living these values. You will begin to see these changes in your external life; these changes will only support your true heart with love and honesty.
3. **Gratitude**—Take a moment each day to focus on the things for which you are grateful. Dr. Wayne Dyer recommends affirming your appreciation to all that you are and all that you have. "Change your thoughts, change your life," he says.
4. **Learn to Trust Your Intuition**—Make peace with the reflection of your heart. Quit the "yeah, but" or waiting for the other shoe to drop; your ego wants to plant the

seed of doubt, so be prepared and have an out clause. For me it is going back to step 1.
5. **Un-Forgiveness**—Forgiveness may be the single-most important aspect of healing and moving forward. Forgiveness is solely for you, overriding any proof that leaves you right or wrong, moving past the grudge, and just letting it go to God. So let go of all the rules surrounding forgiveness and start "un-forgiving" yourself. Know that you are always doing the best you can with the information you have. You know your intention no matter how that has been translated. Allow forgiveness to make space in your heart.

*

These are just a few of many tools that will help us at least choose a path. The simple ideal of conscious living, starting to live from your heart, and forgiving from your soul are major accomplishments.

I leave you with a message paraphrased from Matthew 13:31–32 and Luke 17:6: A mustard seed is small, but it's alive and growing. Like a tiny seed, a small amount of genuine faith in God will take root and grow. Almost invisible at first, it will begin to spread, first under the ground and then visibly. Although each change will be gradual and imperceptible, soon this faith will have produced major results that will uproot and destroy competing loyalties. We don't need more faith; a tiny seed of faith is enough if it is alive and growing.

CHAPTER 8
DIVINE ONENESS

NOVEMBER 1, 2011

At the end of most yoga classes, teachers will seal their hands at their heart in a sacred position called *anjoli mudra*. This practice is wildly popular when followed by the spoken word *namaste*, which means "the light source in me bows to the divine light source in you." This represents the belief that there is a Divine being or Source within each of us, and it is this divine source called oneness that we should solely reflect in each other.

Oneness is a concept that is simple yet very difficult to put into practice. When we look into the eyes of our friends and family, we often see a mirror of difference, and it would be safe to say it causes a great divide of judgment and sarcasm for many. However, with this simple intention, it draws you back to the basic truth that we are all one.

We are all created by the same divinity, no matter what form of rituals you may follow or religious beliefs you embrace. Evolving to understand oneness, it is rather normal that we would go in the opposite direction to see the differences before we can understand and complete the full circle, which brings us back to the truth. The truth simply means your full evolution to enlightenment.

There are many truths and a great deal of wisdom that will auspiciously blaze our trail as we awaken on our journey. Each lesson is either the experience of our self or reflected in that of another. However, the lesson learned is always about becoming more consciously connected, living within each breath, without fear, and free to choose life.

Our ego will have us believe we know how others should live their life and what they may do wrong, and set by our standards, we believe we have the answers to make it better. This is brought forward by the great judgment of the ego, your individual "I" maker that sets you up for a great deal of suffering.

Allowing just enough confidence with empathy to make you believe you are right but then just one step away within that reflection comes forgiveness. We can only love and forgive, sharing in each person's journey, setting down the torch of judgment, embracing the experience as a learning lesson of our own.

Understanding the ego is a challenge that may take a lifetime to even scratch the surface and many lifetimes to understand. However, breaking through moments of sweetness to see the truth (enlightenment) with a light that warms your entire soul and the connection to God's guidance is proof you are on the right track. Then the moment may be gone, but all you need is that one breath because it is that breath that will lead you to the next step of evolution.

As we complete the full circle, oneness may be described on certain days, such as 9/11, where we completely go beyond all form, race, and ethnicity and just love one another. We love beyond the special relationships, such as our mothers, fathers, family, and friends. We love because it is how we are guided to live. Can you imagine a world where we see the same love for our mother as we see for a stranger? This is the love that breaks down the walls of hatred and judgment, and embraces universal love. This is the ultimate *love!* This is the love Jesus spoke of in biblical times. When we are willing to set free of our boundaries and just see the goodness in others as reflected in ourselves, this is when we will have encountered oneness.

There will never be enough pages in a book, a blog, or speaking forum to share how blessed I am to have all the love and support pouring in daily. It has taught me that my own judgments are really just a weakness I see in myself. Through oneness I am choosing to set aside my mirror of opinion and just be part of each person's journey, as you are part of mine. The light that shines within in me is a reflection of your truth and love, which connects each of us on a plane that we don't always understand.

As I stated earlier, the world is designed to divide us and set us apart by creating as many boundaries as possible. The boundaries become anything that may set us apart, such as our job status, societal class, how we define our success, etc. However, when you think about your true nature, a state of being "naked" (meaning without your job, clothes, house, toys, all the things you believe define you), all you have is your soul. This is where and when we ask the difficult questions: Are we happy? Have we listened to God's guidance? Or do we care more about external successes? There is no right or wrong; we must honor where we our in our evolution (our truth).

It is the most common lesson we learn, but still one of the most challenging: How would one feel if he or she lost everything—job, home, life as it was previously defined? This is when we see firsthand how much value we place on these items, which naturally will be a distraction from soul growth. We continue to define our successes on how big a home is, how powerful our job may be, etc. Again, there is no right or wrong if, for example, one has a huge home; it is how much value is placed on it. This is why a shocking challenge often changes people quite a bit, placing them on a different path, with new awareness.

In April 2011, earthquakes struck Fukushima, Japan, with such a blast that it sent waves around the world. As thousands lost their lives due to the tsunami that hit the coastline caused by the quake, one of the biggest concerns became the Daiichi nuclear power plant that was melting down.

As we watched stateside, we saw videos of people courageously helping others, risking their own lives without a second thought. You saw the fear and you could quickly see how it was put out with the love of people working together to save their homes. Neighbors helping neighbors, strangers helping strangers; there was no limit to the beautiful connection that was exemplified through what turned into months of concern.

At the time of the earthquake, one of my best friends, Elise Maudsley, had just been stationed at Yokosuka Naval Base. As Tad and I first heard the news, we panicked because we knew her husband, James, was out to sea. The news immediately deployed information about the earthquakes.

When I spoke on the phone with her, it took everything inside me to not cry and beg her to get on a plane that night. As it worked out, she got on a plane the very next night and took up residence at our house for a few months. I cannot even begin to tell you how wonderful it was to pick her up at the airport as I watched them scan every bag for radiation. It was just a crazy time, and the only thing that kept it all together was *love*, pure *love*!

The first night Elise and her daughter, Olivia, arrived there was a sense of relief, but still the energy of loss hung over them like a dark cloud. She told us stories of being stuck on a train in Yokosuka and how everyone stayed calm as they helped out elderly and children. She described in detail what it felt like to be pushing Olivia in her stroller, as the sidewalk became a "bounce house." It was absolute horror, but we were just so grateful not only that she was back in the states but that she was hours away from where the worst of it had happened.

We continued to watch the news of the melting nuclear plant and prayed for all those who were stuck without food, water, or shelter. James, her husband, was part of the biggest relief effort to provide Japan with first aid and food, so it didn't go unnoticed that he was there, dealing with all the dangers that go along with such a big relief effort. I saw the sadness and worry in her eyes as Tad and I comforted her. She was so grateful to be safe, but she felt so sad for the atrocity that many of the Japanese people were going through.

On top of it all, it was her birthday that week, so she was thrown a difficult life challenge, yet in the face of this challenge she remained positive. I knew once she settled in a bit we would make the best of this time and take her mind off the situation. She was learning firsthand the lesson of being "naked." I sat by doing my very best to support her.

No one knew what was going to happen, whether Elise would ever go back to the home she created in Japan, which housed all her material possessions. Everything she had—pictures, memories, the love of a new space, and the dreams of a journey through the lands only seen in pictures—could be lost. All she had was one bag of clothes for her and Olivia.

As I knocked on the door to wake her for dinner, I saw her kneel over her bag as tears streamed down her face. She said, "It's just so overwhelming for Olivia," who was asleep trying to adjust to the major time difference. It always amazes me that mothers put the feeling of their children far ahead of theirs; it is the beauty of nurture, and Elise is an exceptional mother.

I reached down to offer my hand and then a hug to assure her all would be okay. She asked how I knew because in the moment it looked bleak for so many. However, here implies the lesson that we are not our things, our memories, or our hopes—we are love. If we have love, there will always be support, and that is what matters the most.

Looking back, their unexpected visit was actually one of the most fun and exciting things that came from such a devastating situation. Olivia is two weeks older than Sawyer, so for all intents and purposes it was like having twins running around the house—complete and utter chaos. Elise and I were a great team as every night, after a long day of taking the kids everywhere; we sat down to watch our bad TV shows with mommy treats and a bottle of wine. "It was the best of times …"

The night of her birthday a group of friends came over to surprise her with a cake and loving, support. A few friends picked up a beautifully decorated cake and some birthday cheer as we prepared a small surprise.

As we sang the birthday song to her, she broke down, her hands covering her face, trying to protect the last attempt to hide her overwhelming emotions. She had been doing her best to hold it deep within her heart, but in the wake of love she felt the strength we had to hold her up even if for only a moment. This allowed for her to let go long enough for her to cry into her beautiful cake. She was so grateful to be amongst such kindness and support that it easily ignited an emotional overhaul. I mean she'd just left her whole life, including her husband, in a disaster-torn country and spent twenty-four hours flying with a two-year-old. I am surprised it took the two days for her to break down.

Elise is such a special friend, and it was difficult to see her facing such a tough experience. However, I also saw her courage and bravery as she faced this basically as a single parent. This was the lesson she was handed, and we both learned so much. It is in the moment that we sometimes forget that growth never stops, it always continues, and although we may get breaks, it never truly stops. Additionally, this is the strength that military families sacrifice for all, while their spouses are keeping us safe at home with our freedoms. Regardless of what one thinks about politics and the like, there is one thing for sure: men and women all over the world in the armed forces support our country for all that it stands for in the Constitution with great pride.

Elise and I first met at the captain's meet and greet at Great Lakes Naval Station in Illinois. Through slow conversations and many similarities, we became great friends. There are many memories that are just filled with ridiculous laughter, laughter that goes beyond just a chuckle—we are talking about fits of laughter, a pure belly laugh. Laughter that works out certain muscles in your stomach you didn't know you had and the proof is it hurts for days.

We are like sisters. We look like sisters, we act like sisters, and our relationship will forever be bound in love. Our similar beliefs were just one aspect that connected this friendship, but it was pure love and life that was the real connection. While I was going through trials and tribulations struggling with a serious back problem, she would always help out with Sawyer.

I will never forget the day I had an appointment with yet another spine specialist. As I sat telling Elise what the appointment was for, tears streamed down my face, as I felt like I hit my wall and just couldn't handle it anymore. When I looked up from my snotty "cry–storm," I saw her crying too. She felt so much hurt because of my hurt, which is such a reflection of friendship that there are no words; this is special.

Elise and I got into all kinds of great trouble together, especially the night we "thought" we got pregnant. It was a night filled with dancing, Captain Morgan's rum, and acrobatic yoga. I remember looking toward Tad and James as they rolled their eyes at each other, while we continued to dance all over the kitchen to our "theme song," "Fireflies" by Owl City. After our dance fever we decided to start an acro-yoga session, with Wendy at the helm of instruction. Wendy began "flying" each of us (one at a time) into the heights of this beautiful expression of yoga, taking us right to the edge. That night we shared the love that we all have for life, and the next morning the foghorn rolled, but it was worth every memory.

Shortly after Elise shared with me her news of pregnancy. I was so excited for them and this new journey they were about to embark on becoming a family. Elise and James got pregnant quite easily. She was filled with sympathy and empathy toward our plight and challenge that we faced trying to have a baby.

After Tad and I got engaged, we were over the moon to find out we were pregnant. However, our dreams of a family were squashed quickly the day I went for my first ultrasound. I was told I was having an ectopic pregnancy as after six weeks there was still no egg in my uterus. It was a difficult day, and in the moment I felt very little support from the clinic I was working with in Boston. I felt more like another mom who would silently cry because the nurses and physicians had become numb to the outcomes and more concerned with protocol.

I was in shock and not given any options other than a treatment, which would basically abort the pregnancy by blocking the folic acid to the fetus.

This felt so wrong and was so upsetting that I remember crying for days. My mom and dad were so supportive and spent the weekend with me in Boston. As my mom began packing to head home, my dad asked me if I wanted him to stay an extra night. Honestly, I remember feeling so numb that I wasn't sure if I wanted to be alone to feel bad for myself or wanted him to be there. As a last-minute decision he stayed, and we waved good-bye to my mom as she left to prepare for a long workweek ahead.

That night at about three o'clock in the morning I awoke to the fiercest pain I may have ever felt in my life. It was like a knife in my side. I immediately headed to the shower, as water has always provided me great comfort. This was when I noticed a large amount of blood on the shower floor. I yelled for my dad, and he quickly went into rescue mode. He got me dressed and helped me out the door. I was in so much pain that I didn't page my doctor's service; we went right down the street to Newton-Wellsley Hospital. I could barely walk even with assistance as Dave (techniquely my step-father but played a fatherly role my whole life so I refer to him as dad) began taking care of business. He knew this was serious and was not about to wait another moment.

They quickly took me back and got an IV started. Once I was a little more comfortable I was able to share with the staff that I was diagnosed with an ectopic pregnancy. The OB on call was paged and was in the room in fewer than two minutes. He did the ultrasound himself and was quick to share the news. Emergency surgery was the only option because the fetus was getting bigger in the fallopian tube. I remember hearing the devastating news, and I knew what was coming next. He was going to tell me he had to take out the only tube I had, my last chance for a spontaneous pregnancy, because it would be too damaged from the ectopic pregnancy. Previously, I had explored in vitro fertilization (IVF) on my own with the conclusion that it just wasn't for me, so this news came even harder on my heart.

Dr. Tom had the face of an angel and the compassion to match. He held my hand as he uttered the news of what needed to happen. "Holly, you need to have your fallopian tube taken out because it is going to rupture."

My heart sank; back in 2001 I had to have my right ovary and fallopian tube removed due to a very large cyst. I knew if he took my tube out that it would be impossible to have a baby naturally, as both fallopian tubes would be gone. I looked into his gentle eyes and pleaded with him to keep the fallopian tube intact. He took a breath, and a moment before he looked at me and said he would do his best. I took one last look his way as they rolled me into the OR.

Dr. Tom sat there for a moment while he mulled over the situation. This was difficult because the standard of care is that the tube comes out in this situation. Studies show the importance of removing the tube as it can cause future problems, not to mention the fact that the tube is 90 percent of the time unable to carry an egg from the ovary to the uterus because of tubal damage. This is important to understand because this medical situation left me with very little chance to have a baby naturally.

It was a difficult day. Tad was in Italy for another two months before he came home for our wedding. It would be at this time that we would move to Great Lakes, Illinois, for his final command before he retired as a boot camp instructor. For now, as he started his day back in Naples, Italy, he had no idea that our chances of having a baby dwindled even further.

While I was in surgery my dad had my phone and with some divine guidance figured out how to make an international call. Tad was already in his early morning meeting, a meeting with security clearance, so it was only interrupted upon emergency. When my dad spoke with the clerk he explained the situation and the meeting came to a halt. Tad later told me that his heart sank when the clerk came in with a call for him because that was never good news.

My dad informed Tad what was happening and he was in shock. It was a very tough moment as he was worried about me and was sad to hear what happened with the pregnancy. He clutched his fingers between his eyes and took a breath. We had just taken almost three weeks to travel through Germany and Italy, but he knew he had to be with me. He spoke with his boss, and again this is a testimonial to what an amazing man Tad is. Without having any vacation, his boss rushed him out on the first Military flight to Boston.

When I woke from surgery, my dad was next to my bed and had a big smile on his face. Then I saw Dr. Tom shortly after, and he told me that although he was able to save the tube, it would probably never be viable. He would later tell me during my follow-up visit that I should really consider IVF because I had such healthy eggs. It left me with very little hope for having a baby because I knew in my heart I would not do IVF.

After several hours in recovery, my dad loaded me into his truck and brought me back to my condo in Boston. What a difficult night; all I wanted was to hear Tad's voice. When I called his office his line went straight to voice mail. Then I called the "other line," and one of his shipmates said he was in a meeting. I was still groggy and decided to go to bed. The seven-hour difference was always something of a struggle but was one of the factors that made us stronger in our communication.

That night I dreamt of him coming to my door and taking away all my sadness. He wrapped me in his arms and I felt nothing but pure love. It was amazing and felt so real that when I woke up I was surprised that he was not sleeping next to me. The next morning I called my mom to tell her my dream, and she just laughed with empathy, as she knew my heart was hurting.

Over the next several hours I moped around the house, and each movement was made with an extreme level of gentleness, calculated with precision and forethought because stomach surgery affects more movement than you ever thought possible. After a few episodes of *Dog the Bounty Hunter*, I was ready for a nap when the doorbell rang. I slowly walked to the door and opened it to see a dozen roses and then an amazingly handsome man peek around the bouquet. I released a huge breath and just fell right into his arms. My tears were uncontrollable and my heart felt full. I felt like I could drink up all his love and I would be healed.

I couldn't believe he was here; he definitely pulled off the surprise of the century, which is not easy with me. I usually have an intuitive sense about these things. We usually had to go two to three months between visits, especially since I had just spent a few weeks with him, made this such an unexpected present. We just cuddled into each other's sweet kiss and embrace. I felt safe and knew that no matter what happened, he would be there for me. I truly trusted that God would create our family the way it was meant to be. I was blessed to be marrying such an amazing man, and that is being modest.

Even though this was a sad time, we took advantage of the situation by putting the final touches on our wedding. It was to be a simple, old-fashioned "hand fasting" that has come to be interpreted literally, as the symbolic act of tying a marrying couple's hands together with a ribbon. The idea is that they are bound in love and light instead of a contract. When the wedding came it was a perfect day, which would be attended by our entire family and closest friends. It would be a day filled with great memories and sweet good-byes as days after, we would begin our trek to Great Lakes, Illinois, to start a new life chapter.

After the move, and once we got settled, life changed quite a bit. I made some of the biggest decisions in my life. I felt like God was giving me a blank sheet of paper to truly reflect who I was and who I wanted to be. I enrolled in a yoga teacher training class at a studio where I had practiced only a few times. The classes were brilliantly woven with spiritual philosophy and the ideal of enlightenment. It was beautiful and in just a number of days so many yogis extended themselves to me, I felt so welcomed at such a warm kula.

I was bouncing with each step, and my smile was bigger than the Cheshire cat's at the new opportunities being presented. I felt so connected to the teacher training group, a small group of nine woman who all came together to share their deepest insecurities and life challenges to make way for this new knowledge—a new way of living, "living yoga."

We would all come together for a full weekend of training, every other weekend. Although it was so exhausting on a physical and emotional level, we learned so much from each other. It was as if it was designed divinely by a greater power so each of us could surrender, embracing the practice.

After the first few weekends we all began to notice a few things that didn't seem right with the teacher. She was the owner of the studio and choreographed these radiant classes, which seemed so authentic to this path. However, in just a short time we all began to observe things that were not marked by yogic living. She would become very mean and take moments of the training to embarrass one who was struggling with the material. She would become defiant if we asked questions that may have gone against the grain of what she was teaching. She had "her way only" policy, which didn't seem to match the philosophy of yoga. I began to hear rumblings amongst the other students, so I took it upon myself to do some digging. I reached out to a couple of students who had taken the training before us and was shocked by the information they shared. There was more drama in this studio than on *General Hospital*. How had I missed this? This felt like another challenge that would keep coming up in life until I set it free.

I wasn't sure what to do; my heart was filled with the passion for teaching. I could see my dreams of opening a studio and creating a space of healing moving further away from me. I quickly made a decision to speak with the teacher directly, which was a new direction for me as confrontation was not a mastered skill. Prior to our "meeting," she actually directed several personal attacks toward me, and this assured me that a difficult decision was looming. I was told she had not given a number of students their certification once they were done with training because they didn't do the work according to her standards. First, there was a lot of work to do for this training. Second, after handing over a large sum of money, I would not tolerate threats like this.

When I confronted her, she ran me in circles trying to get me to chase my own tail. I knew what she was doing and wanted no part of it. A few of the other girls had already gone to different training classes. This was a point in life where a cycle would stop. It was a big moment for me, not going along with something because it is what you are supposed to do or because it was difficult to be kind with honesty. This training was not going to serve me in becoming a great teacher; I knew the answer in every cell in my body and I made the choice to move to another class. This may not seem like big deal, but in the moment of it, the question of making a good decision while being wrapped in emotion made it a difficult choice. However, once I cut through all the cords it was clear, and I felt like I had a huge win.

This was where I met Wendy, who lovingly and empathetically took me into her teacher training even though it had already started. Her kindness was beyond what I expected, and I knew a friendship was forging. I was proud as I lovingly broke a cycle and made a choice that was right for me. This is not always the easiest option in life; sometimes it is easier to move away from confrontation. In the end I knew this was right and as I moved toward the right decision, life again restored an ease that only comes when you are traveling in the right direction.

This teacher training was great, and each weekend I would learn so much about this beautiful tradition and myself. I would surrender another layer that wasn't serving me and listen to the experiences of those around me.

Life was filled with so much joy. For the first time my hopes and dreams matched my life goals. I felt like I had it all; I was blessed. I was meeting so many amazing people through Tad's work and the yoga studio. I was surrounded by pure love, and there was no negativity or drama of any kind.

I realized it was a choice, maybe subconscious, but nonetheless a choice to invite drama into my life.

Tad also loved his job. Every eight weeks he would be given eighty recruits to break down and build up as a strong unit to move onto a Navy Ship. It was so amazing to hear about them in their first weeks and then attend their graduation. There was never a graduation without tears as you watched these proud men and women stand tall in support of their achievement. Tad was incredible; he gave every ounce of energy to these young adults as if they were his own children. He wore every hat imaginable and was the catalyst that would change several lives when they wanted to depart the training. Still today he gets e-mails of gratitude for what he did for many of them. He loved his work and was so humble, I couldn't be any prouder.

While we were out in Great Lakes, we both felt a significant healing from the experience of the ectopic pregnancy. However, it wouldn't be long before we found out we were again pregnant. I was so excited and didn't waste much time on worrying. Each day I would practically marry my hand to my belly, willing this baby to grow. Each day I felt so blessed as a baby really was the only missing piece of the puzzle. It would be later that I learned there were so many puzzle pieces, just not put together.

After six weeks I had an ultrasound, which revealed that the fetus was in fact exactly where it needed to be. Tad and I were over the moon. But it was only a few weeks later that I noticed some bleeding. I called our doctor and he said a certain level of bleeding is normal during pregnancy, so I was relieved.

That night Tad and I drove to the city to hear the music of Gary Allan, Leanne Rhymes, Keith Urban, and Kenny Chesney. We had amazing third-row seats and the music excited our souls, a space that reflected a pure knowing that seemed to mimic on some level of enlightenment. It was a space without worry, filled with pure love and trust. If we were in this space all the time, we would never suffer or question the challenges we face, we would just understand it as a lesson of evolution.

The next morning Tad headed to work, and I just didn't feel right. Throughout the day the bleeding got heavier, and I just knew something wasn't right. I called my friend Lynsey and asked if she could take me to the ER.

Lynsey and Joe have known Tad for years when they served overseas in the navy. Throughout their career they developed a very strong connection as "family." When they all were stationed in Naples, Italy, they started a tradition they called "Friday night festivities." It was a celebration of life and of God, pure fun. If I wasn't there they would set a place for me at the table and put the computer down so we could Skype throughout dinner. It was really a fun experience and made this time of separation much easier.

When I called, Lynsey picked up the phone and immediately heard the terror in my voice. She dropped everything she was doing and came to pick me up. We headed to the urgent-care center where we were meeting Tad to hear the news we all were wishing we wouldn't: I was having a miscarriage. We all cried together over another loss.

After a few weeks I realized Tad and I were pretty disconnected. We were like two ships passing in the night, focusing on our daily lives as not to disturb our broken hearts. Then finally it came to a halt after a few misguided statements. We both fell into each other with tears streaming down our faces. It was a loss, and we finally acknowledged what we feared the most: we might never be parents.

We spent the night together just holding each other, apologizing for how silly we had both been, and then through slow comments we began to talk about our situation. We concluded that we would have to trust God. I asked for one more try, and he was skeptical because each time it was so painful. However, he agreed. We decided that after the "third time is the charm," we would begin gathering information on adoption. This was a very special night as we came together as one, a united front.

My follow-up appointment was the next day, and the doctor told us that due to only having one fallopian tube, we only had a 1 percent chance of having a spontaneous pregnancy. It was difficult to hear again, but it was information we had already processed, which left us in the arms of adoption. However, I wanted to try one more time. I knew the statistics, but I didn't care. I was ready to surrender, and if we were meant to adopt, then that would be the way it would go.

Tad and I were quick to make a vision board to call a baby to our life. Whether I carried the baby or the baby came from another mother, it didn't matter. Either way, the child was coming from God to our hearts, and that was all that mattered. We wanted to share our love and build a family unit of love.

Another month passed and it was so fun to listen to how happy Elise and James were with all the experiences of first time pregnancy. I knew Elise would be an amazing mother, and I felt such joy in my heart for her and James.

Within that same week I got my menstrual cycle. I went downstairs with a beer in hand to tell Tad as we watched the remaining Sunday football games.

Tad was my light, reminding me that whichever way we have children is God's plan, and we needed to hold true to that in our hearts. It was such great advice to get me out of my pity party moment. I could always look to Tad to see the most positive side of any situation. He is a great husband, and that is yet another blessing in my life.

Oddly enough, the next day my period stopped. I thought that to be extremely weird but didn't put too much thought into it. As the days passed I thought, *Wow, I have never had a one-day cycle in my life; what's going on here?* I called the doctor to explore the possibility of a cyst, and considering my history he asked me to come into the office for some tests.

That Thursday morning I got the news of my life. I was pregnant!

It was very early, but I was four weeks' pregnant, and so far all looked good. I had to wait another two weeks before I could get an ultrasound, assuring the baby made it down to my uterus. However, patience was on my side, and what seemed like an eternity turned into the most amazing day of my life!

I remember running outside with my ultrasound pictures in hand yelling, "I'm pregnant." When I told Tad, he held me in his arms for what seemed like hours. We both couldn't believe it—it was truly a miracle.

We decided we were going to hold off telling anyone until eight weeks, but because I was showing at six weeks and people were starting to ask, I had to let the cat out of the bag. I shared the news with almost everyone; however as it is such fun news to share I wanted to surprise everyone I could. The next day I called Elise and asked her to meet me at our favorite Thai restaurant. After we ordered, we began talking about her pregnancy. She was glowing and just so excited about how their life was about to change. I smiled, thinking how much both our lives were going to change and that we were going to go through this sacred journey together.

She was sharing news about her most recent appointment, and I asked when she was due. She told me, "Around the second week of May."

Well, I said that was great because it looked like we would be delivering around the same time.

We just kept talking and then it hit her: "*What did you say?*," elevating her voice to a roar, and everyone in this very small space was looking at us.

I said, *"I'm pregnant."*

We hugged and laughed, dancing for joy for the road that lay ahead. It was a very special moment, which would mark the many more experiences to come.

We had our babies within two weeks of each other and each had our own experience based on our needs. In addition, my friend Hannah had her third baby the first week of May, so we were moms in the making with a threesome of babies.

Coming full circle, you can see the importance of oneness in friendships, in families, and with strangers. We are all here to learn from one another, but as we awaken we need to keep ourselves physically and spiritually healthy. Surrounding us with those that see the importance of love being the bottom line in this game of life.

Sawyer is a miracle! This was a period that marked my trust in God. Just when they statistically said it was near impossible, God blessed us with a baby. This was really the first time I ever fully surrendered and trusted God's guidance. It has taken many lessons to engrain this into my heart as I still find myself pondering on decisions that take me away from surrender.

The lessons that unfold while you are on your personal journey of evolution are amazing. With the many writings that have graced the walls of every library in the world, we see before our eyes the trip to enlightenment of those before us. We hear with each work, each experience, ideas, and tools that will help us wipe away the fear and negative emotions while opening our heart and soul to love.

This is one of those stories—a poem where the author is unknown but not forgotten:

> One tree can start a forest;
> One smile can lift a soul.
> One candle can erase darkness,
> One laugh can conquer gloom.
> One hope can raise your spirits,
> One touch can show your heart.
> One life can make a difference,
> Be that *one* today.

CHAPTER 9
A WAITING GAME

NOVEMBER 4, 2011

Each day of the first week, treatment was so anticlimactic. It was over in most cases in fewer than twenty minutes, and then the whole day was mine. I would talk with the nurses and read, but one of the greatest things on my mind was watching my white cells drop.

Yes, of course I had a chart. I envisioned my white cells dropping lovingly to zero, the Loveolution heading right into God's hands, and then going back up strong with intent. I pictured each cell filled with beautiful light, serving my body as a guard and light worker in defense of any attackers.

Every so often I would wonder why my body had turned on itself—but had it? Or was that a reflection of my mind? The medical community has no idea where leukemia comes from, how it starts, or why some respond better than others. Why do mostly children become inflicted with this dis-ease? So many questions supported by very little information. It is important to move past the whys and go to the hows. How am I going to get well? Answer: I am well!

I believe I am already well and whole as I represent God's reflection and plan. To hold this thought against such strong physical suggestions can be difficult. Again, fear takes the main role and directs the play.

I'd always held this thought. I was specific and stern to request that physicians discuss options on how I would get better, never discussing and planting seeds for the symptoms. Although this seemed a difficult request it was always respected, which made conversations easier for me to embrace. However, probably a lot more thought went into how they would approach me with medical recommendations. One of the nurses told me they wrote my wishes in my chart, but I think they just had a secret symbol for difficult patient on the door. Whether it was that suggestion or my beliefs, I breezed through chemo. I was in remission in two weeks, which took us right up to Thanksgiving. Of course they would not give me full word until I had my fourth bone-marrow biopsy, but I knew in my heart my cells were following the light of my soul.

The following days were filled with much excitement as two friends from Chicago were flying in to be a part of the Loveolution. Wendy and Colleen were already in the air as I checked the clock every ten minutes; needless to say I was excited about their visit.

My family was amazing, but I missed my friends. I thought my best friend, Emily, would be around more, but after her first visit I didn't hear from her for quite sometime. We all deal with challenges differently, and I truly respect that each individual will fill you up how he or she can when you need it. This was the first time I truly respected putting myself first, as I had no space to worry about how someone else would handle my circumstances.

I finally fell asleep for a minute until I heard, "You have visitors." Seeing Wendy and Colleen's familiar faces was so refreshing. I felt their love coursing through every cell in my body. Their energy was filled with great excitement, and we had lots to share and much catching up to do. Colleen was most grateful that the trip was smooth. as her fear of flying, like any fear, tried to steal the very essence of joy and love she was trying to create.

Behind the love in their eyes I saw a small amount of surprise, as it was difficult to see one you love change so much in so short a period. I comforted them with my heart and through my eyes. Both received this secret code and understood all was well.

They walked through the door and can probably still feel the strength of my embrace back in Chicago today. There was an immediate sense of comfort and the sharing of love. There was much to celebrate and much to get caught up on since two weeks is a long time in the life of a single yoga teacher and healer.

We spent the night laughing away, and it seemed not a moment had passed since we last saw each other. We were still three silly girls laughing about the trials and tribulations of each other's lives.

We were always trying to set Wendy up with every opportunity that presented. In this case it was one of my doctors. My friends were asked to leave the room as to encase a "sterile field" for Dr. Slater to put in a PICC (peripherally inserted central catheter) line. During his time in my room I told him all about Wendy, and his assistant and I egged him on to find the courage to ask her out.

I believe Wendy was some type of Lady Grace in a previous life, and some of that energy has carried over to this life. She has a secret in her eyes that is magical and drops most men to their knees. However, in the same sentence, with the wrong partner this can go terribly wrong. I have witnessed some of her partners take advantage of her kind heart and beautiful sense of adventure in life.

After an hour of discussion he was definitely interested. As he walked out of my room, my friends greeted him. I watched carefully as he locked eyes with Wendy and immediately turned into a twelve-year-old boy, not sure what step to take. He looked down at his pager, his security blanket, pretending to have work to avoid his sense of adult shyness. It wasn't meant to be, but we did spend the next hour looking up his credentials on Google and looking him up in the hospital directory. Ah, girls, it doesn't get old. I suspect our next act may have been prank calls.

We spent the next hours talking about what I had missed over the past few weeks. I was surprised how much went on while I was tasked in my little room. They both lifted my spirits high into the sky as I saw the truth (an evolution of enlightenment), in their eyes that they believed I was well.

Next on the agenda was some healing. Colleen prepared to do body work, while Wendy caught me up with the Chicago yoga community and her recent experiences. She shared with me her dreams of teaching and what directions she hoped to travel in her life. All of us are passionately connected to yoga as it has changed many to be greater, kinder, stronger, and understanding of love and forgiveness.

Colleen and Wendy are both beautiful women on the inside and outside, shining with such nurturing love and healing energy. Colleen has many great gifts, and she has this ability of speaking her mind in a very calculated way. Wendy is a little quieter, an observer, waiting for the exact time to share her opinion while intently listening in on conversation. In addition, she has a gift for teaching the practice of yoga, and for that Colleen and I will always be grateful.

She taught us to embrace the beauty inside ourselves as yoga teachers.

Of course the alignments, poses, and philosophy are extremely important, but if you don't know who you really are, then you are just going to copy a teaching style, which defeats the whole purpose of leading and awakening.

Colleen also has many gifts, gifts that embody great intuition and a craft for physical bodywork. She began doing some bodywork the first day she arrived at the hospital, starting with reflexology, and the experience left me in shock as I felt my body zinging all over the place. From the very first moment, after the shock of such disheartening news, Colleen knew on several levels that this was my journey of awakening. She knew I was going to be well but that it may not always be an easy road. There couldn't be any more truth to that statement!

Colleen possesses an overall psychic sense and wisdom that is representative of an old soul. We have talked many hours about the challenges that build our spirit and soften the ego. We have shared the importance of each and every experience, which aids in the awakening of every spirit. The important purpose may be one moment in time, it may be a role, and it may be a spoken sentence that changes the path in an instance. Whatever the experience, it may affect so many people around you, like a sound wave, spreading itself across the universe.

It is stated in the Bible that holding an intention of wellness is how Jesus healed. Colleen and Wendy both are healers and their presence was reassuring, filling my space with significant amounts of comfort. It was indeed an epic weekend.

As I thought about how much fun I was having, something triggered a string of thoughts that took me back to my old home in Chicago, again realizing how quickly I left the east coast for Chicago five years earlier.

I will never forget that morning as my mom lay in bed while the sun still slept, and she thought about her daughter getting on a plane to move halfway across the country. It was a difficult good-bye for both of us.

My dad drove me to the airport, and I felt tears stirring the whole trip. I love my family so much and am so blessed to have my mom and dad, who have always support me on all my endeavors.

In addition, there is a connection between a mother and daughter or mother and son, which is like no relationship we know. My mom is my home, my answers, and my script. Now I was going to explore and meet the naked version of me, a blank piece of paper. I knew working in the pharmaceutical industry for as long as I did and in the many capacities I experienced was not my life purpose. I knew that this move to Chicago, which I thought was a state at first, was an opportunity to explore my inner soul on many levels. The biggest lesson I learned before we even got settled into our rental home was that your baggage comes with you, literally and figuratively. I got my chance at a clean slate and began taking as much time as necessary to clear out all old baggage.

It was so liberating as I could feel emotionally and see physically what was truly a part of me and what was not. It was like a spiritual spring-cleaning that led to a feeling of freedom and strong sense of being alive. However, you can only clean what you are really willing to see, so this was a juncture to see my soul in its purest form, to see my truth completely without judgment. It felt amazing, and I recognized that I was not all that different from what I thought was my truth. I did recognize the many mistakes that I had never given the forgiveness they deserved. It was time to surrender and let go.

This got me thinking about home. Home is always in your heart space, so no matter where you are physically, you are always home. The trick becomes who is surrounding you in your physical space. If true friends surround you, and there are no expectations or labels, then all is good. If you are surrounded by people who didn't get the memo that you have changed and are working toward awakening, then you can feel stuck.

This thought took me to the yoga community, and it reminded me of the word "kula," so I wrote that night, when Wendy and Colleen left for their hotel, in hollysloveolution@wordpress. Their visit provided an inspiration of thoughts:

Kula

*

The Sanskrit word *kula* refers to a community of the heart, where a group comes together of its own free will to intentionally support the union between power and consciousness. The union supports each individual in love and lifts up the idea of oneness. Learning becomes the internal bond between the space and those who occupy it; the love synergy keeps such a woven lock of support and confidence. To be part of a space like this is simply amazing. It may happen in your neighborhood, in communities from coast to coast, but the one common bond, even in the differences that each space may share, is that it is protected and sacred, filled with love.

This space becomes an opportunity to share your vulnerabilities, fears, and desires without needing to have reinforcements from your ego. It is just trusted that the energy of the space will support this journey for you to soften your ego and reunite with your true self in spirit.

I am extremely blessed to have found a kula in the Yoga Effect Studio. It is a space that has much love, many ideas, and words spoken just through a glance. It is an external space that warms the transition to your internal ideals for healing and love. Anna, who embodied this vision, started the studio just about a year ago. This sacred space now just continues to evolve in the direction that it needs to in order to support the community.

Sitting here in Boston, I meditate upon the energy of teaching classes and the joy of students as we all come together to learn from one another. Teacher and student is the title, but the learning has no boundaries. As I continue to heal I am beginning to broaden and identify other "kulas" that exist for me in life.

My family kula is one that goes beyond words. Coming from a very large family, it is amazing to think of all the blessings each member brings to light. Family can certainly take on many meanings, as we all know there is not one that is perfect. However, it is the uniqueness that we offer and tolerate, bridging the gap to love that is the lesson of oneness as the described above "kula." No matter how we see each other and what we may believe best for each other, love is always the driving factor within a family.

Family is a word that has always had conditions, but when you open your eyes you realize family is simply the people who love you unconditionally. Understanding that these "people," when the label has been cast aside, are no longer defined; they can be friends, teachers, or strangers. They love you for your journey, your faults, your lessons; it is put to the test time and time again.

It is when we let go of the idea of perfection and all the annoyances (which are just mirror effects to begin with anyway) we sometimes set the trap for ourselves and then we break through to love. We support each other the way we know how, and with a string of love we connect to one another, weaving the ring of the family circle.

Over time, as we pull the veil down one layer at a time, the circle will continue to extend through trust and love and will abolish judgment. We will learn, when we are ready, to overcome disappointments, love, and deep forgiveness.

Wendy and Colleen spent the next few days doting over me with bodywork, love, and much laughter. Every time a nurse came in she asked if she could have a treatment since my room smelled like a spa with the most beautiful essential oils and aromas.

It was a difficult good-bye, although I knew I would see them again soon. They would visit when I got home from the hospital and was ready, and I would visit them in Chicago. They were always in my heart and alongside phone calls and e-mails, and we always picked up right where we left off as if there was never a pause.

*

Exercise: See where you fit into your community? How strong is your Kula? What can you do to let go of insecurity to connect to your Kula?

That night before I went to bed I got a beautiful e-mail from Wendy. It is a beautiful prayer that has brought comfort to me daily:

Daily Prayer

May today you have peace within.
May you trust in God that you are exactly where you are meant to be.
May I never forget the infinite possibilities that are born in faith.

May I use the gifts I have received and pass on the love that has been given to me.
May I be content knowing I am a child of God.
Let this presence settle into your bones and allow your soul the freedom to sing, dance, praise, and love.

It is friends like Wendy and Colleen who have made this journey what it is. The list goes long as there are so many who have been a spoke in the wheel of my life. It is today and every day that I want you to know how much you mean to me. You all know who you are. Thank you and much love always.

CHAPTER 10
EXPECTATIONS OF THE HEART

NOVEMBER 8, 2011

It is not always easy to understand why we all have so many expectations of others and of ourselves. Judgment and its expression has continually been a difficult concept to embrace since the dawn of time. Judgment being the opposite of love is one of the many tools the ego uses to keep us under control, locked in the handcuffs of suffering. However, during this experience I have learned that judgment and expectation are two words we interlace daily, regardless of whether we take note of it.

Expectations and judgment hide behind the very core of our ego, striking when our hearts least expect. Even with consciousness of judgment, it still slides into many conversations that seem too tempting not to add our opinion. It is not necessarily a bad thing to have expectations and/or observations, but it depends on the circumstances. Unfortunately, what becomes the common mistake is that judgment begins to play a large role in our expectation, which can easily become a regular practice.

We experience all kinds of expectations. In fact, we experience expectations and judgment before we are even born, starting with our birth passage. As the angelic awakening continues opening the hearts of birthing mothers to the innate process within each birth, many moms fight this natural adventure, mostly due to fear and judgment.

Birth can create many emotions before, during, and after. These emotions can wreak havoc on a mom who had a difficult birth experience because of unnecessary interventions or just a difficult birth process. I was recently told of a mom who was in active labor for a whole weekend. As the birth community rallied for the midwives who attended to this mom, she inevitably ended up in the ER with a necessary C-section. Why did this mom, so passionate to have a home birth, have this experience? One may never know, but I am sure old emotion and fear played a large role. I believe this mom marked the face of courage, and it was this strength that became a platform for inspiration. It strikes the heart of many other moms and dads to start asking questions and take back their rights to birth the way they want.

As a doula, I have watched moms give birth in the hospital, in tubs, and in the comfort of their own home. It is a beautiful and natural process wherever the mom feels connected and comfortable. However, there are many people who do not agree with this choice, and because of their experience, consider it wrong. It is amazing when discussing birth with a group of woman of varying ages what surfaces. Women who were subjected to twilight birth, which is a type of birth when the mom is sedated and the doctor just palpated the baby down and finally pulled him or her out. The mom has no recollection of this birth experience and as fathers were not yet allowed into the rooms all they heard were the screams. We could write a whole book about birth experiences from this period of time, but it just clearly makes us understand that we have to take back our right to an innate birth that is healthy on mind, body, and soul.

Ricki Lake, in the documentary *The Business of Being Born*, has brought to light the history of birth and why medical interventions have trended to extremely high statistics in C-section rates. Her research, along with significant statistics relating to births, started a movement for birthing moms to advocate for their birth experience. Many moms have reconnected with their primal desire to have a more natural birth experience. This comes from an understanding that the birth process will leave imprints on the rest of your life; therefore, it is important to be well informed without judgment and/or fear. There is a plethora of books that focus on birth options, risks, and benefits, which truly prepare you for a connected birth instead of a birth directed by fear.

Birth is yet another area in life that is exploding at the seams because women are waking. Just through stepping back in history we can see where things went wrong and how many births emotionally scarred woman for generations. Now women are taking back their birthright, which is a gift.

There are many women who have been called to pave the way to reconnect women to conscious births. One of the most amazing is Ina May Gaskin. Her story is fascinating and brings forth the divine works of Mother Nature.

Ina May, along with a small group of free thinkers, started a commune called the farm, which settled in Summertown, Tennessee. They lived without the influences of the outside world, grew their own food, built their own homes, and delivered their own babies. To me this goes beyond critical thinking; this is a group of individuals who were not hippies, but were so connected to nature and source that they just allowed their intuition to guide them.

With each birth they learned from the point of conception the importance of nurture and nature, not one versus the other. They gained techniques, as each birth was unique, requiring different skills. As each baby entered the world, "The Farm" grew with such a connection that it caused quite a stir. Women outside the commune began asking questions, an innate fire to understand what was lost and how to become once again connected.

Birth can be looked at as a rite of passage and is constantly being judged as right or wrong. We have been given so much misinformation regarding the birth process that we no longer have the correct information to make good choices for our families and ourselves.

Why am I capturing the essence of a conscious birth? This book is about the very challenges that wake us up to our personal truth during our life evolution, experiences that lead us to discover our internal flare, which will imprint a happier, healthier life, a life without suffering. Ina May is one of the many greats who pioneered our return to conscious birthing—birth mimicking a moment of spiritual evolution that in one instance can change your life.

Today obstetrics and gynecology are plagued with the same issues as every other specialty. They are trained clinicians who focus on just one function of the body. As we watch birth statistics trend the wrong way, we look to places like The Farm and have to ask why their statistics are significantly different.

I believe each family should make a decision about birth based on research, intuition, and comfort. It should not be about a political stand, or your ego. It should encompass the understanding that birth is a very important moment in the life of a child and its mother and father. It should be as conscious as possible, supported by accurate information that will leave you filled with inspiration, not regret.

How we make this decision is like any other we make in life; we have to research and listen to our God mind. This is partially based on where we are in our evolution, what knowledge we have, and how society has impacted each of us personally with the fear surrounding birth.

It is a journey, one that we create with God as our leader. I have met many moms who had a hospital birth, followed by a home birth. Each experience was different but evolving with such love that fear was pushed underground.

We know that, as in life, we can't control every factor that goes along with the birth process. However, we can envision our birth, be present during our pregnancy, and be connected during birth.

Working with moms during pregnancy as a birth educator and as a prenatal yoga teacher, I get the chance to learn and witness moms evolve toward a connected birth experience. This is so beautiful, as it is one of nature's greatest gifts. With each baby born unto this earth, we realize that we "Let go and let God!"

CHAPTER 11
CHOICES

NOVEMBER 11, 2011

With any type of revolution or Loveolution, people tend to get very involved and share their opinion about everything. Most often this is done with good intentions, but it is based on a perspective, one that is based on where we are in life. A great example of this would be a simple flashlight. Some of us are in a space with just a tiny penlight, so the view is limited, but there is still a light. Some have a regular-size flashlight, which offers a greater view, and then some of us are blessed with the greatest view of all—there is no need for a flashlight because all the lights are shining bright. It all just depends on where we are in our evolution, where we are with our life experience, and how open we are to learn. We only evolve when we are ready and willing to open our mind and our hearts to new experiences; the next level. I do not think the writers of *The Matrix* were very far off from this spiritual belief.

When I first shared my choice of treatment, there were many strong reactions all over the board. Many understood that dis-ease is far beyond just a physical affliction. It is spiritual, an opportunity to evolve, which is why I have referred to it as a gift.

I completely entrusted God with my heart when trying to have children. However, I was in a different space when this challenge came my way. I was in shock, and even though I thought I worked through a great many of my fears, there was a significant amount when it came to mortality. Trusting in the face of death, the what-if, the idea of it encompasses a great visceral reaction for most everyone.

I researched with every free moment, I leaned on so many naturopaths, and the answer was the same: allopathic treatment was the right direction for this particular situation. It was such a difficult choice, and one that needed to be made quickly. I felt there were two paths opening up for me, and I had to take the one that I was ready to take at the speed I was ready to embrace. After I made my choice I was in a good place to share it.

Reaction is a funny thing, and we do not always have as much control as we may like when it comes to our words. There are moments in life that take us so much by surprise that our filter just seems to shut down.

Some of the reactions were the opposite of supportive, but I understood that as I was shocked, others too had a difficult time with this news. One individual actually said, "Wow, I can't believe you're getting this treatment; I would have thought you would have gone down fighting with natural medicine." I would never fight with any medicine. What is missing here is the respect of choice and truth without judgment.

I believe in naturopathy in conjunction with Western medicine. I have always said if west would meet east, we would have a masterpiece of health. I made a choice based on research, trust, and my gut. I am so grateful to Dana-Farber and the doctors who treated me like a person instead of a patient. However, we established expectations together. I asked that they not discuss symptoms with me, as I believe the physical suggestion can be much greater a trigger than the actual medication itself. They agreed. I had two side effects during my treatment.

The doctors respected my requests and I respected their knowledge and experience. They explained to me why from their perspective this treatment was the optimal choice. I learned on my own why natural medicine would not have had such success in this case. This was not a matter of "my way or the highway," it was a matter of a specific situation. There is truth in "Gray Street," which affects many cases, as it is not black and white. These cases soon become the matter of finding the best match and making space for your body to heal.

There are thousands of cancers that have been healed naturally, but many people do not want to believe this truth because that would not fit into their box, making their belief wrong. It doesn't have to be right or wrong, and we need to move away from this kind of thinking toward a more loving, open thinking.

This is an opportunity where we can respect each other's choices and at the same time offer education in the light of spirit instead of the guise of ego.

We have all experienced a situation where another has judged us because of our choices. It happens daily until you let go and know you are making the best choices you can out of love and truth. It is at this time that you will no longer have concern when you are judged, and people will just judge you behind your back. I laugh as I write this because it is the truth. This truth goes beyond thick skin—it is about letting go, which opens the path to a life of great freedom, which releases suffering.

We need to learn how to live our lives as strong in love as we can. What others believe we should do is simply what you will allow into your space. This is an important lesson, as intuitively you begin to feel when you are being judged or when someone is giving you loving guidance. What is that saying about opinions? Yes, the infamous saying about opinions—everyone has one! This is true, but God will speak through others when you are clouded. This wisdom feels like adoration floating over a cloud-covered sky and cannot be mistaken for the grit and hardness of the ego.

I am not sure how many times I will share my gratitude for this gift because I have learned so much, and as I continue on this journey I become all the wiser with each experience. I have learned to listen, and, when guided intuitively, when to share words. I have been grateful for the difficulties and challenges I have faced as they have turned into healing. However, through these times, love kept me grounded. It is that simple.

I believe you need to have great respect for anyone who makes a choice for treatment of any kind. I have spoke with many who have questioned the entirety of their diagnosis. As I can understand, my showing up with not one symptom of leukemia, only a smear of cells, told a different story.

We need to support each other to the best of our ability during a time of challenge. We need to offer a hand of love instead of a furry of your personal facts and opinions about what you would do.

Currently I am in the process of physically rebuilding my immune system naturally and cleaning my body up from the toxins that I was exposed to during treatment. This again creates an internal conflict of interest for me, as I know in my heart that I am a reflection of God, so there is nothing to clean up. Therefore, this clues me in to understand at this part of my journey (although I believe the soul is perfection), there is still a missing piece to my puzzle. With patience, dedication, and continued life lessons the lights will get bigger and bigger until they are all the way on.

I do my best each day to have continued patience and kindness while I learn and evolve. Like the flip of a switch it may happen when I least expect it, but I believe eternal freedom from the mortal mind/ego will be my next gift.

Through these words you can see how expectations and judgments can easily cause significant harm emotionally. I used birth as an example, as it is one of many great experiences in life that we cannot control and parallels so many spiritual ideals. It takes many moms out of their comfort zone, forcing a spiritual experience even if it wasn't expected. Let's just acknowledge that even though it is something that happens every day, it is a miracle. Every day miracles occur. Some may go unnoticed and some may be celebrated, but either way miracles are a gift of evolution. Miracles are one of the many experiences that signal the wake-up call. It is time to dissolve self-created myths and lead willfully with your choices. There is no reason to be judged for anything. Who cares what society defines as success or if you follow the rules? Dare to be different and find comfort in that difference. The most important thing is that you are here to learn and evolve into a loving being connecting to others as one.

On a slightly different note regarding self-judgment, I sat in bed meditating on expectation as I wondered what my husband and son would think about my now bald head. It was definitely expected, and we prepared Sawyer as best we could. Now I would put into practice the experience of letting go and embracing God.

When Tad sent the text alerting me they had arrived, I immediately felt the anxiety building in every cell in my body. Again, over and over, the thoughts rang through. What would they think? Would Sawyer be scared? Would Tad think I was not as attractive anymore?

Of course they would be fine. I knew this in my soul, but that voice in my head had other plans. I once read an article in *Yoga Journal* about a woman who got breast cancer and her husband gently walked out the back door. I get it, I saw it, it's difficult, but I could never imagine leaving Tad at his most difficult life moment. That is the hand fasting commitment that we made to each other, to love without condition. Quickly I realized it was my reflection creating this fear, and it was a game changer.

That night I was tired but so happy to have had such a fun day filled with love and joy. Sawyer and Tad both love with reckless abandon and both see my heart and beauty. Tad even thought I was sexy bald.

As I settled into a gentle breath, I reflected on the day. Calmly and with spiritual guidance, I wrote in hollysloveolution@wordpress.com:

> "Strength shows not only the ability to persist but the ability to start fresh" (Celebration of Freedom).

*

Today was a great day! Two of the greatest men in my life, Sawyer and Tad, came to visit me for the first time together. Sawyer had not been up to the hospital yet to visit. I had much concern about the physical suggestion of illness and how he would be impacted by the whole experience. How would he see his mommy in her new environment? A little boy with so much energy, how would he feel about the fact that his mom could only play in a very small room? These were questions that were rolling through my head as Jennifer, the day nurse, helped me complete my head shave.

Once I noticed it coming out far too fast, I thought it would be fun to do a traditional "Joan of Arc" haircut. So I took to my hair with a pair of scissors, and you would have thought I was actually a trained hair stylist. Well, that was probably just what I thought, and I'm sure there would have been a lot of painful looks walking out of a salon.

At the time it was so freeing just to use my hair as a canvas, getting to create without any fear of the outcome. I knew the shave was coming next, so this was just a middle step for fun. And fun it was, as I continued to angle and shape each cut to be free from the next, there was no direction, just pure fun and adventure.

When the adventure was over, I have to say it was cute. I could pull off the ultimate short hairdo. So what had ever stopped me before from having such a super short fun haircut? Answer: expectation. It isn't so much about the haircut as it is what the haircut symbolizes.

We begin early in life to create and cultivate what I call "the wall." Actually, it starts from the moment we are born. All the people in our life write on these invisible walls, imprinting and leaving their energy mark on best practices of living. I must say these imprints mostly come from love and best intention, but they are simply opinions; we know everyone has one. We should embrace and admire these intentions from others as it soon will be our time to landscape. This becomes the realization that, in our adulthood, we need to begin construction to our walls. Breaking down the wall only to leave the love becomes important in creating freedom. This freedom allows us to maneuver into new territory that will gel and support radiant experiences without holding us back. All this from a haircut! Seriously!

Later that morning was the head shave. I didn't think it would be that big a deal. I had already cut my long hair off with no attachment whatsoever; I did the Joan cut, and then the chop block. But the emotions that streamed from my heart as I watched the final stage of my hair fall to the floor, piece by piece, was beyond my anticipation. It was almost as if I was silently crying for each piece, as this was a rebirth in so many directions.

The first look in the mirror was hard; I "thought" it classified me as "being sick." It was the first time I felt forced to share my journey without having space to hide, leaving every last insecurity open to air. However, the struggle was that I am *well* and wanted people to hold that image of highest divinity for me, as I needed to do for myself.

I too have been filled with empathy and sympathy when I see people externally showing a challenge. This is so subconscious and deeply ingrained within us that it really takes conscious effort to change. Again, this sense of pity comes from love but does not offer much positivity on the receiving end. Sympathy and empathy certainly should be something we feel because it connects us with our human oneness of caring, but then it must shift to empowerment. This person's life will never be the same, and it is a great blessing that will shift the shape of his or her wall.

We have all had internal struggles, and depending on what they are, the outside world may or may not ever have known. Think of what an impact this struggle made on your life, and then imagine if you shared it fully. Maybe it would be scary or freeing but nonetheless empowering because of the support and love that would help you in your moments of weak thoughts. This was just confirmed for me as the day continued.

Sawyer and Tad arrived at Brigham and Women's by two. The light in Sawyer's eyes when he saw his mommy was compared to that first glance we shared at birth. The love is just bound so deep that it has its own language. However, what happened next was unexpected. I took off my little beanie hat to show Sawyer my new haircut, and he thought it was the funniest thing he had ever seen. He was laughing and rubbing it like the Blarney Stone. He just thought it was awesome.

All the worries and concerns were for naught because in that moment I learned a lesson that I hope I learn every day, for the rest of my life: Sawyer only saw my heart. He didn't see a haircut or cool mommy clothes (or bad ones, LOL). He didn't see the things we plan or teach him to better his life. He just saw the love in my heart that grows every day for him, the familiar love that he kisses and hugs each night.

Through the eyes of a two-year-old, life is love, which is the emotion that molds them during their young life. As each child begins to grow, there are more people participating in the shaping of the wall and impacting it in so many ways. Don't get me wrong. I subscribe to the village, but the village needs to have the same foundation: *love*.

As we grow into our adulthood, our walls get bigger and stronger; much more is written, oftentimes too much more. The dry-erase marker doesn't work as well, and there are even some nails that have left deep marks.

However, just the awareness that we can choose the décor of our wall can be the jolt we need to make the choice to reconstruct and recreate, allowing a new sense of freedom and simple possibility, holding dear the experiences that have shaped us, but allowing for new molding as we can create any reality we want. Through awakening we learn to let go of the writings that are no longer serving us and make peace with allowing in new experiences.

What an amazing day of love and lessons. The day was a big milestone in this adventure. In addition, the doctors stopped by while my family was there and shared how happy they were with all the great progress I had made. Little did they know I was working hard, each day a strenuous drill, to overcome fear and reside in fearless faith. This becomes the act of going beyond awareness of our greatest fear and overcoming it.

As I was going through my daily challenges, my thoughts like a ball in a ping-pong game, I realized once again the blessing that went far beyond my scope of experience. Behind the scenes my physician group was working hard to make sure they handled my care intricately and with great allegiance. Their dedication was so amazing. On this particular Sunday, Dr. Geo came in to check on me. It would only be a few more days before I went home.

That night I felt encased in love.

*

Exercise: I challenge you to wake one morning with the intention to write down every judgment you say out loud, and then two days later write every judgment seed that is planted that we choose not to release with spoken word. It is truly amazing when we see on paper how many thoughts of judgment we have in a day. However, with just an intention (*sankalpa*) and choice to release these judgmental thoughts we can rise above and see the love that is there for all of us.

CHAPTER 12
SIMPLE MATH

> Who would stand before a blackboard, and pray the principle of mathematics to solve the problem? The rule is already established, and it is our task to work out the solution. ~Mary Baker Eddy

NOVEMBER 14, 2011

Last night I stepped out of Brigham and Women's Hospital to take my first real breath of fresh air. Even with a mask on and the smell of the city, it was a very, very sweet breath.

Tad looked at me when we loaded up the car and said, "Are you ready to go home?" Words that never sounded so good.

We set off to head back home, driving through the beautiful city of Boston. People rushed to get on and off the T, and I wondered, as I looked at them, why they were rushing. Maybe they were rushing home from work to see their family, a date, a night with friends. It was amazing to wonder what was happening in someone else's life after you reflect upon your own. In addition, the energy any city creates is exciting and mysterious. We all have something exciting, and for me it was heading home to see my family and sleep in my own bed.

On the way home, Tad and I caught up on all kinds of things and just enjoyed being together. As I reached for his hand on the drive, I realized how much I missed his touch and that which I already knew—what an amazing man he is.

As we got closer to home I couldn't help but let a few scary thoughts creep into my mind. The last four days in the hospital were mentally tough and were a challenge on the ability to recognize doubts and fear; so again, last night was a challenge to keep those doubts and fears at bay.

A tool that I had been using regularly these past few days was to surrender all my thoughts to God. Not even process them, not try to figure them out; just completely let them go to God. It is a great tool, shared by my dear friend Hilary, which works almost always.

Last night was no different, but what was different was that in return I got a clear thought back almost immediately. This was already decided: I am well. I just let the thought flow through me because it felt so great. In this moment it was hard to believe I could ever think otherwise, but I was going to hold this space for as long as I could because it was truth.

Walking through the door to the most precious face and clapping hands, "Mommy is home!" was one of the best moments in my life. Sawyer is just such a love and made my homecoming the best.

Also, my parents made such space for our family and in doing made this a much easier time for us. They made so many arrangements that it felt like we were walking into the energy of "our home." Seeing them all together in the doorway was a picture so perfect it will luminate in my mind for many years to come.

After just a minute through the door, Sawyer proceeded to run around the house in about ten seconds to show me all the things I had missed as time has no concept, especially to a little boy (including bedtime). But last night was special, so we continued to enjoy each detailed session, never walking away from the moment.

After getting settled in, I made my way to my old bedroom. I lived in my parents' house for about a year after college, so it brought back so many memories of just starting out in life. Tad and my mom bought a new mattress and fresh sheets; I felt like I was sliding into the sweetest sleeping environment ever created and bound with nurture and love.

Sawyer was fast asleep in the other bedroom, where he and Tad would sleep together for the next year. Doctors prepared us for the transplant and recommended I have my own sleeping arrangements. This was fine as they were in the next room over, but in that moment I reflected on what a journey this was for Tad and Sawyer.

Tad just started a new job, and Sawyer left all his friends and loved ones behind at a moment's notice. I know how I felt, how the sadness seemed to drink me up—how did Sawyer feel? I didn't ask him, as there were bigger emotions to address when I got a little stronger. A conversation I would have with him alone so no one would be alarmed.

That night as all the lights were out and I was tightly covered in love, I thought about how this voyage came to be. The path of divinity laid out each step as a stone, making it as easy as a path to travel while looking at the scenery. My family and friends shared great love and support. The emotions I had worked through to this point unleashed a great deal from my past and all this in just six weeks. It was a lot to lay my head upon, but I soften my eyes and relaxed any tension in my face. I sent away any negative thoughts again for the third time that night and prayed.

My first morning home, Tad let me sleep in and get a little more adjusted to being back in Massachusetts. I felt good, but was moving quite a bit slower than my normal, which is probably for the better. I know this will make Colleen very happy as she is always trying to show me the way to serenity and calmness. She couldn't believe that even with treatment I continued to move way too fast all the time.

This time I was happy to heed her call. I spent a great deal of time reading. Some of the reading was books people sent out of love, some I had on my wish list, and then there were the books that I called work. *Science and Health* was one of those books that made you critically think about many concepts. I will offer a short and sweet summary of an amazing woman who changed and continues to change the lives of many.

Mary Baker Eddy wrote *Science and Health* in 1875. After healing herself from a very serious accident, she made an amazing discovery, Christian Science. This was based on her system of healing, and her commentary on the Scriptures. It is an amazing book, although it is what I would call slow, thoughtful reading because each chapter is filled to the brim with concepts and bright paths to light and healing.

This first morning home I was reading *Science and Health* and came across a paragraph that really made so much sense. After much thought, I wrote in hollysloveolution@wordpress.com about this profound quote:

Simple Math

*

"Who would stand before a blackboard and pray the principle of mathematics to solve the problem? The rule is already established, and it is our task to work out the solution."

It hit me like a ton of bricks; the problem is already solved: "I am well." It is up to me to show the solution.

This just explained and ironed out about thirty-five years of past challenges and life lessons. Knowing the problem is already solved gave me such comfort. I can make this really hard or I can just sit with the idea that the problem is already solved and feel gratitude that the solution is there whether I believe I know it or not. I am the image and likeness of God.

It was such a strange feeling to know something so strongly but not really have all the pieces put together. It was a blind belief knowing I was healed. All of the "proof" to support this was happening all around me, and I had a deep gut feeling that supported this beyond any physical essence.

I will not say it did not create a lot of confusion for me because I was living in two worlds, one where I knew the truth unequivocally and the other based on fear.

When I shared with a few close friends that I was not sure I ever had leukemia, they thought I was crazy. Maybe. However, when I woke that one special morning feeling a sense like I should go get my blood tested, it was an extremely fearful thought. I even doubted myself and asked Colleen as she entered the door to watch Sawyer if I should even go to the appointment.

It wasn't the usual intuition that one may have when he or she should take a different route home or want to call someone who has been on his or her mind all day. This thought was riddled in fear ... "What if something is wrong?" We know miracles exist, but are they miracles, or are they the God-given ability to heal ourselves, as some believe? There are a lot of answers surrounding this and a significant amount of research based on the laws of physics.

Gregg Braden has spent his life researching this paradigm of false limits. He used science and its many laws of physics to peel back the misunderstood layers to uncover many truths of the universe. In his book *The Spontaneous Healing of Belief*, he covers a significant amount of science, along with mind and bodywork, to prove the great boundaries we have placed on our healing ability. I too felt this as I questioned what was really happening.

I recently told a friend I'd had an understanding of how saying something like, "I am not sure I had ALL, based on a number of things," caused concern for many. However, when you begin to know the whole picture of what happened in the beginning and how this came to be, you too may question the exact thing that I did. This was not a plan of wishful thinking to avoid pain, it was something much deeper.

When asked if one believes in God, the answer is most always yes, but many of us have never seen God. However, we believe with every ounce of our being that God is love and truth. So may there be more?

CHAPTER 13
AFTERSHOCK

> God doesn't give you the people you want, he gives you the people you need, to help you, to hurt you, to leave you, to love you; to make you the person you were meant to be.
> ~Author Unknown

NOVEMBER 14, 2011

Relationships are such an interesting and amazing part of life. We foster all kinds of relationships, from our parents to our first boyfriends, girlfriends, teachers, family and more. Every relationship is so important in one's growth, including the evolution of relationships, such as learning how to be a better partner in a relationship, and this is just scratching the surface. This also means learning how to distance oneself from certain relationships with honesty and kindness.

Having the ability to identify which relationships best serve your life is important so you can clear your heart and listen to Spirit's guidance. This can be a difficult task because as it is important to discover relationships that serve you the best in your life, we discover those relationships by being in many relationships that do not serve us.

Most if not all relationships are built on a foundation of love. As we all have had relationships that ended differently than maybe we would have hoped, it is important not to get caught in the trap of control because you will be the one to suffer.

"If you love someone, set them free. If they come back they're yours; if they don't they never were" (Richard Bach). This saying has been around for a while, but it's still one of the most difficult to practice. It trails the very essence of freedom that many of us have forgotten. Many of us continue to attach to any relationship that makes us feel loved, grounded, and whole. However, we should be turning inward to connect to self-love, which will accomplish the same goal.

We are always changing and being challenged by the relationships in our life, especially friendships, because this relationship embodies many truths in life to be successful. With such a variety of friendships, over time, you learn how to honor and balance the relationships in your life.

One of my favorite yoga classes that I have ever taught turned to the sacred stage of life and relationships. This stage metaphorically shows us just how important it is to have balanced relationships in one's life. Just as I experienced the class the day I taught it, I invite you to embrace hollysloveolution@wordpress.com as I wrote my memory of such a great experience:

*

> I started the class with a deep breathing exercise as to allow everyone in a very gentle space of freedom. Once I felt a shift in the room, I then asked each yogi to envision a theater. This theater may be colossal, with grand curtains and gold stairways, or it may be simple and sophisticated. Either way, it was yours to be as creative and imaginative as you wished, designing a stage that would be a great depiction of your life, representing the intricate moments you relate to the most.
>
> As I could see the breathing slow and the faces soften, I read an anonymously written poem titled "Life Is a Theater."
>
> "Life is a theater, so invite your audiences carefully. Not everyone is spiritually healthy or mature enough to have a front row seat in our lives. There are some people in your life who need to be loved from a distance.
>
> "It's amazing what you can accomplish when you let go, or at least minimize your time with draining, negative, incompatible, not-going-anywhere relationships, friendships, fellowships and family!
>
> "Everyone cannot be in your front row.
>
> "Observe the relationships around you. Pay attention.

"Which ones lift and which ones lean?

"Which ones encourage and which ones discourage?

"Which ones are on a path of growth uphill and which ones are going downhill?

"When you leave certain people, do you feel better or feel worse?

"Which ones always have drama or don't really understand, know, and appreciate you?

"The more you seek quality, respect, growth, peace of mind, love and truth around you ... the easier it will become for you to decide who gets to sit in the front row and who should be moved to the balcony of your life.

"If you cannot change the people around you ... can change the people you are around!

"Remember that the people we hang with will have an impact on both our lives and our income. And so we must be careful to choose the people we hang out with, as well as the information with which we feed our minds.

"We should not share our dreams with negative people, nor feed our dreams with negative thoughts. It's your choice and your life. It's up to you who and what you let in."

As I read this poem, I saw tears sliding down people's faces. Breathing had become so still to make space for this wisdom.

While I went on teaching the class, I then read the poem again while they were going through asana yoga, but this time I added my hearts window.

I shared that I wished we could have the whole world in our front row, as this would be considered oneness. However, at that time in humanity our world was divided by the ego, by right and wrong, by Democrat or Republican—the list of boundaries and labels went on and on. There was such a strong divide that slid through so many areas of life that all we could do was offer love and forgiveness.

As we awaken we should make life simple by taking the path less traveled, which is the path that matches your heart regardless of what others think. You will be judged no matter what path you take. Love is the bottom line, and the more you feel warmth in your heart, the more you will understand that we are all doing the best we can. In this space you will learn to identify the right path the first time it comes around, instead of being presented with so many difficulties to press you to the other path.

We all need to listen strongly to the Source that guides us with understanding and acceptance that friends will always flow in and out of our lives. This includes the relationship you have with yourself, as you will continue to evolve, finding your place on the stage of the sacred theater.

Practicing this ideal is difficult since although some friendships have longevity, it doesn't mean you are evolving together. It would be perfect to believe we can always make it work, but sometimes it is meant to flow out of your life, which is a blessing on both ends.

*

There is another poem, author unknown, that I believe reflects the beauty of relationships. It is called "Reason, Season, or a Lifetime." I am not going to include this here, but the title pretty much opens the door to the reality of every relationship in your life.

While I believe this poem is quite accurate, we need to move past labeling and just allow relationships to take the role they are suppose to while they are in our life. I believe people come in and out of our life when they are divinely guided. Whether it is a chance meeting that left you with a thought that was life altering, or a lifetime friendship that continues to bring love. Either way, we need the wisdom to let the beauty of the friendship be free-flowing with light.

The Lifetime friendships is by far the most sacred of all relationships and evolve with time and heart. They are there in support through good times and bad, divorce, marriage, raising kids, moving, illness, and job changes— the list will go on; as life continues to change, so does the friendship. It has no bearing on how long you have been friends, nor does it keep track of what one has done for the other. A lifelong friendship is a gift.

However, what gets tricky is that there is not a map, which teaches you how and when it is time to lovingly move forward in life with or without a relationship. As a society, the acceptability of "white lies" has become more of a convenience to avoid making difficult choices. Think of how many times in life, had you been honest from the start, you would have avoided controversy and bad feelings. If you know your intention is of love that is all that matters, as you cannot control someone else's reaction or lack of reaction.

There is no question that relationships can be very difficult to manage, but when there is an external challenge it makes it even more difficult. Illness is somewhat different, and many don't know what to say or how to deal with this type of news, which is fine because in the moment I didn't either. Again, our culture doesn't exactly embrace the mortality road map, which teaches us how to deal with emotions that teeter on the line of death. It seems tools that correlate with death are avoided at all costs unless it becomes part of life's circumstances.

On the other side, for me, most people supported me with such love it was amazing. It was so fascinating to know how many people wanted to help and be there for me. Friends of friends sent me prayer gifts and support, and people texted all the time, which just represented how much love we have for another and how quick we are to connect to someone we barely know. This is all in the same breath as someone knowing you since childhood and deciding he or she cannot be part of your journey.

I have spoken with many people who have experienced a very difficult moment in life, which shifted their inner circle of friends. Usually this fostered a shocking loss of a close friend, or even "best friend." Getting such a shocking diagnosis will forever be the cornerstone that changed the course of my life; I will always refer to it as a gift that keeps on giving. It also has shifted those in my "front row," which now I see is a blessing, making room for more peace. It is these difficult experiences and decisions that help us grow.

As I stated previously, friendship is a sacred relationship that brings forward so many lessons of learning and sharing. A friendship isn't about who has been your friend the longest, it is about who came and never left your side. With each person I speak to that has a similar life challenge the common theme is that they see the reality of the relationships in their life. It is almost as if the truth can't be hidden.

I too experienced a very close friendship that ended when I got diagnosed. We were very close, supporting each other through life's difficult moments and embracing the celebratory experiences. We were godmothers to each other's children and often gave each other a great deal of guidance.

About a year before this journey started, she sent me a beautiful e-mail sharing how much she admired my strength and ability to love. She went on to share that I was like a sister to her and she felt so blessed to have our friendship. I mimicked her call and felt so blessed to have such an amazing friendship. In that moment I believed it was a lifelong friendship.

It would be months later, after I got home from the hospital, that I would realize some pretty difficult aspects about our friendship. She had been facing some tough life challenges for a couple of years. However, no matter who we are, we can't escape the soul growth that comes from experiencing life's challenges. In the big picture we can see these challenges are crucial, though in the moment this is much harder to embrace.

Once I got home from the hospital, it became clear she would not be able to offer support. In my heart this was such a shock. I would never have thought, but when I got weak so did the friendship. It is sometimes by accident that we learn compelling information that can change a relationship quickly. Regardless of the landscape of her life, as a true friend you would always have some level of support out of love for a true friend going through such a major life challenge.

After a process going from anger to understanding, I went back to what I knew: that we are all doing the best we can. I have learned that it is not our job to decide if the actions are good enough, it is our job to decide whether the actions are still serving us.

I thought long and hard about this specific chapter, as many have had this exact or similar experience. In fact, I think it would be safe to say that at one time or another we have all experienced some type of friendship ending. After a great deal of thought, I have realized that sharing the details of my friendship will not be the catalyst that offers healing or perspective for anyone else. Each circumstance is different—some are more hurtful than others—but in the end the most important factor is that you made or are making a decision in love to end a friendship that was not serving either of you. You opened your heart to set you both free and honor your truth; this is brave and courageous.

There is no doubt that good-byes are difficult, but I feel it is important with every relationship in life that it is never good-bye. Even though the relationship has ended, through freedom and love you may find friendship another day. It may just be a sweet hello, it may be a letter of support during a difficult time, or it may just be a memory; either way you need to celebrate the many memories and have compassion for such a brave decision. It is in these moments that we start on our path of evolution, journeying to the center of our soul.

With all that being said I will add one thing that may be an important facet to honoring your truth. In a decision regarding a relationship, we each have our own perspective as to how and why we arrived at a choice. A true friendship is one that honors all the elements of life: love, trust, forgiveness, kindness, and truth.

We have all had friendships that are not balanced; I call them the "vampire relationships." They are unhealthy for both parties and usually do not last long. These are the friendships for "a reason" and don't always have to end on a sour note but seemingly do. It is so important to forgive the situation and be grateful for the learning. Letting go is a big part of ending any type of relationship. No regrets, just lessons learned.

Honor all the relationships in your life as they are or should be a reflection of you and your heart.

*

Exercise: How do you know when it is time to give out new admission slips to your front row? Well it really isn't that easy, but there are for sure signs that help us see if a relationship is healthy or energetically draining.

Consider your feelings when after time spent with a friend. Ask yourself these questions:

1. Pay attention to the environment of the friendship. Is there a lot of belittling and do you find yourself feeling unsupported and/or defensive then there is an imbalance in this relationship. A true friend will offer honest advice, but this is after listening lovingly. It is a natural balance that cannot be learned.
2. Be wary of the friend that consistently gossips. This is a difficult area because gossiping and sharing information about another friend, how they are doing, any life changes, isn't gossip. We all know that gossip is the judgmental version of how we think that person should

be or live. Gossiping is a difficult thing to cut out of your life, even at the most innocent level, but once you make the choice to remove it from your life it feels so good. I want to clarify gossip is negative, ugly, and inside you know it is wrong. This is very different from catching up your circle of friends or a community you belong. Gossiping leaves you walking away feeling very bad, feeling like you got sucked in, so there is a very distinct difference. One last thing, if a friend gossips about someone else, be sure she or he will be gossiping about you.

3. Does spending time with your friend make you feel defensive or upset? Do you spend time justifying your own behavior around your friend instead of feeling excited to be together?
   Are you happy with this friendship or do you leave feeling energetically drained?
   Do you feel the friendship has a natural imbalance and feels more like work?
   Has your friend betrayed your confidences?
   Does your friend really listen to you and offer loving guidance, or is the response "I know because…
   Do you have the same core beliefs about parenting, spirituality, and can you disagree about a matter lovingly?

4. Finally, write down what in your heart is a balanced healthy relationship. What characteristics are important to you and what do you need from a friend. Just like any other relationship in life there is always effort that need to be maintained. With friendship the only thing that is truly holding it together is love.

CHAPTER 14
A DAY OF THANKS

> Tell me and I'll forget. Show me and I'll remember. Involve me and I'll understand. ~Confucius

NOVEMBER 16, 2011

In our family, we have a tradition of telling stories before we go to bed, when we are tired, or simply to ride on the tails of imagination. The most famous of all the stories is "Scratch, Itch, and Whatchamacalit." This is a traditional story that Tad's father told him when he was little and Tad introduced to Sawyer when he was around three.

It is a story about three ants, Scratch, Itch, and Whatchmacalit, and an anteater named John Q. Snoppeye. These stories encase so many adventures where the ants have to escape the clutches of John Q. Snoppeye. They travel all over the country, through dinosaur land, to the moon, back from space, and their favorite spot, 44 July Lane, where they go play with their best friend, Sawyer David. These tales are so entertaining and exciting, filled with pure imagination and creation. Sawyer has always taken part in creating the story, allowing his pure imaginative version be a staple with the three ants, which takes them all over the world. It is very exciting and a nice family tradition that we will keep passing through our family lines.

One particular night, while I was healing from my first treatments, I was having a very difficult time getting nausea under control. Usually doing breath work, along with anti-nausea medication, was all I needed. However, that night I lay in bed, tears rolling from one eye pooling in the other, and Tad sat next to me to offer love and support. He began to rub my back and talk about his day to further take my mind off the situation. It had become a joke that when I didn't feel well, I would ask Tad to tell me a story. He began with the three brave ants, but that night I needed something more. Making up stories on the fly is not Tad's strongest point, but he has passion and experiences that alone tell the most amazing of stories.

That night as I lay still, Tad searched his personal inventory to find an experience that had wings of inspiration. He began with his journey to Iraq. Over time, Tad has shared some of his experiences about the navy, but this night was different. It was as if he was ready to bare his soul about a time in life that was filled with challenge.

Most of the men and women who went to Iraq or Afghanistan came back different people. They all learned quickly the gift of living in the present moment.

Tad went to Iraq and Kuwait at the beginning of the war in 2003. It was obviously a very scary time, as going to war is filled with the challenge of the unexpected, carrying guns, always watching "your six," (which means watching your behind) and sleeping through desert sandstorms—not to mention the spiders and snakes. The word war itself holds so much power that it alone is enough to play mind games.

It is believed by many spiritual teachers that war is the result of an imbalance of male and female energy in the world. I am not sure what my take is as history continues to repeat itself through the election of leaders who abuse power to an extreme, taking away the very foundation that most countries are founded upon, freedom.

I am sure the experience of war will have changed Tad's life forever. I never will fully understand what an experience like this could actually be like. Even trying to put myself in his shoes, I cannot fully understand what each service member experiences during his or her journey during wartime. So I listened …

Tad, like many men and women who join the service, feels a strong connection to country and the protection of freedoms. He was proud to serve his country, no matter what the cost, to help ensure the freedoms we enjoy today. Throughout the years, he has shared many of his experiences overseas and on deployment. He has had an amazing career, and I love when an opportunity presents itself to share his experiences, especially those that opened his heart and soul.

However, there have been experiences that put him to the test. On his way over to Kuwait City, he had to take a commercial flight from Manama, Bahrain, to Kuwait, Kuwait City. He obviously stuck out like a sore thumb being on a flight that was filled mostly with people of Middle Eastern descent. As he walked down the aisle to find his seat, a women spat in his face. I was in shock when he told me that, as I cannot believe anyone doing such a thing no matter what his or her emotional reaction. This has nothing to do with race, this has to do with humanity, and I struggle with the idea that anyone could do such a thing.

In true representation of who he is, he went and took his seat with no reaction. I am sure it bothered him, but he understood and respected what she may have been feeling. He had a higher purpose and was not going to drop to that level.

I have no intention of discussing wartime politics, but it is interesting to hear people talk about the war as if they served, as if the very essence of their opinion was based on experience. There is so much that we do not know, so how can we come close to having such strong opinions if we don't have all the puzzle pieces to put together?

Tad began sharing his story as he stroked the little stubbles of hair that were starting to make a comeback on top of his head. He said, "It was one of the first nights I was in 'theater,' and the alarms called for protective posture"—meaning full chemical suits had to be worn at all times, so when the air sirens engaged, they were ready. These sirens were to announce that patriot missiles, missiles designed to implode the opponent's missiles, had been launched.

It was early in the morning, and he was doing his best to resemble what we'd call "sleeping with one eye open" when the sirens blasted. He got his gas mask on and headed for the bunker, which had been dug five feet into the ground. He looked from left to right, watching his fellow servicemen in full suits and gas masks, waiting for the all-clear sign. When he shared with me what that moment felt like, it was so powerful. It was certainly consumed with a little fear, but mostly it was a feeling of connection to his fellow servicemen and a strong call to duty to serve his country. He felt proud, as he should have.

This to me was such a powerful story of living in the present moment, which is not something we get forced into very often. In that moment Tad did not know what was coming his way, but he naturally engaged in the emotion, which represents the gift of the present.

He embraced life, and although there was probably some level of fear, his emotion to serve his country overcame any connection to it. No one has a guarantee in life, but there are definitely situations that force us to recognize that life is a delicate balance. We are blessed to see these precious moments and face them with courage. These situations truly are a gift because they show us that living in the present moment is the beginning of awareness, the beginning of expanding our truth and starting to live consciously. It opens the door to gratitude and grace, truly embracing such blessings in our life.

As I will never know what it feels like to be in the military or be involved in wartime, through oneness I got to experience many of Tad's gifts that shifted him to living and having gratitude for each present breath. I listened to many of his experiences, without judgment of politics, of war, without my opinion. I listened to the emotion of his experiences and with this I too shifted.

When we begin to set free from the future and embrace our past, we slide right into the present. We enjoy each breath more when we surrender to how we believe we are supposed to live, and then we truly experience conscious living!

Tad always has told me anytime you are in an airport, always thank a serviceman or servicewomen dressed in uniform. It is not easy as it takes you far outside your comfort zone because you do not know what the reaction will be or if it is your place. But please trust that you cannot imagine how far a simple act of kindness goes for someone who is serving our country.

Thank you all to the servicemen and women all over the world who have served! I have learned much from your experience.

CHAPTER 15
THANKFULLY GIVING

> Don't be afraid that your life will end; be afraid that it will never begin!
> ~Grace Hanson

NOVEMBER 24, 2011

It is difficult to recover from treatment when you know you are on a schedule for more treatment. The power of suggestion, I believe is paramount, but now I know it goes far beyond my limits of understanding.

One night, during my first inpatient stay at the hospital, when I couldn't find sleep if it hit me in the head, a couple of the nurses took over Tad's job telling me stories about healing. One of the nurses recently went through her personal experience with healing and offered stories of courage and hardship. She also told me stories about patients who had strong visceral reactions to treatment. For example, one of the chemo agents is red, and this woman would literally throw up every time she saw a stop sign because it was so bright red. I am sure over time this went away, but what an impact. I was so blessed to have avoided such reactions, and I am sure that had a great deal to do with what I allowed into my space from the beginning. I established "my rules" right from the start, learning we must always advocate for ourselves.

I was packing my bags and preparing Sawyer for my departure, which this time would only be one week at the most. It would be my third and final treatment before the transplant. However, this time was a difficult time to be in the hospital. It is never easy to hear the words; "You will be in the hospital during Thanksgiving." However, when they are followed by "you are in remission," it makes it much more manageable.

As you can imagine, our family had been celebrating since the first mention of remission, which was showing at two weeks post-treatment, although they would not give the official word until all bone marrow and blood tests were complete. It was amazing and could not have happened at a better time.

Today we celebrate and cherish Thanksgiving with family, as it will forever be a personal reminder of Gods gift to our family. It is a day to ultimately give thanks and gratitude for all the blessings we have in our life and a day to overindulge in food. This day is as rich in history as it seems strong in tradition. I believe sharing gratitude is important every day, but Thanksgiving represents an intention of gratitude that can not be missed.

Sharing in gratitude is one of many tools used to get out from underneath one's self. With this you see that life is precious and we always, no matter what the journey, have a multitude of things for which to be grateful. There is always a glass-half-full approach, *always*!

After a long week in the hospital going through what would be my last round of treatment, I got the good word. On Friday, November 25, Dr. Woods told me I was free of the Loveolution and was in complete remission. I can't think of any better news for my family on a day of such giving.

It was shocking, and there were many tears because this was the start of my new life. I saw all my dreams fleeting back into reality and my fears continuing to quell.

Right after they uttered the word remission, they didn't waste a moment before they began talking about the bone-marrow transplant. I just wanted to revel in a moment of sweet success, to bask in the amazing achievement, but the transplant team wasn't wasting any time. It was as if the oncology team had passed the torch and had made it clear that it was an optimal time to do the transplant, as I had been in unofficial remission for weeks. In addition, I was healthy and everything was showing to be extremely positive as we continued to get more amazing news on this special day.

I was preparing to head home from the hospital when things got even better. It was a gift so special that it would forever change the landscape of my life. My only biological brother was a match for transplant.

My heart stopped; tears were uncontrollable. My brother and I have not been extremely close, but it wasn't due to lack of love. Shad and I are very different people, but we have always been there for each other.

My mom took my hand in hers and we cried tears of joy. She said she knew he was going to be a match, as if someone gave her an intuitive vision how this would play out. It was potentially a 20 percent chance that Shad would be a match. I would fit his profile so strikingly that we were a ten out of ten match scale, so I consider this another great blessing in life. From recent research and understanding, the process of transplant is extremely complex, but having a related donor match makes the whole process much easier, as it is your genetic line.

When Shad and I spoke for the first time, he couldn't possibly understand how thankful my heart was that my brother was choosing to save my life. Believe it or not, many donor matches choose not to give, which was a shocking statistic for me.

I am sure he could hear my voice share a certain unspoken sense of kindness and love. No matter what the process of a bone-marrow transplant, my brother fought to make sure I got what I needed. I can only imagine what it feels like to the have the opportunity to save a family member, to give life. He actually told me he would do whatever he had to do to save my life, as it was not even a question.

I may have questioned this twenty years earlier as we fought over the TV or silly things sibling rivalry creates. We never had a close relationship, but this act spoke volumes of the love that truly connected us. This is a representation of the unspoken truth of love that is innate for those in our life.

Imagine a world where this kind of love existed for everyone, regardless of your relationship. The commitment and love to walk through this process shows the deep ingrained love that leads us to enlightenment. That love flows far faster than any negative thought or judgment could ever dream.

Family and friends alike can be the circle that causes us much angst when we get caught up in all fictitious parts of life. When we let the ego guide us down the road of "we are right" and "they are wrong." This is different from knowing when to release a relationship, but oftentimes we combine the two.

I believe we have chosen each other to learn and to heal, rendering the same path, but sometimes riding in different directions. The more we focus on the truth, tearing down all the boundaries, loving with veracity, and forgiven with ultimate light, the more we begin to heal.

Sometimes it takes an "illness" to wake up everyone to the gift of family and especially that extension to each person in the world. However, within that same situation many ignore the call and continue with life as if the words were never spoken. These are often the hardest lessons.

Bone-marrow transplants are very different from what many may think. Many believe that it is a very invasive procedure that has risky outcomes. As it may have been in the past, today it is a very different process. It is quite simple, as it masks the similarity of a blood transfusion, but an epic blood transfusion it is. The donor sits for roughly eight hours with a tube in one arm and a tube in the other. The blood goes through a machine that swipes all the whites cells and then gives back the rest of the cells in the opposite arm. It takes what it needs and gives the rest back—now that's love!

As easy as I made it sound, the other end is very dangerous and difficult. For the donor they give much time for testing, and then the day of donation is a long one.

For the recipient, it is an entirely different story. After being put into remission, the recipient receives chemotherapy and radiation to drop the white cell count back to zero. Then you receive the new white cells from your donor. There is a list a mile long of things that can go wrong and a list of common side effects. However, for today I wanted to enjoy my family, who were all in my hospital room celebrating a beautiful day. With Sawyer snuggled right into me while the rest of my family talked about the blessing of the day, I made plans to head home. It is a snapshot to be remembered forever.

The following week after my Thanksgiving stay at the Brigham, I met with Dr. Sieffer, who would be the first to give me as many details as I allowed. Everybody has a different experience, he stated right from the start. He told me we would discuss more details as we got closer to the transplant date and I agreed. The list of concerns seemed to be a mile long as Dr. Sieffer put his hand gently on mine and told me he believed I was making a good decision. I put my other hand on his and went through my whole speech about only giving me necessary information.

This was not the first time he showed his true heart, moving past the realm of staunch doctor-patient relationship. He was real and treated me like a person, not a patient. When I asked him if I were his daughter, would he recommend it, he gave me a humbling, honest answer, stating that it would be too emotional for him to be in those shoes.

He was making a recommendation outside of personal emotion, which was the best help we could have going through this experience. It would be almost impossible not to allow emotion to be part of a decision. That to me was the true sign of someone who wanted to see me live into my nineties.

Amy Jenner, the transplant clinic nurse practitioner, seemed to be Dr. Sieffer's right hand, and they made a great team. She was a little more open and answered each question with a certain level of honesty and positivity.

When I first got home from the hospital it was bittersweet, because each week I had to make the trek to Dana-Farber to get blood work and any other necessary tests in preparation for the transplant. Tad usually was the one to take me to my appointments and would work while we waited. On days that he needed to go into the office, someone else would always step up to take me.

Tad works for United Natural Foods, Inc (UNFI), and I am still amazed how true they have acted upon their family values mission statement. If UNFI had not been so supportive, I cannot even begin to imagine how many additional difficulties we may have had to face.

So many amazing moving parts have backed this journey. Therefore, it would have been a huge struggle had my loved ones not stepped up to help when it was truly needed the most. This is when you really understand the blessing that goes beyond healing.

My uncle Johnny (I call him UJ) and I have always been very close. Since my days in high school, where I challenged him to his first experience at parenting when my parents left him in charge during their vacation, through every big life event, he was always there to offer love and support. He happened to be the person who took me to the particular appointment where we discussed the transplant in full detail. It was a tough appointment, without question.

UJ picked me up at the crack of dawn and off we drove to see the city lights. By the time we reached the city, the sunshine lit the backdrop, waking everyone to start his or her morning routine. As we got closer to the hospital, we drove past the Christian Science reflecting pool, which is absolutely beautiful. It was a constant reminder how strong the power of the mind is. Each time I drove past I said a prayer that I would be guided by my soul and not my ego mind.

As I have been to the Christian Science Center, it is a beautiful experience with many reminders that we are reflections of God. The reflecting pool outside is the final reminder that we are perfect without error.

This particular day alone was scheduled to be a long one, fitting in as many appointments as possible in preparation for the transplant. The first appointment was with Dr. Sieffer, as he asked me to read the list of risks and complications that could occur during a bone-marrow transplant. In addition, I was asked to read the side effects that have a higher likelihood to occur.

I could barely see through my tears when I looked up to see UJ's eyes. He too felt my fear and wished he could take it all away. Dr. Sieffer had a very empathetic quality, but his goal was to provide me "a cure" that would result in my living a very long life. If I were a betting woman, I would not mess with his stubborn side, so I was counting on it.

I barely made it through the laundry list and then had to sign my life away. So that was done, but my tears had decided they were not. After spending a good amount of time with me, Dr. Sieffer gave me a hug and told me he believed I was moving in the right direction. Even though I just read the outline of a transplant out loud, I do not believe it fully registered, which is probably how I got through it.

Dr. Sieffer told me to take as much time as I needed to clear my head before leaving. I know this was a very difficult appointment for UJ as well. He was just thrown right into the mix without any warning.

As my tears kept flowing, UJ had no idea what to do or how exactly to comfort me. One of his favorite nieces was in the middle of a crisis, a big crying mess, so my funny uncle told me a secret. Actually, he told me a very surprising secret, which I promised I would forever keep between him and me. What made it so fun was that no one else in our huge family knew his secret. For some strange reason it made me feel a little better as it is always fun to share a secret. Surprisingly, a short laugh and huge hug helped me pull it together.

UJ and I always had the exact words for each other, and this became an inside joke. Each birthday I can expect a card riddled with hilarious information about "The Keddy Family" at their finest. It was perfectly created with love but so funny that each year this has been one of the things I look forward to during my birthday week. I am blessed to have such an amazing extended family, and UJ being at the top of this list, I was grateful.

As we pressed onto the next appointment, I looked at my schedule and realized we had some very difficult things to face that day. Slowly I felt the color drain from my face as I thought forward. Then I remembered I could only be afraid if I was thinking about the future. I then caught my short breath and extended it out as far as my ribs would allow. Taking in the air (even hospital air) was a blessing in the moment as it gave me the clarity I needed to be present. It would have been easier to run away into the future, but I needed to face this with all I had.

Next we made our way down to the radiation oncology floor to meet with Dr. Krasner. This was one of the most difficult parts of the transplant for me as I was hoping I would be able to evade it by the skin of my teeth. However, they wanted to do it as a safety precaution.

Dr. Krasner's fellow came into the room, and as much as you understand it is a teaching institution, sometimes it feels like you do not want to talk with a medical student. I know we all start somewhere, but still. However, that day I did not want to be someone's beginning, an experiment of words that are the hardest to be heard. In that moment I needed solid facts, clinical trials, and statistics that I could sway into my favor. I mean really, every statistical analysis can be done to show whatever you want it to show; I needed it to show that radiation was going to be like a day in the sun.

However, the fellow, who didn't even introduce himself, had other plans. I felt the tears getting ready for rally number two, and UJ had to sit in the waiting room because he had a phone call he had to take. I was in a crisis moment and the phone rang, and when I heard Colleen's voice my body released into the chair. My tears were jumping over one another as I assaulted my phone with words, trying to explain how I felt about the radiation.

She gave me some great insight in dealing with this integral part of treatment and it worked. She began to talk with me in her loving, kind voice, and I again felt connected. This was a tough day, no doubt, and you can see how the most divine people show up right when you need them, even if they are thousands of miles away.

I finished with the appointment and blindly signed all the paperwork, again signing my life away. At least this time I wasn't forced to read aloud all the risks/benefits that I would be facing. It was time to put that meeting behind me as I already encased it with love and light.

I met UJ out in the waiting room, and up we went for my fourth bone-marrow biopsy. They gave me some medication and told me to wait about fifteen minutes for it to kick in. I was waiting and it kicked in all right. I began sharing my life story with the tech that had done all my biopsies thus far.

It was a quick procedure, as it should have been. He had pretty much drilled a hole in my bone four times previously, so there should have been a straight path right to the juice of the bone marrow.

While getting the biopsy, more details from my morning blood work came in, and for the first time I needed to get some platelets via a blood transfusion. The nurse began to get everything in motion for me to go up to the seventh floor to get two bags of blood. As we headed toward the stairs, I took a moment to gather my gratitude, which shows just how blessed I felt during this process.

Most transplant patients, especially at this point, need many transfusions leading up to and following the first year after a transplant. I was blessed, and there wasn't a moment that I let this be forgotten, and I will never forget.

After I got blood, UJ and I began our drive home. We were both exhausted from the day, but I cannot fully express what a blessing it was to have him there through each step of the way. I felt as if he divinely was the one to take me because his humor for life and our family was just the perfect mix I needed to get through the day in one piece.

CHAPTER 16
A GIFT AND A POSE

DECEMBER 5, 2011

We may not always be able to anticipate what life is throwing our way or how we will react, but making the best of each situation almost always becomes a blessing. Becoming a yoga teacher was such a special experience and learning moment in my life. The choice to embark on the path to becoming a yoga teacher was met with all kinds of emotions. I was basically offering myself up in the rawest form, releasing fear and insecurity. This was a big part of the process to make space for the gifts that yoga would teach me.

Prior to the teacher training I was an avid yoga practitioner, and like most was drawn to the path through the idea that yoga offers intense physical fitness that may be gentler on the body. Over the years, I have observed yoga in many forms, but for me this practice or philosophy is continuously teaching me to connect, evolve, love and forgive; it is a way of living. Simply said, yoga is not about touching your toes, it is about what you learn on the way down. It was this awakening that I looked forward to each time I stepped on the mat and took what I learned into my daily life.

Another one of my favorite parts of yoga is that you are always a student first, and becoming a teacher only smoothes out the circle, as you begin to share the teachings through your own expression. In addition, learning and evolving as a student, lovingly teaching others to soften their ego and open their hearts allows the practice to melt and mold their life; it is such a beautiful experience.

I have gotten the opportunity to watch yoga spill into many lives and wash away so many negative emotions and experiences, clearing space for the practitioner to fill up with love and peace and begin the process of changing the way we think and/or live. It has been such a blessing as I have learned and been inspired by so many yogis.

From the eight-limbed path, the asana Hatha, physical poses are what attracts most students; I call it yoga's front door. Every pose is guided with breath, creating and opening a space, which allows a natural flow of energy. This is a calling that fills one up with the most powerful vibrations of love while at the same time softening the ego. Every yoga pose is constantly evolving and presenting the yogi with a different set of challenges on a physical level, and when ready it is taken deep into the soul.

That night I sat in bed reflecting on my last appointments and shivered at the thoughts. I needed to release all the false thoughts and fears, but breath work wasn't fully doing the trick. At that point I got out of my bed and planted both feed solidly into the ground. I began moving through asana, dedicating each fearful thought to each movement. After ten asanas, I moved into child's pose, allowing the wisdom of movement to melt into my heart. I then utilized my breath to make space for love and forgiveness. Forgiveness for self and love for all—it was a great awakening, an even greater moment.

"A gift and a Pose"

*

I climbed back into bed and wrote in my blog: "A gift and a pose."

When we move into a pose, we explore, starting with breath and alignment, but then move into a much deeper experience. We move deeper into the pose until we find the sweet space where our mind softens in combination with the physical essence, making way for the connection to spirit. This feels like the brightest, warmest light guiding us to the seat of our soul, which divinely balances the mind, body, and connection.

One of the many poses that offer a unique connection to this feeling is triangle pose. A triangle has three equal sides that in yoga form represent the mind, body, and spirit. This pose teaches us to be strong, and through strength seek balance in all aspects. For me, this pose has always presented many challenges, which is really exciting, as each challenge will present an opportunity to evolve in the pose and life. While in triangle pose, a practitioner creates a beautiful line of energy from the hip to the crown of the head (one angle).

Oftentimes, when creating this line or angle, we sacrifice another angle, losing internal and external balance. As a teacher, I have watched so many yogis struggle and/or suffer within this pose. Going too deep to the floor with your hand closes off your hip, your foundation, if not planted strongly, will offset the support you need to work the upper portion of the pose, and a hundred little subtleties in between this metaphorically represents life so adequately, which is why it is one of my favorite poses.

Why do we choose to struggle or suffer at all? There are so many ways to make this pose more accessible to each yogi, but the point here is that mirroring triangle pose, in life we often choose to struggle or make things more challenging following the guide of the ego.

After observing many triangle poses, I believe that on the outside we want the pose (our life) to look picture perfect as this is our (society's) idea of measure. We are challenged by the belief that if it doesn't fit "perfectly," then it might not be right or we are doing it wrong. Naturally, if we do not allow time to learn in the pose and surrender to the pose we will never understand the true essence of the pose in its entirety; the same can be said for life. Forcing oneself too deep into the pose before you are ready will create imbalance and throw off the "tri" angle, weakening the basis of the pose.

Triangle pose has always been a great teacher, showing me guidance on the inside and outside. A pose for the soul.

- I have spent every class in at least one triangle pose and have spent many classes struggling with how I think the pose should look. After years, I realized by surrendering to the pose and to the practice, my body would naturally soften to a place where I would find a spiritual openness.
- Triangle pose was a place where vital life force would lift me up to an awareness going far beyond the pose. In this place I feel the breath connecting to my heart and

- moving throughout my entire body; the earth beneath my feet feels like it is the only support I need in the world because we are all one.
- When it actually comes to the idea of the "tri" angle, or mind/body/spirit, I have realized the greatest gift of all: the spirit is love, the spirit is God, God is the spirit, and God is love. The spirit is the only angle that we need to believe is perfect in its divinity.
- When we know this, all the angles in our life will be in perfect harmony. We will begin to listen and be guided by this internal spirit instead of our environment. We will embrace the loving nature of life and soften all the boundaries that we have created and have been created for us.
- We will forgive always without reason, we will love stronger as it comes from an internal fire, and we will embrace the true idea of peace that runs through each soul. We will recognize oneness for its true definition and apply this to everyday living, identifying the ego as the plan that keeps us believing we are separate.

*

May we all embrace this gift, peeling back the layers of our veil and connecting to our divine spirit.

CHAPTER 17
TRUST AND DIVINITY

DECEMBER 10, 2011

Each week I can guarantee at least one trip to Dana-Farber in preparation for the transplant. There has been so much coordination with insurance, completing tests, meeting the whole team. I have to say it has been a bit overwhelming, but again I am thankful that all has fallen divinely into place. My brother has been an amazing support, as has been our whole family. However, it is important to move beyond your expectation and just allow.

As things were moving forward smoothly at the perfect pace, I got an unexpected phone call from the transplant coordinator at Dana-Farber. Tomorrow was the day planned to begin a transformation as I was to be admitted to the hospital to begin preparations for the transplant. That all changed with one phone call as my brother had a cold last week and his white count was still not where it needed to be to start the process.

I cannot even begin to share the intricacies of this process; they do not leave any Ts uncrossed, which becomes a comfort as well as a curse. This news shook me to my core, as I was *ready*. It is like preparing for a race—you prepare mentally and physically, and then you are ready to go. I sat back in my chair, my face white as a ghost, and I looked at my dad. I said, "They are icing the kicker."

I took a few deep breaths for the panic to set free and got myself grounded. After I settled, when I connected to natural breath, a divine message was sent. I remembered a yoga class I taught about trusting the flow of the river, releasing all resistance, and trusting in divinity. I was reminded in the order of patience during manifesting for the highest good of all those involved with this process.

This now became an opportunity to put these ideals into practice. As I was definitely disappointed in the change of plans, I had to trust that this was part of God's divine plan. This was the challenge, to trust that it would serve all of us in the most appropriate way for the highest good.

Once I embraced this thought, I felt a strong flow of peace enter my body, although there was a small part of my ego still trying to take space. I smiled, as I was happy to identify the voice of the ego and transcending into the God mind, which was filled with trust and love.

I consider it a victory when you can tell the difference between God's guidance and the mortal mind/ego. It simply gets easier each time, and the ego voice becomes softer and softer, until eventually there is no distraction.

Your soul is filled with love, and there is no opportunity to allow fear into your experience, as it will just muddy the waters, allowing emotions such as frustration and anger to fill the pool.

Now I am taking this time to work on my vision board and get a few more things done until we get the new dates. I have followed God's lead right down to the research that helped in this decision. I will continue to follow his lead and enjoy this time. I have no doubt that I will look back, as I have numerous times before, and say, "Wow, the timing really worked out for our best interest."

Last night I was doing some reading, and as I was preparing for bed, I came across an article about limiting beliefs. It couldn't have been more appropriate to support the journey of that day. When we try to force or entirely run the show, we end up creating many boundaries that limits our beliefs instead of flourishing them with infinite possibilities.

Limiting beliefs may be learned from or influenced by school, work, family, or a number of sources. These limitations not only make you feel frustrated and confused, they often keep you stuck in a place where you cannot manifest the experiences you really want. In addition, you hold on to the way you believe it should look.

"Manifesting" is a new-age term that gives freedom to the essence of our reality. As we are all here to serve a higher calling, it is within our power to create our own reality. However, this is where conscious living comes into play. Some ideas that will allow a more conscious environment are as follows:

1. Truly love and embrace yourself, as you are constantly learning and evolving. Do not be prisoner to your past, as you are your present. The past is only the lessons that have shaped and evolved you.
2. Embrace your power; worry less what others think, and know you are always doing the best you can.
3. Keep warm your relationships. Understand that you are a reflection of those close to you. It is love when you know that a relationship is no longer serving you; we are all in different places. Give without expectation and always be learning. Listening to others helps you have balance. Defending your position will just keep you stuck.
4. Forgive daily. Understanding the other person's view even if you see it differently; this is called respect. When it goes beyond this we must forgive and move forward in our evolution. This is always a challenge because we have been taught to forgive but never forget. This again is an idea that will keep you struggling in thought. Allow the experience to shape you, but move forward lovingly.
5. Surrender. It is not your job to get everyone running at the same speed. When you listen to your inner guidance, you will know when to share.

These are just a few ideas that will help you clear a path to manifest, which means to call into your life. It takes time, practice, and most importantly patience. As I have read many books on manifesting, it has been loving patience that has opened my heart to the many possibilities.

There are two parts to manifesting: calling upon what experience you would like to bring into your life through emotion, and then sealing it with the intention of divine timing for the highest good for all involved. While in the first step it is important to recognizing what your limiting beliefs may be and how they are affecting your life. Unfortunately, many limiting beliefs feel so normal that we no longer even notice them.

Clearing out limiting beliefs is just as easy as inviting a new thought into your reality. It takes time, recognition, and patience. Once we bring forward our awareness, it sets us free and we feel lighter in our soul.

The first step in overcoming a limiting belief is understanding exactly what it is and what it does. A limiting belief is a boundary that you created out of insecurity, fear, etc. so that if you fail you have already set up your recovery mat. We must identify this limiting belief that is blocking you from moving forward. Just to have a deeper understanding of what limiting beliefs are, I have listed a couple of examples:

I am too old. Empowering thought: I am on time, exactly where I should be. I am ready now to move forward, embracing divinity.

I don't have time to go back to school. Empowering thought: I will walk one step at a time to see how I can make more time for a new adventure. I will trust the Divine.

I am not a good enough writer to author a book. Empowering Thought: Each writing sample gets stronger and my ideas come faster. I can write a book.

As we see these old thoughts can easily hold us prisoner to our ego, which love to keep us wrapped in boundaries. This is where it is crucial to allow yourself to break down your old wall and be free in creation.

After you identify the limiting belief, you need to challenge it. Asking yourself is this true, do I have evidence to support it, and is my empowering belief really the truth in this case. You will be amazed.

Many great spiritualists and intuitives believe you can have the life you want by creating it. Using tools such as vision boards, meditation, and visualization as just a few of the keys to establishing a great life without suffering, which ultimately leads to enlightenment.

Today, this is a way of life for me, as I believe we all should have a mission statement for our life, filled with detailed intentions. This moves beyond the idea of a goal and drives us right into a state of knowing. Unless it is your time to return home, you have service to do here on Earth with the guidance of God. However, God does not want us to suffer, so you can have everything your heart desires.

This paragraph may be the most important thing I share in this book: we must prepare to hear the voice of our heart, which is God or Source. Allow yourself to forgive those who you believe have hurt your heart without judgment of right and wrong. If you don't listen and embrace God's love and the love of all those around you, most **importantly your self-love**, you will suffer.

How do we get to this place? The above suggestions for conscious living are a great start. In addition, there are a number of tools and exercises that release any and all previous suffering while awakening your heart. Simultaneously, you are tearing down any wall that you may have subconsciously and strategically put up since you were born. Part of this great awakening we hear all around us is awakening our heart to pure self-love and forgiveness.

I believe breaking down your "heart wall" is very important because we all need to identify the emotional hurts we carry. This will set you free to evolve in greatness. This may seem like an easy suggestion, but I assure you, as I continue to work through this process, it is hard. This means you love yourself fully and offer forgiveness to self without needing a partner to accept it or make it right.

Exercise

*

Sit down in a very quiet place and take several extremely deep breaths. Allow your jaw to soften along with the muscles that line your face into your neck. Relax your shoulders, moving right down to your hips, legs, and feet. Lastly, encase a bright light around your spine and from the tip of your neck down to the tailbone, and free each muscle and tendon so that each vertebra may be free. Swing to the sweet sound of your inner song. You may actually feel the muscles soften around a specific area or just feel very relaxed.

Next write down on a single piece of paper all the events in your life that have been extremely hurtful. This may sound like a daunting task, but when you really sit down and think about it, the list may not be as long as you may think. Allow yourself to specifically identify the times in your life that you were emotionally tipped over and never had resolution. Even if you had resolution, did you wholly forgive the situation? This may take some time, maybe a day or two, but work on it and just allow it to be. There is no right or wrong; releasing as many boundaries as possible will be a platform here.

When you feel complete, say some version of the following:

"I have created a boundary that is not allowing me the freedom to dream, creating my reality with God. I have created resistance emotionally and physically and am ready to surrender this fear of lack or love to God. I am moving forward in a reflection of light filled with self-love and self-acceptance."

At this time throw away your paper or keep it if you want to refer back, but either way, let it go. Once you have finished this or a similar exercise, you will have identified what areas you need to let go to create beautiful things in your life. If you wonder what your life service is, you will not figure it out listening to the walls of hurt around your heart. So this first step starts your new journey with freedom and self-love.

This is one of many exercises that will address life's challenges and identify if we are still holding on too tight. In addition to embracing any limiting beliefs we may have and making space for conscious living, we will begin the process of determining our ego from God's guidance.

Let it begin!

CHAPTER 18
FEARLESS FAITH

Feed your faith, and your fears will starve to death.
~Author Unknown

DECEMBER 20, 2011

As my journey with the unexpected continued, wrapped in the Loveolution, it proved to be an even wilder ride. The past two weeks preparing for the bone marrow transplant were filled with unexpected twists and turns.

On Friday afternoon I got a phone call from Dr. Woods telling me my brother had not yet been cleared for transplant because his white cell count was still a little low. They were concerned and wanted to do further evaluation for the benefit of him and me.

However, this meant that the transplant could be pushed back for an additional six weeks, and I would need to go into the hospital in four days for more treatment. This was a thought that I could not believe or bear to even think was true.

I felt my heart drop to my toes, and the tears immediately rolled down my cheeks. Why? Why was this happening and what did it mean? I was ready to rock and roll, to begin this process, to have a beautiful rebirth; ready to embrace this amazing adventure, taking in my new spiritual shift, the beautiful lessons learned, and move forward. With this news I began to doubt my choices and felt extremely let down. The days to follow were filled with difficulty, almost as if this was the final challenge to make sure I was ready.

I called Tad on his way home from work to tell him the news, still feeling the tears welling. I got off the phone pretty quickly to sit in thought as to what my next plan would be, when I got a text. I ignored it at first; feeling a little sorry for myself, and then got a feeling I should check it.

Tad sent me a message: "Feed your faith, and your fears will starve to death."

The words rang through me with such light, and in that moment I knew everything was going to be okay. Tad has been such an amazing partner during this experience and has always had the most divine words to lift me up exactly when I needed it the most.

I took a deep breath and called Dr. Woods right back and at the same time paged Dr. Sieffer, the transplant doctor; I was planning my own conference call of sorts.

I took the driver's seat and looked forward to the road God was paving for me. You see, in that moment I realized that I had been wavering with my thoughts and preparation. It was time to walk through to the other side, but I was still trying to go around.

Upon talking with Dr. Sieffer and Dr. Woods, we arranged a new plan. I asked if they would do one more blood work up on Shad Monday morning before I would have to be admitted.

If his white count had improved, then we would move forward with the transplant for this Friday, February 3 as planned. If not, I would enter Dana-Farber Monday afternoon for an enjoyable five-night stay, and they both agreed. I could tell they both had extreme doubt in their voices and were basically doing this as a courtesy, but nonetheless they set it up so it was done.

Dr. Woods actually prepared me, stating, "It is highly unlikely that his blood workup will change enough by Monday, so be prepared for this." I had no expectation other than following divinity.

Shad and his entire family had a cold about a week before he went in for testing, so I was not overly surprised by this news. Under "normal" circumstances you would admire the body's ability to heal, but if you are going to be a bone-marrow donor, the white count needs to be within normal range.

Shad was amazing during this process, as it had not gone without a significant amount of frustration during preparation and planning. He went above his call and nurtured his body, giving it the optimal chance to heal. Not only did he research what he could do to elevate his white count, he actually drank green juice. Shad was giving me such a gift, and this was one of many amazing examples of how blessed I truly am.

When Tad got home from work, he shared some strong feelings with me in an attempt to make sense of this situation. While he was driving home, he got really angry with God. "Why does she have to go through this? Why can't it just go smoothly?" Then he got a direct answer: *It has gone smoothly.*

We have been so blessed right from the beginning of this journey starting with remission within two weeks of treatment. While Tad began to think back to all the love and support that brightened our path, he realized how blessed we have been. He felt ashamed for having been angry, but it was an opportunity to be reminded of how smooth this journey really has been and how loved we are by so many.

When he was sharing this with me, I felt bad for being upset. When we reflected together, we realized there has been nothing but blessings all around us. It is hard to always understand the whys, but when you see the growth on so many levels, you realize how grateful you are for the experience, no matter how crazy it may be.

Sometimes in the moment it is hard to see and embrace the beauty of the lesson. It is my power to create the vessel, while I flow down the river of divinity. Deciding that you are not going to hang on to the shore, allowing a free flow, is so important yet so difficult to put into motion.

I have realized that I have always embraced the divinity of time, and this should be no exception. I embrace my fearless faith, unwavering support, and love that have been delivered in so many colors.

Tonight as I write in hollysloveolution@wordpress.com, I have my head back in the game. I trust and I listen; I am ready to flow with this journey as I envision a rebirth. Please pray for the river to divinely flow to the transplant.

"Create a flow."

*

I see my life as an unfolding set of opportunities to awaken. It has been nice to have time over the past weeks to reflect silently on this journey since October 6; it has just been incredible. It is interesting how life can change on one inhale and at the same time teach you more than you ever thought possible on the exhale. Life will never be the same, and for this I am grateful.

A few mornings ago I drove myself into Boston, which was so freeing! I think we all forget as we grow in life what little moments of independence, like driving, give us on so many levels.

Metaphorically, this is yet another great reflection into life. We can all remember the day we got our license. As we travel back in time, you may or may not remember all the practice and preparation. All the exciting thoughts of the freedom and cherishing what new experiences this will bring to life. We are overcome with a great sense of achievement and pure joy when we conquer this milestone. Then as time moves forward, this thing, once thought of as a gift, can become a burden or annoyance. In addition, it fosters a space that can create a great deal of anger and frustration with others. It can set up the platform to judge as we establish what we believe to be right or wrong. Something so simple yet so big we forget.

I was reminded of this freedom and mini lesson as it gave me just enough time to rock out to my favorite country tunes, which was a perfect start to a beautiful day.

When I got to Brigham and Women's, I was waiting for the valet parking attendant to get my ticket while I overheard a conversation between two men sitting on the front wall having a cigarette break. They both looked as though they had very intricate stories to tell.

One was a newcomer to what I think is one of the best cities in the world. He was sharing his journey and fears about moving to a city where he didn't know a soul, but on some level he felt at home.

The other man shared a story of his recent recovery, going into details that brought tears to my eyes. He shared his trials and tribulations and how he knew this was a challenge he was going to overcome. He caught that I was listening to his story and seemed excited to have an audience, as he was exceptionally proud of his work so far, as he should be.

However, his rock bottom was hard to hear. He slept on park benches on cold winter nights and tried to sell his only coat for a hit. As I sat there listening with admiration, I was amazed how much the three of us had in common. We were all facing a challenge that demanded strength, understanding, and courage. The common thread weaving together our stories was faith.

As I was leaving my car, my smile spoke volumes, as I nodded in the young mans direction. I then made my way into the hospital to the second floor to get blood drawn and wait. It was a nice morning to just be and place a compass on all the other stories that were sitting around me.

It brought me back to my senior year in high school; a simple quote, which at the time seemed to make so much sense: "Don't go with the flow, create it." When I wrote this in 1994 it seemed simple; I wanted to create my future.

It would be years later that I was introduced to the wisdom of *The Secret*, learning about the law of attraction and manifesting. I can't help but think that somewhere along the way I jumped in the DeLorean and planted this quote for myself to find during this specific time in my life. But as I sat in thought, I have come to realize that there is a big part of this quote missing that brings it back full circle, with no beginning and no end.

As I sat in thought, I pulled out my journal that was a constant companion on these trips to Dana Farber. I began to write about the missing piece that would forever change the foundation of this personal quote.

There is a divine flow to life without question. Some believe we choose our path before we come earth side, others believe it is God guiding us, but whatever your belief, there is no doubt that we have all felt this flow with the ease of our breath and the wisdom that has guided us to the next step in life.

It was that moment that it all fit together like a 5000 piece puzzle that had been in the works for years. Divine source is an amazing, vast river with constant flow; we are the boat. As the divine flow of the river changes in life, it offers the opportunity to learn and overcome, evolving closer to our soul's authenticity. This becomes an amazing chance to put your knowledge in motion.

The river may sometimes offer a solid flow, nice and smooth, and sometimes the river is fast and commands constant attention. However, each time this flow changes, we are presented with the challenge to create and manifest our vessel.

In addition, we can create the shoreline and the items we may need to make the journey more successful, but either way we play a role in the creation. Where is gets tricky is when we start kicking and screaming when the flow gets a little wild. We start trying to grip to the shoreline to stop the flow, instead of focusing on what we need to get through the challenge that stares us straight in the eye.

When I sat quietly and looked at the many different scenarios I gave this metaphor, it all began to make sense. During every journey, at some point, we try to throw out an anchor or jump ship. However, the river is going to keep flowing whether we embrace this or not.

Most often the reason we are trying to escape this divine flow is fear, but once we overcome the mortal thoughts we begin to focus on the vessel and the depth of that vessel (the soul). Then we shift, and the sail catches wind to bring us back to life. We embrace the challenge and see it for the blessing that it presents in our journey.

For me this blessing has brought much forgiveness and love to a level that I am not sure I can quite explain. Maybe there are no words. Trusting that the river will divinely flow and present the chance to understand that love has no boundaries, love is *all*. It just takes one hug to wipe away a day of struggle.

The power this emotion embodies has given me the strength to trust the river to evolve in truth without judgment, spiritually cleaning out every element and experience of my soul to start fresh. A rebirth with new senses to connect with God's voice dismisses the thoughts that are loaded with fear and judgment. It all comes full circle, and each time you take a trip around you peel back a layer of the veil, which navigates you to freedom.

On my way home my mother called, as she was nervous about me driving alone to Boston. She is so cute because throughout this experience she has never been worried about anything except for my driving alone to Boston. She has been such a rock, especially when I have wanted to throw out the anchor. So as I drove home I realized that if I could again acquiesce time and go back in the DeLorean, I would change my senior quote to, "Embrace the Divine flow while you create each breath toward awakening" (Holly Peckskamp).

CHAPTER 19
THE POWER OF PRAYER

> So oftentimes it happens that we live our lives in chains, and we never even know we have the key. ~The Eagles

JANUARY 14, 2012

Monday morning arrived, and I paced around the house wondering if I would wear out my new slippers before Dr. Woods called with the news: Would I be driving to the hospital for a transplant or another treatment? Each time the phone rang I jumped up to answer, only to be met by telemarketers and donation collectors.

I did everything to keep myself busy and keep my head clear of any negative thoughts. I did a meditation by lighting a beautiful candle, staring into the flame, imagining myself driving to Boston for the transplant as if it had already happened. In my mind I celebrated what a great experience it was and how excited I was that it was over.

It was past noon and I was wondering if they forgot about me. It was like waiting for the man of your dreams to call and ask you out on a date. I stared at the phone, willing it to ring.

Within minutes, the phone rang and it was Dr. Woods. My heart sank to my belly as all weekend I prayed and envisioned Shad's cells being in the perfect range. When we spoke on Friday, she reiterated to me that she was just being honest and not trying to bring me down, as she understands there is a specific level of mental preparation for a transplant. However, it was her medical opinion that it was unlikely his white count would change in two days.

I just had a gut feeling she was wrong, so I would wait for the lab to confirm. When I heard her voice on the phone my heart sank even further. *I guess I am going in for treatment*, I thought in the back of my mind.

She said, "I know you were really mentally prepared for the transplant, so we need you to come in by five to be admitted for treatment." "Treatment to start the process of the transplant." Oh, she got me so good! I screamed at the top of my lungs while tears ran down my face. I haven't been so excited since I found out I was in remission.

It may be hard to understand, but this was unbelievable news. I was ready mentally for the transplant and did not want to have any more treatment that wasn't attached to the transplant process. It was divine timing, and I again knew that all would be as it should. It was another lesson in my bag that has shaped me to be as patient within the present moment as possible.

I had spent the entire weekend making new vision boards filled with images that reminded me of health because I believed that I was in full health; the transplant was just part of the process to learn more about love and forgiveness. This is where my yoga training and knowledge was really going to play a large role.

Through my experience studying yoga, Buddhism, and other religious doctrines, I have learned that prayer is a calling inside you, which transcends fear, hate, and anger, really any negative emotion. You tap into an internal wisdom that does not work under a tit-for-tat code; it just thrives under *love and forgiveness*. These two simple words represent release from our past and unity in our present.

We pray to heighten our awareness of one another and to create the feeling of collective consciousness working in peace. Tonight as I sit here and pray, I feel one with God. I believe I am already healed because I am made in his image; therefore, I am whole; there can be no other truth. The mind likes to tell us otherwise, but as I said before, it is getting easier each day to identify the voice that is my ego and softly send it away.

This may seem to contradict the previous statement, but if you take a few moments you will understand this to be true. Our soul knows our mission and or service in this world, no matter who you are. However, it is our mind that likes to block any foresight we receive from our soul. Again, it comes back to our soul knows our full line of destiny when we are born and when we will die. Of course death is something that we don't want to think about, because it brings forth the reality that we are not invincible and someday we will all die. The more validation we have now that heaven is real will help many of us deal with these truths, stories like "Heaven is for Real" and "Proof of Heaven: A Neurosurgeon's Near-Death Experience and Journey into the Afterlife." These stories confirm that there is something more, a more divine experience awaiting us. The beautiful part is that many of these stories really validate similar messages, which help as we are creatures of continuity.

When I pray for my family, friends, and myself, I envision a world of people serving their highest good, a world that has been reconnected. I believe and see what I am praying for as if it has already happened. I believe and embrace a world that respects religious freedom because it brings us to the same place, utilizing different roads. We are all one, here to serve a higher calling.

This understanding of prayer, unending love, and complete forgiveness came all on my journey that started in a yoga class in Boston. A class I thought was going to make me more fit. The blessing with yoga is that it will happen to you whether you are ready or not, almost as if it is happening behind your back until you are ready to see it in full.

Many have asked me what tradition of yoga I study. I am particularly fascinated with the eight-limbed path of yoga, and you will see why in just a moment.

Yoga is a tradition so rich in life philosophy that you can learn from many paths. It is believed to be almost five thousand years old; so much of the yoga we see today has been derived from this first history. I believe yoga is so strong in value that it is important to take a moment to write further.

Most importantly, Yoga is NOT a Religion, it is a philosophy that gives you stronger guidance to live your life in service to God. To live with kindness, love, and without suffering.

There are many styles of yoga, such as Kundalini, Anusara, and Iyengar, and the list goes on. However, the important thing to understand is that all these styles, although offering a different perspective on the physical poses and even a slight tilt on tradition, they are all cut from the same cloth. The hope is to reach enlightenment where we achieve a state of oneness. Many religions offer similar types of ideals, but again, yoga is not a religion, it is philosophy.

The Eight Limbs of Yoga is a beautiful philosophy that guides you through life and can sit side by side with your religious values. It is simple in thought, but not so simple to achieve. Below marks an overview of the eight limbs, which offer guidance in your inner evolution. As you read each limb, you may embrace the simplistic ideal, knowing this may be "the key we never knew we had." This is a path of connection and love.

The eight limbs flow as follows are written in their Sanskrit version:

1. **Yamas** is social and ethical behaviors, which include how you treat the world and those who live in it. They are moral principals and some have referenced them as universal commandments.
    a. **Ahimsa**: Do no harm. Nonviolence.
    b. **Satya**: Tell no lies, not even white lies as this is just a lie you tell yourself is ok to share. Truth.
    c. **Asteya**: Do not steal.
    d. **Brahmacharya**: Moderation and balance.
    e. **Aparigraha**: Free from all greed.
2. **Niyamas** is the inner discipline and how we treat our self.
    a. **Shauca**: Cleanliness, meaning clearing away of internal negative states or mental states of being.
    b. **Santosha**: Contentment, seeking happiness in each moment.
    c. **Tapas**: Heat in the body, making way for discipline.
    d. **Svadhyaya**: Self study as inward reflection.
    e. **Ishvara-pranidhana**: living with the awareness of the divine.
3. **Asana** is the physical postures, which present steady and easy.
4. **Pranayama** is breath control, which allows for a steady state, is creating more space for breath.
5. **Pratyahara** is sensory withdrawal. This occurs during breath work or meditation, your body goes inward releasing the hold on your five main senses.
6. **Dharana** is Concentration.
7. **Dhyana** is a quiet stillness beyond meditation.
8. **Samadhi** is bliss.

The ultimate goal of the eight-limb path is not to achieve these elements in order or at the same time. It is your path, but ultimately the goal is to be free with love and peace. The eight limbs are an extension of your religious beliefs so that you can open your heart and live a more conscious life.

As you can see, the defining force behind each work, this path offers the keys to unlock some of life's greater challenges, making life much brighter. It highlights a better way to consciously live in regard to self and others. It has been referred to being similar to many religious doctrines, but it stands alone as a path either followed with your choice of religion or without in order to seek enlightenment. It has been this path, along with many teachers, that has shown me the light. I am thankful for this wisdom, as it was the seed that began a beautiful garden.

This path helped connect me to the path of many modalities as I placed my heart in the hands of healing. I was ready for this transplant! The first few days at Dana-Farber were difficult as my mind was constantly trying to go off the path that was already created. I was met with memories from this past October and all of the emotional lessons that entangled me to have a stronger understanding of this journey.

Soon after walking through the bustling, revolving door to floor 4C, I saw Mel, one of my favorite nurses, whose energy reached for the sky. She came to work with nothing but love and left it all on the floor before she went home, a beautiful gift for her patients. She gave me a big hug, and we got right down to the schedule with no time to waste.

I made a commitment to myself to embrace this transplant as an opportunity to intertwine all of the new changes and shifts that God has opened to my soul. This is a rebirth that will open spaces for me to serve God and to truly live life without fear because I have set this intention to do so.

I will always live with my heart fully open, listening to the call, and having great joy with friends and family. Lastly, the transplant is a reflection upon how I already felt (I am already healed inside); now it will just shine outward.

It is difficult to say that leukemia, a disease, would be a gift. However, I am grateful for the essence that it has shown me through my eyes, heart, and soul. Please do not misunderstand; there have been so many days of fear, tears, and confusion. But these challenges have given me great insight to love, to understand that all is love, love is home without condition.

I see who I really am on my internal reflection, and scrolling back through time I can easily see when my internal reflection was not love, and life was a struggle. The yogis call it suffering, and can you believe the answer is right there inside you? *Love and forgive yourself* while leaving fear, guilt, and shame in the dust. I cannot say this enough with the hope that a seed will plant for you.

This leads to the big day, where Shad will share his beautiful cells with me. I believe we are all connected in a soul dimension, but now Shad and I have this special opportunity to do so through physical form. It is amazing that I have thought and worked through so many layers that I would have to write a book to explain it all. However, the one thing that often comes up is prayer.

Mode of prayer is such a beautiful thing, and we should each pray how we believe and feel is right for us. Moreover, I do believe that there are so many elements to prayer, which expresses the opportunity to take us so much deeper to our connection with source. I am sure we can all think back to a time where we were reciting the "Our Father," or a common prayer. Within the spoken words there was not much emotion, more just words spoken as a duty to our faith. In the same breathe we can remember a time under similar circumstance where we felt each word jump off our tongue, spreading the love to the other parishioners while feeling an astonishing sense of oneness.

Prayer is amazing; there is no right or wrong. However, I have discovered that prayer, just like everything, has more opportunity when you truly believe with strong emotion what you are praying for, each word ringing a strong vibration through the universe. In addition, prayer is backed by quantum physics, which encases the law of attraction. Prayer is very important to me, and I believe prayer is about the intention, a private conversation with God. I was raised Catholic and spent my younger years learning about the Bible at Sunday school. My mom has such strong faith, and this she instilled so deeply in me that I will be forever grateful.

Learning this expression of religion at a young age was a great foundation, but as I grew older I felt that I didn't connect to it. We all have to find the religious path that guides us to be one with God and the journey to enlightenment, which is another part of the process.

I too began my journey trying to understand faith and questioning many things. It soon led me to the path of Buddhism, which is a philosophy more than a formal religion, and I immediately felt a deep understanding to things that had never made sense.

I understood the age-old adage that you have to love yourself and there should be no guilt in doing so under any circumstance. In addition, loving others without judgment or expectation is a must. This is extremely difficult when you really think about it. Oftentimes, when we are in the moment, we get caught in the draft.

I am so grateful for all the thoughts of prayer and love that have been sent my way. I love you all more than any word can ever convey. I believe all your prayers in combination have been a very large part of my healing, and I will forever be grateful.

CHAPTER 20
IN PROGRESS

FEBRUARY 6, 2012

The first week of the transplant was similar to previous treatment. In order to prepare you to receive donor cell, they need to stave off all your white cells, and they do this through aggressive chemotherapy and radiation treatment.

I had a particularly hard time with the radiation because of the statistics connected to sterility, but I made peace with this and moved past, knowing that if we wanted to grow our family, God would find a way. During treatment I envisioned a beautiful light encasing the radiation, offering healing.

After a session of radiation I went back to my room and was alone for about an hour. Tad and my mom worked out a tight schedule so that I was barely alone. I was only alone at night because hospital policy stated no one could stay through the night during a transplant. This was a blessing because as much as I appreciated their care, they had to wear a mask and gloves the entire time in my room. Trust me—an hour with a mask on is difficult, so just imagine eight hours.

It was also nice to have a little time alone because at night I was tired and usually fell right to sleep. I prayed a lot that day, asking for guidance and knowledge on cleaning up my body from the treatment that was an essential part of healing.

The phone rang and it was Pat Hatwan. He just happened to call to check in and see how I was doing. In this moment I just needed his assurance and that was exactly what he gave me!

In the depths of my heart I knew I was well, and this plan of detoxing just became a way to solidify this deep knowing.

Pat was one of the first few I called at the beginning because I knew he and Lynn would have loving guidance, offering more than just medical direction. I spoke with him regularly to get feedback on the decisions I was making. He would always offer his guidance but riddle it with, "Now, Holly, you have to listen to your gut, all the knowledge, and go the direction that brings you closer to health." Even if I chose a different route than he suggested, he always supported my choices with love. Pat and Lynn are a lighthouse of support in my life, and I am grateful for their love and true friendship.

One night during the first week of treatment, which was preparing me for the transplant, Tad kissed me on the cheek and off he went up the street to the Marriott. Tad and my mom rented a room there for the entire month I was in the hospital so they could be close by at all times. They all really played such a huge role in my healing, as my stepfather, Dave, played a major role in Sawyer's care. I call Dave Sawyer's keeper as I entrusted Dave, whom I love very much, to protect Sawyer during this time and always. Dave is an amazing grandfather, so I feel blessed that Sawyer is a gift.

I was really tired and decided to do a little reading before I went to bed, when a nurse walked into my room. She said she was my night nurse, but I had never seen her before. Most if not all of the nurses on the floor are the same because they have oncology/transplant experience. She was looking through my online files to make sure I didn't need anything when she looked me in the eyes and said, "You know you can heal yourself." She was of Asian decent and saw all my vision boards, so I thought maybe she practiced a similar faith.

I asked her what exactly she was talking about. She said, "Your vision boards are a part of your healing, but once you get to a space that has no limits or conditions, a space that is the ultimate connection your body will follow the wishes of your soul." I asked her how to do this and she said, "Pure faith." Almost as if there was not any doubt that I was a reflection truly connected to the center of my soul.

She walked out of my room, and after about an hour of thought and writing, I went out in the halls to look for her because I had a few questions about the spiritual bomb she just dropped.

When I asked the other nurses where my night nurse went, no one knew whom I was talking about. The night nurse was not on yet, and when I described her, they again did not know whom I was talking about.

I am not sure who this woman was, but that night she left me with beautiful wisdom and the faith to get through the most difficult days of the transplant that lay ahead. I was so grateful for these thoughts because they became great tools that I used regularly when the going got tough.

CHAPTER 21
HAPPY BIRTHDAY TO ME!

FEBRUARY 9, 2012

What a night to celebrate … last night at 10:00 p.m. Shad's cells were brought over to Brigham from Dana–Farber, and what a beautiful sight they were! Shad had checked into Dana-Farber at 8:00 a.m., and until 4:00 p.m. he sat in a chair donating his stem cells.

He is a hero on many fronts, but I saw and felt something different for the first time. I felt a strong sense of oneness, a connection to my brother that exceeds space and time; a light that would guide me.

Shad made this choice for me because he loves me and I am his sister, but in this story there was a point that they told him he could not be my donor because his white count was too low. He fought for me, pushed through a number of hoops until he had a date for donation. His white count came back up, and here we are today. It just reveals how connected we all are to one another. My mother gave birth to me in 1976, giving me a beautiful life, teaching me to live from my heart, among many other things. Last night Shad gave me a "rebirth," which taught me that we are all one in heart, love is all, and it is time to live without fear, which means surrendering to live with an openness to continue evolution.

Before the cells were integrated, we had a chaplain bless them with a beautiful stem cell prayer. I also asked her to share words from my heart. They are as follows:

"I surrender to you, God. I open my heart and my light to your service. I release all fears and false ideas that come from my mortal mind and embrace divine truth as I am made in your image; therefore, I can only be of love.

"I am blessed that my brother, Shad, has given me this amazing gift, which reassures me that we are all one.

"I lovingly accept his cells and his love to work in harmony within my body.

"I envision all these beautiful cells working together in the highest vibration of love.

"I can feel the healing energy flowing through my body every breath I take; *I am healed.*

"I surround myself with authentic and loving people who share my journey of growth and awakening.

"Shanti."

And through those words I felt tears of joy trickle down my cheeks as I stared into the eyes of my mother and Tad, and there was nothing but love present. That was a night I will never forget as I felt all the prayers and intentions coming forward from all of you who have been supporting me on my journey.

As the cells started entering my body, I felt an awkward sensation in my bones, but they reassured me this was normal as the cells were making their way to the marrow. After my mom and Tad guided me with breath work, I settled in and envisioned these cells entering my body with great acceptance and love. It was a feeling that left me without words but a mystical time.

I felt so protected in this miracle that it does not have to be understood. I embraced the love. We talked for a short while with the nurse, sharing spiritual stories and laughing. It was an amazing night; my heart is full, and I am grateful for the Loveolution.

CHAPTER 22
TOUGH LOVE

FEBRUARY 11, 2012

After the transplant was complete, I was monitored very closely by the transplant team for the long list of side effects discussed prior to signing my life away. However, all was going great. It was as if everything was happening just as they said it would and in some circumstances even better.

Every morning the doctors came in with their crew of students to give me a look-over and a quick exam. It is a different generation of doctors, and learning is very different from allowing yourself to examine the whole picture. But I didn't mind; I understood they were learning, and hopefully they would be a part of creating a better future for treatment options. I have to say that they have come so far in treating blood disorders, it is amazing.

This again brings forward the question I will never know: Where and how did the Loveolution come to be a part of my journey? Regardless of where we are spiritually, if what we believe is real on a physical level, we must honor all beliefs.

It may be easier to describe this metaphorically to the overhead projectors teachers used and maybe still do today. The teacher would place the questions down on a screen, and after projecting those first questions, he or she would place another transparency sheet down on top of the first. This second sheet would then project onto the white screen the answers to one question, and as each sheet was laid on top of the projector, it would unveil yet another answer.

I have met those who are on the "final sheet"—all questions answered, and they see the whole picture; this I call "truth." This beautiful truth will come with divine timing, when one is ready, but there is one thing that is certain: once a layer is peeled, once you have seen the truth, there is no turning back, which may create challenges in and of itself.

This all brings me back to the most interesting part of this particular day, which was again the fact that I used to work at Brigham and Women's Hospital as a pharmacy representative. So as I metaphorically understood the overhead projector analogy, I felt like it applied to me especially in this moment.

I knew many of the physicians who walked the halls daily, along with many of those who were involved with progressive research at Dana-Farber. Therefore, it wasn't a complete surprise or coincidence that I knew the lead physician on my inpatient transplant team. It was yet another coincidence that divinely proved another hurdle. The research doctors on the transplant team would only be on service a couple of weeks out of the quarter, so again I asked, what is the lesson in this? Was it forgiveness? Letting go? Both?

It was certainly interesting as it brought forward many memories from the past. Many of us have experienced a job that we haven't connected with and knew was not a part of our life's purpose. We have all done work that is a potential stepping stone to jobs in the future, shaping us for our true calling. However, working for several pharmaceutical companies after college was definitely the wrong path for me without question.

I will always remember the exact day that I officially admitted to myself, although I had known after the first year, that I was working against my inner beliefs and integrity. The calling force happened to be a magazine called *Hospital Representative*. I was walking back to my car to drive to my condo in Boston and it fell to the ground as I was juggling my mail. When I bent down to pick it up, I saw the cover and literally gasped, as I couldn't believe my eyes. My initial thought was of shock because now I knew they did not even feel the need to hide it anymore. The cover read Can Medication Adherence Save Sales? When Patients Don't Take Their Meds, Everyone Loses. I thought it was a joke, or maybe I hadn't read it right the first time, so again I read it, immediately turning to the article before I even opened my car door.

I don't think I have to explain any further because I believe the title says it all, but when I asked a few colleagues their thoughts, they didn't offer much reaction. I was shocked, it was out there, and they weren't even trying to decorate it or dress it up. It was that exact moment that I knew I was done, but I felt trapped as I was living single in Boston, and I couldn't just quit my job—or could I? On my way back to my condo I made a plan, a plan to make the best of a tough situation, a plan to transition with wisdom and experience to the right path. I would do the work asked of me at my job, but I would also open as many doors as possible. I would use this opportunity to learn, to watch, to listen, and to take this information to create a change. I was now an undercover representative.

It is amazing when you dig in the other direction, letting go of any opinions you may have, what will jump out at you. Who was willing to share just a little more information than maybe they should was a surprise. This was where it becomes an ethical challenge. I believe there are a number of medications that truly help people bridge a gap to their health. However, selling drugs, and getting bonuses on how much you increase sales, means you must increase an illness market.

Within that same statement, this work showed me the intricacies of the pharmaceutical and medical worlds in combination. It is a dynamic balance between greed/corruption and care/healing. There are so many incredible people and ideas, but with an industry this big, there is big money and big politics. It was seeing all the sides in their rawest state that gave me the bird's-eye view that you would never get unless you walked the shoes.

There was such conflict that arose almost daily, but within this conflict came the brilliant lessons that showed me how to share this information. I watched the medical industry change right before my very eyes, and the role of the doctor struggling to maintain a humane standard of care was unbelievable on many levels. The story of corruption and greed has already been told and continues to be told if you are ready to listen. However, being exposed to the inner workings of any hospital, you learn a great deal about the backside of medicine.

This was always my greatest struggle because most physicians I worked with also acknowledged the changes that threatened the very essence of the Hippocratic oath they swore years ago as they stood before all they loved. I believe many physicians have the best of intentions to honor their creed to first do no harm. However, as with any big industry, there are a lot of power plays that creates a significant amount of discourse. In most cases you can tolerate the idiocy of politics and corruption, but not when it deals with innocent lives of doctors who work hard every day to help find a healing course for their patients and the patients that trust their doctors advocacy.

When I first got diagnosed, I was doing the best I could to grieve and stay focused, being an advocate for myself. However, this proved to be much more difficult than I ever could have imagined. I thought back to my days as a hospital representative and remembered "Dr. X." We didn't have a super-close relationship, but it was close enough that I believed he would reach out to me with a few answers at such a difficult time. When I paged him, he called right back as he didn't recognize the number and was so surprised to hear my voice. It may have taken a moment to remember me as it had been about five years, but through the plea in my voice, he quickly went back in time to remember a tall lanky girl with ideas that posed a different voice for medicine.

After that first call, several attempts to page him and numerous e-mails went unnoticed; I did not hear back from him. It was a slight knock to the ego, but I didn't have any time for that as I was going to be guided to health either way. One thing he did mention was that I needed to get an appointment to see Dr. Steck (in Chicago), who is one of the best. Funny as divinity played yet another piece of this puzzle, I already had an appointment with her through the previous physician who had been a student of hers. Chicago was where we met with Dr. Steck, and she lovingly sent me to Boston, organizing a whole line of patient care above and beyond her call. She will never know how grateful my whole family was for that appointment as she was a big part of the bigger decisions.

When I got to Dana-Farber I sent Dr. X an e-mail and got a very impersonal response. I decided at that point that my idea of knowing a familiar face was unnecessary, and I needed to move forward, knowing I was going to create this experience the way I needed it to be. Until the morning he became the lead inpatient doctor on Dr. Sieffer's transplant case.

Yet another "coincidence" in this beautiful road that has been brilliantly paved with divine steps. I thought quickly of *The Four Agreements* by Miguel Ruiz. The four agreements you make with yourself are:

1. Be impeccable with your word.
2. Don't take anything personally.
3. Don't make assumptions.
4. Always do your best.

These four simple statements hold so much power and emerging energy to stay in a positive state of love that I quickly forgot the disappointment I felt regarding Dr. X. I knew he didn't owe me anything, but I thought that regardless, one would step up in the name of humanity to help anyone facing these circumstances.

Each morning the team of doctors, a combination of fellows and interns, would knock on my door to see my progress. They would give me the once over and look to my chart, watching my numbers go up, each day with a light that moved me beyond hope. I again pulled myself together in the name of faith and believed I was well.

While the weeks went by quickly, I will not act as though there were not difficult days. Dr. X unintentionally remained a continuous challenge as he constantly planted seeds that were sometimes hard to remove from my garden of hope and faith. I have to say that this took me by surprise, but I worked hard to let it flow, as it wasn't worth my time or my truth. This was the perfect place to insert the four agreements, the perfect tool that allowed a quick release and a balance of energy.

I felt very blessed by the care I received at Brigham and Women's, knowing every day, every lesson was another layer of the onion peeling away, freeing my soul.

It was around this time (two weeks post-transplant) when I started my journey into "Holly's World." This was a common joke amongst family and friends when I would decide to ignore the world around me, creating my own experience. It is a world filled with bliss, love, and zero challenge. It was usually short trips there, but sweet nonetheless.

I would journey so far beyond Holly's World to the center of my soul to find the courage and strength to learn through this experience. I went so far that I do not have much recollection. I had developed a common side effect of transplant, and this required some additional medication. I was certainly in a different place, and Tad didn't miss a beat. Even though he took every moment seriously, filled with dedication and love, he wanted me to have some recollection of the whole experience. So in the decade of the iPhone, Tad took video, and I will assure you from watching, I am glad I do not have much memory of one particularly difficult week.

Some moments were very sad as I sat on my bed, covered in blankets, contending with a high fever, rocking back and forth in a meditative state.

I was extremely focused on my health and knowing I was healed; this I didn't forget.

One night I woke and thought I was in my freshman college dorm room. It totally looked like it, and the nurse, who was one of my favorites, laughed with me, guiding me back "home." She was the best. She sat and talked with me for a long time because she knew I was scared. She was hardcore and had a heart of gold. She is an amazing nurse and I was so grateful for the incredible staff of nurses on this floor.

The following week was filled with similar types of humor. I went on to tell Tad, about my time in seventh-grade home economics class where not only was I apparently an amazing baker, but I could sew too.

On my foggiest day, I shared my excitement about winning first place in a home economics cook-off. It would be the "Twisted Beret Rice Nut Treat" that won me the victory.

Over the week, as my fever slowly decreased, I continued to talk about strange things that Tad would just write down so as not to forget. I told him about a Spartan game that I had to "pass." I would share intricate details about what gear was needed and whom he needed to contact to get the best gear. I explained the plan as a play by play to show how I was going to overcome each and every obstacle.

The most interesting day was when I told Tad we were going to have twins. I said it as if we were talking about the grocery list, just very matter-of-fact. I told him our daughter was going to be a spitfire and described her as if I had just met her. I didn't talk much about the other twin, and I don't believe I revealed the gender. However, that was the hardest two weeks of the transplant, and thankfully I don't remember them. Unfortunately, my mom and Tad do remember each detail as I suffered through a very challenging time.

Once these two weeks passed, I grew stronger each day. I was alert and back to my normal self—well, as normal as one could be under these circumstances.

At this point I was just looking forward to going home and leaving the hospital, but the last four days seemed never-ending. Each night I would go to bed without a sign of a fever all day, and then around three or four in the morning, I would spike a huge fever, and that would shut down my chance of going home. You need to go twenty-four hours without a fever.

It goes without saying that the last four days of my stay were the most challenging for a number of reasons. The last day that I thought I was going to be set free, I heard the words, "One or two more days." I felt the tears slowly trickle down my face, as I didn't know if I could bear one more day.

Each day, as Tad and my mom came to visit, they brought up the mail and gifts people sent. I will never forget the day I received a gift from a very kind woman, whom I have never met. It was from my friend Colleen—her sister had a great relationship with a friend who'd started a "survivor pin." She started this after it was given to her, and so far it has been in the hands of seven survivors. This woman didn't even know me but cared enough to pass on pure love and intention. I was so touched, and this undoubtedly gave me the strength to get through the next two days.

I am glad they didn't send me home until I was ready. However, when I got the thumbs up, I was out the door and didn't look back. I was blessed in my healing never to have been readmitted into the hospital. This is rare, but I believe my thoughts in creating this healing journey played a role.

I received many beautiful gifts and kind gestures; these thoughts of kindness were exactly the thoughts that made me "feel" well! They helped me believe I was healed. A community of prayer and healing is quite powerful.

I knew when it was time to pass on the survivor coin, it was an intuitive thought that came through guidance, and I shared it in Holly's Loveolution.

"Small Blessings Illuminated"

*

> Today was a sacred day as I gave my survivor/courage coin to another who needed it. This coin marked a strong staple in my healing as it reminded me, during many challenging times, of the love and kindness that comes with small blessings. A woman I do not know and have never met sent it to me when I was in the beginning of treatment. She heard my story through a friend of a friend and wanted to share her gift. The coin has now been passed to the eighth person who needed the courage to know she can heal, moving past survivorship; the courage to live beyond the thoughts of fear and move right into the ideal of love. The woman who gifted the coin to me will never really know how

much her kindness touched me, but I have a feeling she wasn't looking for anything in return, just setting the intention to move it forward for love.

When I woke up this morning the first thought on my mind was passing along the coin to my friend. It was as if someone was telling me this coin needed to be her new home while she traveled through her journey. I was excited and ready to move it forward as I had a couple of weeks filled with all kinds of small blessings and observations, truly understanding how far a very simple gesture takes the most surprising recipient.

It started almost two weeks ago as I questioned strongly the level that humanity was teetering. I was observing behaviors that left me lost in thought, wondering if people really are as disconnected as it seemed. People only caring about their own life, "looking out for number one" I think the saying goes.

It went from a woman at the grocery store trying to juggle her three kids that were clearly done with their rainy day adventure. As onlookers passed by I could feel the judgment fill the air, the stares and dirty looks ... to the record-breaking number of doors that closed in my face because the person in front didn't care enough or was too busy to hold the door. I was just observing and wondering, I have been in a sort of lock down, so now that I am in full swing, I am just observing with what feels like a new set of eyes.

As I took note of these simple yet disconnected events, I then began to think about why we are disconnected? Is it because we are always thinking really about ourselves or are we attracting that type of energy toward us? I am sure there are many opinions as the idea of humanity can't be summed up in one sentence, but I was simply just observing. It was in that moment I realized how many people live unconscious lives.

That night I prayed! Prayer is amazing once you let go of the "how to" and just allow yourself to talk with God. Many think this may be weird because he doesn't answer back, but doesn't he? He gives us wisdom through thoughts, he gives us signs, and he opens doors. However, this is all done with our action, when a door opens you will not have the experience if you don't walk through it.

Going through this journey I have pealed a lot of layers off my life, this includes relationships that were not balanced. The more I am honest with myself I am blessed with observing all the greatness that is in my life. I have stop forcing relationships that do not need to be and this is out of love. From the moment this intention is set, it melts out into the world like a wave, not really knowing exactly whom it touches.

Much like a seesaw, this past week I have observed so much kindness that I was almost in disbelief. At the grocery store with just 1 child who was ready to be done with the "shopping experience," I realized that I picked out avocados that were cracked. The woman standing in front of me happened to notice and told me to run with my son to get 2 more. She not only held my spot, but when I got back to the line she had unpacked my whole grocery cart. It immediately shifted the once felt frenzy, to simple love. The day after as I ran my errands every door was held for me and one nice man even complimented my now very curly hair that sometimes creates a feeling of insecurity. It was so kind and I accepted his compliment with an open heart! Small blessings, small gestures and acts of kindness kept pouring into my life, which made me feel a connection bound in simple love.

It was not these past observations that moved me to send the coin forward, however, it was these acts that reminded me how special a gift it really is. Through intention and intent we can shift an outlook, a bad day, a bad year to love. So as I once thought that humanity could not be described by just one sentence, I realized it can be described in one word: LOVE!

Many blessings

Do something nice today just because!

*

"O Lord, your power is greater than all powers. Under your leadership we cannot fear anything. It is you who has given us prophetic power, and has enabled us to foresee and interpret everything."

—Dinka Prayer (Sudan) of the African traditional religion.

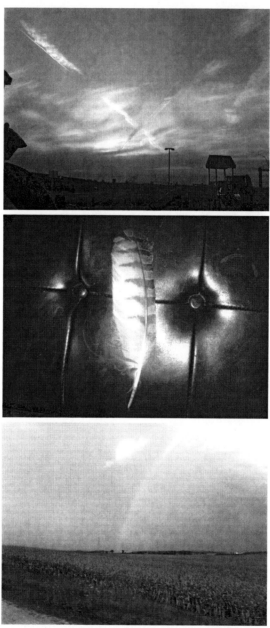

The week I got diagnosed was very stressful, but when I was clear I asked God to show me a sign that I already was well. The first picture is my last night in Chicago, as I asked for a sign a cross appeared in the sky. Then on the way home we saw a rainbow. Days before I was diagnosed I found this Hawk's Feather on my front lawn, a sign of a life changing journey upon you.

This is called "golden rain" when caught in a photo. Your aura is so bright that a camera picks it up. It can also mean there are angels with you.

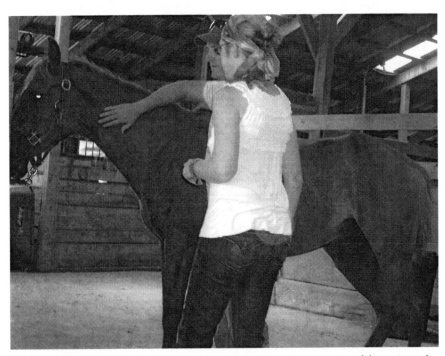

I had a dream that I broke my back on a white horse in a previous life, so in order to get over my fear we went riding. You can see the angelic orb on my low back.

I asked God for a sign while I was driving and in the sky an angel appeared and then it turned into an orb with a purple circle around it.

In the story I tell you about how I found three pieces of the butterfly on three different places and three different days. This was a sign from God that all was well!

Always asking God for a sign and it doesn't take long to create your reality!

Zugspitz Germany where Tad surprised me with an amazing engagement

My brother, Shad Tessier, who donated bone marrow and saved my life.

It was 2 months before diagnosis and the steps
were set up to support this journey.

When Sawyer first saw me with my bald head he just
laughed and hugged me, seeing nothing but love.

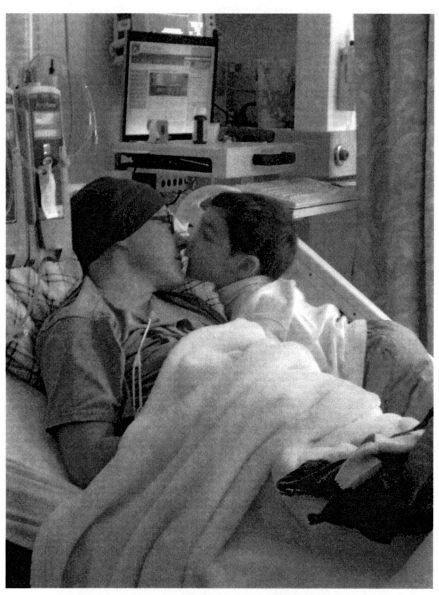

This was a day of great thanks with love as we found out that I was in full remission and Shad was a match for transplant.

Working out everyday, even when I felt like I couldn't go far.

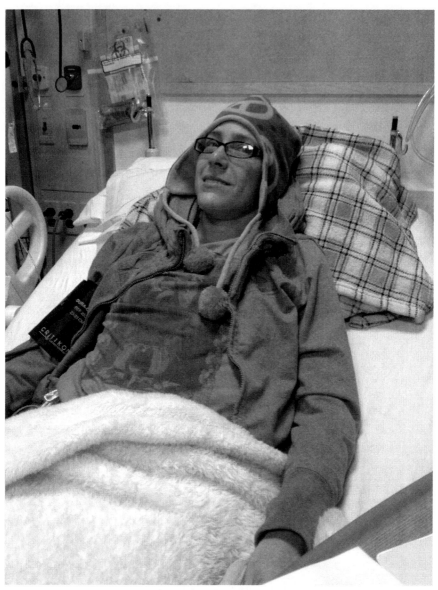

This was a very emotional night as a chaplain blessed the cells and I wrote a poem to manifest a full healing.

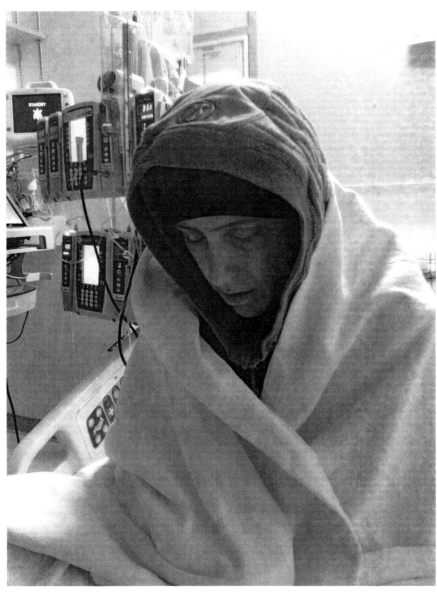

This was the two weeks that I didn't make a whole lot of sense, but I saw the light on the other end.

There are very few pictures of my when I lost my hair but as you read in the book it was a process and in the end I felt proud.

This is one of three vision boards that marked my walls to keep me positive and aligned with health.

The amazing Yogi's honored me with a prayer vigil.

As I healed after a year I was able to take a trip
to Denver with my family. So blessed!

Sawyer and I did yoga everyday, he was a great teacher.

Sawyer connectes and grounds himself in Tree Pose
(Looks like he is being supported by the tree behind him).

Sawyer is so connected to his soul that he knows exactly what he likes.

This is the coin that followed me to be a continued sign. When I would give it away, I would receive it as a gift. The survivor Coin I gave to another after I "survived".

This was the night of the "Light the Night Walk". The beginning of my healing!

CHAPTER 23
HOME IS THE HEART

> I long, as does every human being, to be at home wherever I find myself.
> ~Maya Angelou

MARCH 20, 2012

I have been home for about two or three weeks, the hands of time lost somewhere between the hospital doors and the cheeks of an angel. Sawyer didn't miss a beat; it was as if I was never gone. The funny part is that in retrospect, the six weeks during the transplant seemed like a distant memory when I got home, which probably puts Sawyer and me on the same page with "time."

As I settled into a home routine, I realized the next few months would be filled with many challenges as I got back on my feet. This undoubtedly would create an opportunity for strength and growth not only for me but also for my whole family. I embraced the transplant and let go, surrendering to the guidance of God. This would be the final stage; now it was time to heal emotionally. It was time to brush off the fear, put into action all the wisdom that came from such an intense life experience, and move forward. As you can imagine, being in the hospital for such a long time was filled with all kinds of experiences. These experiences in the moment were neither good nor bad, they were just part of the journey, mental images I have chosen to sweep away long ago.

During all the ups and downs, all the ebbs and flows there was one special night that will forever be engrained in my memory. During my time in the hospital, on February 9, there was an anticlimactic moment that I call a "rebirth." Even though every day brings experiences that may evolve us a little more than we may notice, this particular night was a representation of new life, new choices, and new dreams. The most important of all being pure love; I would live with a true heart and love without condition. I would surrender to all old beliefs, old emotions, and old attachments that never served me. I would live guided by God's work, which would mean forgiveness to self. Although I have already discussed the transplant in detail, I believe this to be such a monumental moment that I want to share a few more specifics now that I have had weeks to process what really happened.

It was a night my family will never forget. For my mother, one child saved another; for Tad, a brother-in-law shared cells that will forever melt in love; and for me, a new relationship, no matter how subtle, will continue to change my life. And of course all those amazing, beautiful cells have blended and become one.

Shad donated all day and produced twice as many cells as they required, channeling a successful transplant. The more you get, the better, so the transplant, regardless of the nights that will be a dark etch on my journey, was a huge success.

That night as I saw the cells "come into my room," I had a single thought, a blank sheet of paper. This was an opportunity to make right what I needed to make right, which meant cleaning out my emotional closet, living dreams, and great change.

The chaplain read a blessing:

"**Holy One, we gather this day holding a source of new life in our hands. As we bless these stem cells, we thank you for the donor who so graciously gave them to give another a new chance at life.**

"**As these stem cells flow into Holly, we trust in your care and blessings this day. We pray that Holly's body be fully receptive to this new day of birth and as we go forward. Strengthen and bring comfort to Holly as each day will hold its own challenges. We beg for peace in body, mind, and spirit, so that good energy will flow at the dawn of each day.**

"**Bless all those in Holly's circle of love and support. Nurture their compassionate hearts and illuminate their lives so your light be ever present to Holly.**

"**Walk us into the future, and we pray in gratitude for your blessing this day.**

"Amen."

Tad and my mom both took one glance to see how I was affected by the gentle, inspiring words. As they looked toward me, I felt my heart fill; I felt light in a time where fear was trying to be the leader. I felt God holding me in his arms. Tad and my mom, both under the wings of an angel, would guide me through a new birth. This would be a different type of birth, but a birth all the same.

From this point forward Tad and my mother pretty much managed my care and advocated for me when I was not fully aware. It was a team effort at home and in the hospital that made this journey so successful.

I looked back at my last post and was shocked that Father Time again struck midnight while I was down the rabbit hole. It seems like I was just this week getting my feet back on the ground and gaining clarity. All my cells have synergistically come together and didn't miss a beat. Oftentimes one will need medication to help the body kick start the regeneration process, but I did not need any help (with meds, anyway). All came together through God's love, and each week my cells and body have responded with amazing grace.

What can I say about all these cells being little overachievers? We were really blessed and never took that for granted. I can't thank my supporters enough as it was their intentions, love, and prayers that were one of the strongest driving forces, next to God's love. Without this it would have made this experience that much more challenging.

I wish there was a word that went above the call of thank you, but from the deepest nook in my soul, I thank you all.

As I continue my healing in its earliest stage, I am very delicate. However, my soul feels so strong and bright as it welcomes me back to knowing my truth. Tonight I wrote in hollysloveolution:

"No matter where you go, there you are" (Confucius).

*

> I am slowly putting the pieces back together, and as it gets a bit easier, I am starting to see the bigger picture. I am ready to live. Life will never be the same. My heart feels so full, and "don't sweat the small stuff" is an understatement.

Starting from the moment I walked through our front door, I saw all the work my family did to prepare our home for my arrival. There was such a long list of tasks that needed to be done, such as dusting, carpet cleaning, curtain cleaning—you name it—and it was cleaned. This was all done within the confines of love to support my new immune system, which is much like that of a baby. I took this metaphor literally as I continually call this my "rebirth" and know that I got another chance to move forward with a great deal of wisdom.

Over the next six months I was told to exercise caution, making good decisions with small trips and visits. As each month passed and my immunity grew stronger, I gained more freedom. However, it was the knowing that I am bound to my home that was such a new concept for me. I have always been on the go, and this was a house arrest of sorts, without a police record.

I am excited to use some of this downtime to write and share the insight I have learned. I am definitely looking forward to practicing yoga and riding my stationary bike that my parents thoughtfully chose to give me for Christmas, somehow keeping it from my sight. More importantly, I am ready to live life. I am ready to wrap my arms around this whole experience, push it deep into my soul, and force my ego out the other side.

I don't need to worry about time missed with Sawyer and family because it has all been growing and is an intricate part of this learning journey, which continues from here.

I now have to make this space my home as I am going to be embracing this scenery for a lengthy amount of time. It is all based on progress, but generally along with strict diet, the healing is being home. I can feel this physically—and mostly emotionally—as I begin to step forward in light!

Without doubt this has been an unfamiliar road, which tries to produce a significant amount of fear due to the unknown. Fear it is metaphorically like the monster in the closet—it is not real but likes to scoop up your anticipation as if it were truth. The very thought of it can cause you to feel lost in a world so big, but knowing that you can always be found by beaconing your heart space which will guide you right back home. This was now our new home, and my heart was filled with so many new experiences that propelled great love.

CHAPTER 24
THE MOMENT OF THE PRESENT

> You don't have to see the whole staircase; just take the first step.
> ~Martin Luther King Jr.

MARCH 27, 2012

It is so easy to allow your mind (it is never your heart because if it were, it would only share the truth with you) to overwhelm you with anything in life. Your mind and thoughts can allow you to feel "so busy," double-timing it through life. However, when you sit for a moment you realize the statement "so busy" is the driving force of your stress. When you write down what is stressing you, when you write your to-do list, you might not be as busy as you originally thought. So ringing the words "I'm so busy" all day is the storm around a beautiful day.

Our mortal mind or ego is in a constant state of trickery. It is amazing to think that your subconscious mind is harboring so many negative thoughts, thoughts that do not serve you with the glass half-empty.

Coming from our fast-food society, many of us want to have the end result without walking the one step at a time, listening to our heart making decisions that will bring us happiness. This is just an example of how we get caught in the trap of living either in future moments or the past.

I always thought, after getting a degree in criminology, that it would be so great if I could go back to 1994 and change my major! However, there is a reason this was my path and where it directed me. It took me on a great journey, learning so much along the way, waking up to the truths of the world. Not to mention it brought a few lifelong friends to my life, who still share their love today.

One in particular is my friend Marc Breadheft, who is one of my closest friends. We met in college and knew each other before we really knew ourselves. It was a great blessing to keep an intricate connection as we each personally grew in our own hearts. It marks yet another example of the inner circle of your life and why they have been planted in your "front row."

This friendship correlates to one of the greatest realizations to this point, (as I have had plenty of time to look deep), *I am love*, pure love and that alone is what starts the journey of my souls evolution. It is an amazing lesson learned. When I focus on the truth that my heart is full of love and I have self-worth, fear and control begin to lose their strength. The more I become my true self, the more I forgive myself for the lessons I have been part of along the way, the more I learn that I have a purpose here and will be guided in the direction of my journey, the more I love.

Emotions are the doorway to your soul. Allow yourself to let go of every part of you that you feel is wrong or bad. Focus on the love you have to give, as we are all connected. Take a couple of deep breaths and draw something or someone into your mind that has caused you stress. On inhalation bring in a beautiful red light of love, and on the exhale release whatever circumstance is bringing in stress. Take a moment to recognize that we are all at a different place in our journey and should not be judged, but just know everyone is doing the best where they are.

These are really challenging concepts because oftentimes, if it doesn't feel normal or acceptable to us, we make it wrong. However, we all have a lot to learn from each other, so moving softly to understand instead of judging is a great start.

Many blessings to self-love and self-preservation!

CHAPTER 25
MIRROR REFLECTIONS

"The universal mirror is so honest and accurate that your deepest secrets show up in the reflections you see of yourself. Every person and situation in your life is a mirror aspect of you as within so without."
~ Diane Cooper

APRIL 06, 2012

It is so important to understand the tools that can help you find your inner love and peace. Now looking back, I see how the mirror is such a strong, persuasive tool to help the ego or your heart. It is truly amazing how the mirror, representing the law of reflection, allows for you to really see the depths of your life. It allows for you to see the reality of your emotions and creation, if you are ready! There is no doubt that those who surround us are a reflection of our internal manifesting. Some in our life are a reflection of our continued growth and healing and others are here to teach us. This reintroduces the idea of the theater and who sits in your front row. You may have the same entire front row your whole life, but maybe not. It is when we truly embrace "non-attachment" that we feel freedom in seeing our reflection.

The mirror invokes a deep spiritual gift that has been seen throughout history; Egyptians marked their walls with the very essence of the mirror showing us that this knowledge has always been available to us as we evolve.

Sometimes in life we have experiences that create your inner circle when you don't quite have the strength. Colleen and Wendy are a part of my circle and when they came for their second visit from Chicago thankfully I was home, not at the hospital. It was so great to hug them and know they were going to be with me for the whole weekend, a weekend filled with yoga, reflexology, cranial-sacral and Thai massage; it was great!

The entire weekend was filled with continuous laughter and tears, but it felt so good to get a fresh perspective. I felt like there was a strong undercurrent throughout the entire weekend. A theme that spoke to all of us about the simplicity of life, yet showed us how we sometimes still choose the more challenging path. Simplicity offers you the ability to live directly from the rawest part of your heart that knows the truth about your journey. It is just waiting for you to stop living from the outside, waiting for you to honor your reflection so you can truly hear and feel the personal rhythm of your soul.

Michael Jackson was far beyond his years when he wrote "Man in the Mirror." Take a moment to read the lyrics, and you will immediately realize you may never have been aware of the real message behind this rhythmic melody. I know this has been my experience, where I've gotten so taken by the music that the words become jumbled into each note, and I've missed the very essence of it's expression and meaning.

Michael Jackson along side the likes of Gandhi were two very different men from different times but with the same message; "Be the change you wish to see in the world." Within a few words they each speak of the bravery and courage it takes to make the change you see in your heart, a change that mimics love within you and outside of yourself.

With this message in mind, the concept of the mirror is riddled with a great deal of trickery. It gives us the ability to see our actions in the mirror of others. This is where the mirror becomes a great tool to recognize your own internal judgments; the release of deep external judgments that we can see in the "mirror" will eventually relieve you from the internal ones.

This was one of my very first lessons when I stepped on my yoga mat, in a room that was previously a dancer's dream. It was lined with mirrors on every side, which allowed you to see yourself and others all at once. This just fostered an environment of internal judgment but nonetheless offered a great lesson—we are our own reflection and/or projection.

Every time we judge another we are simply reflecting or projecting that judgment deep within our heart, tucking it away so no one can see. However, it is still there burning a legacy in your heart, so what better to do than put it on someone else, wrapped in a fury of judgment. This is the ego's way of tricking you into avoiding the evolution towards oneness. For example, when we judge another, it takes the light off us and suppresses our commonality even further. The great news comes by way of recognition as you engage in the egos play. This is oftentimes one of the many steps towards awareness in your journey of evolution toward oneness and love.

For me personally it is so mind blowing to realize how much power the concept of the mirror holds, a simple moment of self-rejection when you see your reflection. This is how your ego can interfere with self-love as you are shown how the mirror, metaphorically and physically, can open the door to self-loathing and anger. However, the more layers we peel, the more we use this tool with a sense of truthfulness, the easier it is to hear the internal heart that will guide you to your true passion, your true role.

To help peel the layers back, we must *allow and listen*.

Each day we get intuitive information from God or Source. Some of this information is very simple, such as guiding you home a different way than your normal route and some intuition or guidance is much more complex. We often doubt the very essence of energy that flows to our heart, and can even mistake the voice of the ego for the voice of our soul.

This guidance over time can provide an easier path filled with the sweetest wisdom, instead of continually walking through life with blinders. Starting with your breath slow down each step, allowing and listening to the wisdom from within.

It is when we slow down our thoughts and put away our needs and the needs of others for a moment that we begin to hear this subtle guidance. As we build a relationship with this inner tuition, we are more able to distinguish the ego that creates fear and suffering from our guidance.

As we continue to soften our senses and embrace calm, we will find the fortitude we need for patience. This is the foundation for manifesting the experiences and knowledge that will lead you towards your soul journey, leaving pain and suffering behind.

As my weekend with Wendy and Colleen continued, we discussed and shared the many tools we each use to hear the voice of our heart. I shared my experiences and successes with writing my affirmations and visions on my mirror with dry-erase markers, using both these tools to retrain my thoughts. Going from a space of "I am" and working out the kinks until moving just a little further along, embodying my created reality.

Each morning I start my day envisioning my greatest intentions and gratitude. It is such a wonderful feeling to be connected to Source, which is always guiding us toward our soul purpose whether we listen or not. However, now I know that there was a missing link. I knew what I "wanted" but didn't allow it because I kept walking down the path of the same old patterns. Even though I had a new thought process, I realized if I didn't change my actions, the thought would stay just a process. You will continue to walk the same path, with the same outcomes in life, until something happens to wake you up … welcome, Loveolution.

I am not saying we bring difficult things onto ourselves. However, when you ask God for patience, you may not get patience wrapped in a bow. You may get stuck on the highway for two hours while missing a date. This is where I learned to be conscious with my words and thoughts. Stating, "I am patient" is a much better approach. Wendy and Colleen shared similar stories of lessons learned.

We talked about creating a vision board, which has a foundation supported by quantum physics and the laws of the universe. It is truly an amazing spiritual tool to create a life you love. It can be anything in your heart's desire, knowing God wants us to have abundance, which simply becomes what you make of it.

We looked over my vision boards from the hospital, which were filled with pictures and words of healing. Prayer blessings and images made me trust the divine guidance that was being centered in my heart. This allowed me to set my course as I navigated change and understanding, love and forgiveness. For these blessings I am so grateful, along with the gratitude for great friendships. All these intentions were surrounded by two very important words: "I AM". It is easy when you are calm with peaceful surroundings. It becomes difficult to truly believe what you want to manifest and listen to God's guidance when the world around you ensues chaos on many levels. So we start with releasing the levels of chaos by eliminating things in our life that just bring negativity. It doesn't have to just be a person, it could be an exercise class we are desperately trying to fit into the wrong part of our day, which may be creating stress on our schedule. It can reflect a support meeting that creates more stress than support. Looking inside yourself and being honest will help you clean up the external things around you in order to create a calm.

Colleen and Wendy, along with a handful of others, have held my hands in difficult moments, helping me get to the other side. They have held the fear, giving me a chance to feel the freedom to hear God's wisdom. Lastly, they sat with me even when they weren't physically present, hundreds of miles from their life to love me to health. These are the types of friendships that make "home" wherever you are.

CHAPTER 26
BALANCE

APRIL 23, 2012

After my visit with Colleen and Wendy, I continued my journey to seek balance and wisdom. I was in the process of creating my home while healing and driving out fear. This was no short feat, but I felt the support of those I love, which gave me a great deal of courage.

I soon realized, in order to create your true reality you must leave fear in the dark, judgment in the past, and open your heart fully to love! It is a choice that is waiting to spread through you and all those you choose to be in your reality.

It seems that this may be a very difficult ideal to hold in truth, but it is the ultimate goal—full love and forgiveness. I was working so hard to dissolve any and all fears that continued to try and sneak their way into my head. With a striking average of sixty thousand thoughts per day, and metaphorically being on house arrest, I had a lot of time to think.

While I saw the challenge that presented, I once again had to reach for my bag of tools and put them to immediate use. Oftentimes it is difficult to clear out old thought patterns and behaviors, but with the use of meditation, affirmation, and envisioning, I was feeling strong. In addition, I always had my family around to support me when these sacred tools were unevenly matched.

It is amazing to see myself as I stand today in full health. It would be silly to say I never wavered from my true beliefs. That I didn't have any moments of projected fear that tried to throw me off course. However, I have known that my true soul has always been there to support me even when I didn't know I needed it. It has been one step at a time that I have peeled the external layer to evolve. Whatever metaphor you want to use to describe your evolution, it is such a blessing to be on the hunt for your personal empowerment even for just a moment.

There will be many people in your life who will always hold you to the time when they knew you no matter what stage of life you are standing; they will not embrace or move forward with your new awareness. However, if you just hold your true reflection and your true heart, they will either exit your life or cheer you on with love.

While I see the importance of balance in every endeavor in life, I know this can be one of the greatest challenges that we work with on a daily basis. I thought a lot about where I see myself today, my naked heart, and I wrote thinking only of one word: *balance*.

I say my no-fear mantra and immediately feel my body chemistry change. Leukemia has been an opportunity to learn about fear and face it. We all have fears, but when you really have to face fear, you need to learn techniques to squash them, or push them so far into the past that they are just a memory that doesn't affect the present.

This is our choice, and I am choosing to move past fear. It doesn't happen in a day, but I have taken huge strides since October. I am facing it head on softly and gently like a goddess, instead of a warrior. I am taking this route because the more I listen to the fear, the more I realize how much of a trick it really is and how my mind wants to keep this obstacle course in full swing. Today, I will love this fear because it has taught me a lesson, the most precious life lesson.

Fear is a beast running its course through most of our lives, I can only imagine what the world would look like if there was no fear, or less fear. Fear does an amazing job fooling many of us as our inner voice; the ego doesn't want us to know the truth. Therefore, we take the hard path because of fear, not realizing that if we listen to our inner guide, life would be easier and filled with so much more love.

When one feels misguided in life, where is the most common place we look? Outside ourselves, often looking to our culture and society to give us a definition of what is right and wrong.

Of course this starts with our parents' mold; however, we quickly take over as early as grade school. This is where we really experience judgment and begin creating our story. Fear keeps you working and living externally so you don't notice that you don't like your job, haven't been on vacation for five years because you don't have the money, or want to lose weight but don't have time to exercise. These are just a couple of examples of many that keep you living in fear, keeping the door closed to living your true life.

I have talked about fear a lot throughout this book, as it is the greatest boundary we have in our spiritual evolution. There are many ways to address fear, but without question it is the biggest creator of boundaries and judgment. It can keep us in the handcuffs of suffering for many years. However, once you begin to identify your fears, you can slowly start to cut the cords that keep you connected to this false reality. You start embracing the ideas that are cherished with love and walking away from the ones that bring forward sadness.

Fear created by the ego will do everything possible to disguise itself from being found. Fear will hide in your dreams as a symbol, preying on your wish of guidance. You begin to believe this "sign" was sent from above to guide you, but if it sparks any creation of fear, you can be sure it was sent by your ego.

Fear hides in our insecurities, deep in the layers of worry, and the one thing that can dissolve the ego's strength is love—pure love with a dash of forgiveness. As I said, fear (ego) is extremely tricky, much like a chameleon, changing colors faster than you can recognize. However, the first step is to identify the level of fear in your life. One at a time, when you are ready, you slowly put the light out and will feel the freedom that becomes a power.

During the many months I was home I decided right from the beginning that I was going to make the best of my time. One night while the house was asleep, I lay in thought. I reached over to my bedside table and began writing in my journal. I listed all the things I believed were fears, but it was getting so long I stopped to work on it later. I was surprised to the length of the list because I have worked through a great deal of fear in my yoga practice. However, what I never really recognized was the layers that run deep under a fear. The idea was that the fear itself was never there until the layers slowly began creating this fear that was trying to work into my reality.

Later the next day I reread all my "fears," and one at a time I wrote why this wasn't truly a fear and if it was how could I dissolve this untruth. This was a lot of work and took a lot of thought, but with each fear addressed I felt an overwhelming accomplishment encircle my heart. I felt free.

Exercise:

*

I already put in a similar exercise to addressing limiting beliefs, but another major part of our evolution is identifying our fears and challenging them. Fear is created on so many levels that it takes continued effort to identify the true fears you have in life. The surfaced fears, such as flying, heights. I am not minimizing the reality of how difficult this is for many, and not to mention life changing. However, there are so many layers to fear that create our fear of flying or heights. One night, as I was reading my journal, I realized that most, if not all fears stem from the concept of our mortality. I could not think of one fear that did not metaphorically or physically result from death, which I found to be interesting. For the purpose of this exercise you are going to take a few days to write down all your fears. After a few days, sit with it and really identify if this is a fear or if those around you have created it for you? Next challenge it!

Challenging a fear can be quite difficult because chances are it has been a generational fear you learned from another. The intentions are always good, but none the less they deepen the strength of the fear until we find a way to overcome it. By challenging it you are asking: does this fear come from my own experience? What is a real example that would support this? When did it become a fear and what was happening in my life at the time? You have to treat this like a court case and you are the leading attorney trying to prove that this fear is simply "false evidence trying to be real", creating as many boundaries as possible so the mortal mind has control. I suggest start with the easier fears, as you will see on your list you may even laugh at some of the things that you are afraid of, which require you to live your live a certain way. For example, I have always been afraid of the dark. So when I was alone in college I had to have the TV on all night, which is a terrible habit producing very bad sleeping patterns.

Once you have started to challenge these fears, set them free, affirming that they have no space in your life. Remember it is a choice, if you want to allow a fear to control how you live. I have listened to many talk about why they are afraid to fly and I have such empathy for this as it is so real for them. However, this is changing the way they live as they can only travel reasonable distances. We can move past these fears and clean the slate once we understand the root of the fear, challenge it, and affirm a new positive thought.

CHAPTER 27
MAGIC RIDE

> "So many people live within unhappy circumstances and yet will not take the initiative to change their situation because they are conditioned to a life of security, conformity, and conservation, all of which may appear to give one peace of mind, but in reality nothing is more damaging to the adventurous spirit within a man than a secure future. The very basic core of a man's living spirit is his passion for adventure. The joy of life comes from our encounters with new experiences, and hence there is no greater joy than to have an endlessly changing horizon, for each day to have a new and different sun.   ~ Jon Krakauer, *Into the Wild*

MAY 15, 2012

Our family is settling into our new but old space, which is bringing to light all we have been through in the past year and life is becoming clearer by each passing moment. It was a showstopper without question, and the fact that none of us saw it coming proves that living in the present moment is quite a difficult challenge. It is a way of life, to break the habit of living in the past or living in the future.

My parents moved into their new condo over on the lake, which is absolutely beautiful. We have maintained residence at their home, which has been such a blessing. It is not easy to share a space with an entire family, including their animal farm, but my parents opened their arms with support and love. In addition, divinity continued to prove its path with love and perfection, placing each stone just a simple step away.

Now as I move further away from the transplant, it all seems like a dream—or is it just catching up with everyone? Either way there have been a lot of tears representative of a new life and continued gratitude, which will forever be a natural part of life.

It was great news when Dr. Sieffer told me my body was 100 percent "engraphed" with Shad's cells. This means my body didn't reject any of the millions and millions of cells that were transplanted to me. My immunity is getting stronger. This is a reflection that I have always been well and that my body is just simply catching up to my soul. In addition, I would never have imagined that while I was dealing with such a life challenge that the most amazing people would show up with just the most divine answers.

As the months passed, life started to seem real again. I was no longer seeing life pass by in a surreal state. I felt that once again I was a part of my life, taking one "new normal" step at a time, my spirit feeling the adventure that was under each step. That may seem like a difficult thing to understand, but through the toughest of days, life lived me. Through those days I began to understand the imaginations we must have in order to override the ego, the love we must have to forgive and leave judgment behind. The courage we must have to trust God's plan and live with power.

When I have a moment of fear, I immediately ask God for a sign or a dream that will give me guidance. Last Monday I had an appointment at Dana-Farber. Each appointment seems to offer a chance to work with my "no fear" policy. I acknowledge what the ego is trying to accomplish before and during each appointment and the "what ifs?" At each and every appointment, I always bring my angel coin to remind me not only of this wisdom, but the false reality that fear tries to create and the worry that is utterly unnecessary. In my efforts to trust, I decided that this coin would hold these intentions. Whenever my mind would go to a fearful space I would rub my thumb over the angel, feeling the wings and the brilliance that flows from a divine being. Immediately my thoughts became surrounded by love and peace.

I hold tight to the coin whenever I am getting my blood drawn, again so I can keep positive affirmations running through my mind. On the back the coin is inscribed with the words *strength, courage,* and *love*. These are the words I want surrounding me.

As I was sitting in my seat that day I was observing all those around me. Many were recent transplant patients; many were other types of

Loveolution. I could tell that everyone was wondering what one another was experiencing, but we all just sent shy smiles to each other filled with love and kindness.

This particular appointment, I watched a women and her daughter help their husband/father into the bathroom and overheard them talking in front of the bathroom door. The daughter was weeping and appeared to be trying to hold it together for her father, but even with her best effort this was all she could muster. She asked her mom how she was so strong and her mother replied that she was just being strong for him.

As I was walking by the front desk I took my angel coin and I folded it in the mother's hand as I promised her the strength, courage, and love it will bring her. I gave her a hug and then was on my way out of Boston. I had never done anything quite like that before so I felt a little weird, but that was just my ego connecting to something that was off the beaten path. It is a similar experience to when we thank someone in uniform for his or her service; speaking to someone we don't know is often outside of our comfort zones. This woman smiled at me and I never saw her again. However, I never expected anything back. When I gave her the coin it was not to feed my ego or make me feel important. This was a sign that I was moving in the right direction.

A couple of days later a friend came over to visit and bring a birthday present. My heart warmed and my breath stopped as I opened the gift—it was the exact coin that I had given to the woman at Dana-Farber just the day before.

Over the past year I cannot even begin to tell you how many similar experiences I have had, even if it was just a voice giving me guidance that went beyond the bounds of "coincidence." The more I surrender and embrace effortlessness, the easier it all feels. Is life hard? Yes, if that is the image we give to it. Sometimes the experiences we go through come out of left field, but we need to learn lessons. Somehow these experiences pick you up and inspire you with wisdom and love, leaving you so much lighter and ready to take life to a new space.

CHAPTER 28
THE TIDAL WAVE

> The ones who are crazy enough to think they can change the world are the ones who do. ~Steven Jobs

JUNE 11, 2012

Healing is a gift. It is terrifying and sacred in one breath, filling you with light, hope, and wisdom in another breath. This way of living is wholly based on love and strength from God. However, on the journey of healing, truly knowing you are one with Source can be the bigger part of learning. Awakening to the truth that your God source connection may be wrapped in a coat of fear and despair is the place where your evolution can start.

My healing journey has been filled with many ups and downs, but what I was not prepared for was the tidal wave of emotions that hit months after the transplant, after I had become much stronger. I had nights spent with dreams that were filled with doubt and fear so strong that I didn't know what my place was in this world. There was a lot to make sense of, and as I've done all along I surrendered to these emotions, knowing they were just a form of fear. I embraced each one and surrendered, listening to the guidance that led me to freedom- another layer peeled back. However, there were so many layers the peeled along the way that it sometimes became overwhelming.

I am so different from the outside and the inside alike. My hair is growing in nice and curly which is an unexpected change. I mean I too got on the perm bandwagon in the eighties, but never expected my long blonde hair to one day be taken over by brown, curly hair. However, it is beautiful and fun and a perfect metaphor for the person I am becoming.

The only sadness that truly came from my hair when I lost it was that I could not hide the fact that I was going through a health challenge. They way I looked fostered an image that I didn't believe. But this was one of my many lessons of surrendering and wrapping myself in love.

I was blessed in my journey to catch my physical body up to my soul, which fell upon the hands of trust. Trust was a big part of healing, and there were many tears that accompanied the days I lacked trust. This has not been a journey of perfection but a journey of falling and getting back up, each time becoming more self-assured.

Each of us is on a journey to evolve to our soul, but it is my belief that on some level we choose how quickly we will evolve through our life experiences. Turning left at the "learning fork" may progress us through a year of learning and turning right could be a more gentle approach that can take twenty years to gain the same insight; it is what we are ready and able to handle. The journey is your experience, your reality to create. Remember the vessel and the river.

"Not everyone will understand your journey. That's fine. It's not their journey to make sense of. *It's yours!*" (Zero Dean). This is an important lesson to embrace in life as once again, it offers a great chance to learn. There is no question or doubt that we should always respect another's journey, including the choices made. However, you will have an opinion about what choices you may make and what turns you will take. There is much to be learned if you listen instead of judge. Observing or having opinions does not have to be judgment. This is where respect, love and kindness plays a role supporting someone going thorough a difficult life challenge, no matter what it is.

I remember like it was yesterday the night my mother and I talked about her reflection of this experience and the strong effect it had on her life in ways that I could never have even imagined. As she shared her thoughts, I was deeply touched to know the growth she felt through supporting me. It is with great surrender that we learn from another's journey. The more open we are to this instead of trying to fix it, the more we will awaken. It is a beautiful process that continues to connect us as one.

My mom and I have always been close, but the experience of the Loveolution really connected us on a very different level. Our relationship deepened into a friendship yet still held the love of a parent. I often asked her advice about ways to guide Sawyer through this experience. There were several occasions when he broached the topic of heaven, as God is always part of our daily conversation and I know that my mom's explanation made the concept of heaven much easier for a three-year-old to understand.

One night while eating dinner, out of nowhere Sawyer looked at Grammy (my mom) and said, "Grammy, how come you are not in Kevin?" It took everything to keep a straight face as we explained that it was "heaven," and no one knows when he or she will go there. It is really when God calls us home, it is beautiful we said. That satisfied the moment, but I could tell there were deeper questions on the horizon. Sawyer then went on to give us his detailed explanation of how we move to heaven. He told Grammy that when she died she would go to heaven, and then Mommy and Daddy, and then we would just all meet-up again in heaven. We just laughed at the simplicity, which was so innocent, yet so accurate.

God's guidance is like a GPS with love, always giving us the best direction. As a parent I felt strength from God as I was able to discuss heaven with Sawyer in an honest way, using a tone that was light without going overboard or creating fear or fantasy. It was the most difficult conversation I have ever had as he looked up at me through his brilliant blue eyes with such admiration. He has so many of Tad's attributes that sometimes I feel I could forget he was created by both of us. That is a bit of an exaggeration, but you can understand what I mean. Tad is an amazing man and father. He gives Sawyer the tools to be a very true soul who honors his own desires in life. Together with much love, I believe we all make a great team. We learned from those who parented before us, we always listen to our hearts, we communicate with each other, and most of all, center our family with God.

One day not long after Sawyer asked me what heaven feels like I reiterated the concept that we all go to heaven at some point; we just do not know when. However, this time I went on to explain that we "believe" it is a beautiful place and this is where we go when our time is over on Earth, similarly when you come home from school. It was quite amazing to see how my son adapted to this concept with such love and curiosity. He asked some very cute and appropriate questions, all the while as tears gathered at my heart.

Later that night before Sawyer went to bed we prayed to God. I explained, again in child language that God is everywhere all at once. He replied, "Like Spider-Man." "Of course like Spider-Man," I said and laughed. "God is part of us, inside our soul, guiding us like a teacher." This may seem like a deep conversation, but it was very light, almost like he already knew of these concepts. I quietly told my son that if Mommy goes to heaven, I too would always be with him. He asked me when I was going to heaven and I again replied that no one knows when it is his or her time, but there is nothing to fear because it is pure love. I asked him to think about how much he loves Mommy and Daddy. He replied, "I love you to the moon and back with zeros." It just doesn't get any better. "Well, heaven is just like that kind of love." That was all I needed to say to create a safe understanding for his spiritual growth.

The obvious, but very difficult fact is that no one truly ever knows when it is his or her time to go to heaven or where the soul travels once it departs the physical vessel. This may be a different belief, but on an intuitive level I believe life on earth is an experience that was designed purely for the purpose of a spiritual awakening. The Loveolution may have been a difficult journey for some because in reflection, it makes you question where you are with your own mortality, a thought that may be too heavy.

There were many lessons learned while traveling the Loveolution, but one of the greatest I have learned was overcoming the fear of death. After the past two years, I have come to realize that we cannot die, as the spirit is always whole. We may leave the physical body behind, but our spirit is always present. While we all may have differing beliefs about death and what happens in the "afterlife," the idea of the unknown creates so much fear that many cannot find peace with it.

It is amazing to see how different cultures celebrate death. However, once you find peace with this ideal you can move past fear into a space of peace. You may begin to embrace it as a process of the journey. Understand that I still have moments of fear regarding leaving my family too soon, but when I center and surrender this fear it floats away to God; I again feel blessed with freedom.

When I got home from the transplant, we had many conversations with Sawyer about Mommy's "boo-boo," which turned into Mommy's "challenge". Amazingly enough, Sawyer was always very clear about why I had to wear a mask outside of the house and that every week I had to go see the doctor. These things became common conversation in our home because we wanted to be honest, wanted Sawyer to share in the emotions and understand that we were embracing this experience. He never once wavered, although he did ask some pretty funny questions, which we always answered as honestly as possible. He was a champion and I am so proud of all the obstacles he overcame along with the rest of us.

Like the rest of us, even with moments of triumph, Sawyer too had a few days that appeared overwhelming, which was very difficult. He would ask, "Mommy, why are you crying?" Upon explanation, I would always say it is okay to feel sadness sometimes. He would then ask, "Are you happy now?" How could I not smile? It would turn me on a dime, experiencing his pure, unwavering love.

Sawyer started preschool about six months after my transplant. I am sure everyone would agree that it is one of the cutest things in the world to see your beloved child take his or her first steps towards independence. The bravery and the courage shine through their hearts like they are superheroes. All children may handle this experience differently, but through this process each child learns how to have compassion, patience, and love.

Just like the first look at my baldhead, Sawyer never even took a second glance when I put on the mask. After the first explanation why Mommy had to wear a mask, he never showed concern. However, for me it was an entirely different story. It was hard to completely let go of what "you believe" others will think. Old insecurities surface to make life challenging and the story we create may or may not be true. Slowly, over time there were a number of similar situations that allowed me to surrender. They were beautiful moments, moments filled with strength, freedom, and self-love.

The first day I picked Sawyer up from school I had my mask on, which warranted a number of stares. My skin grew thicker by the minute, even as I knew that for most people it was just curiosity. However, my concern about what others thought about me melted away each time Sawyer would see my face through the double glass doors. His smile would grow in an instant, so big that I felt the tears come up from my toes. It is and always will be pure love, a reminder to surrender. To this very day I am always amazed at how our children are light years ahead of where we think they are.

As is a theme throughout this journey, trusting in a greater plan is extremely important. This leaves even the smallest decisions filled with some type of greater connection and guidance from God. This is true in every aspect of our life and I truly believe that from the depths of my soul. In addition, my experiences in life continue to point toward this truth.

When Tad and I were thinking of putting Sawyer into preschool it was a difficult decision. The transplant team recommended we wait until I was a year out from transplant before Sawyer enter any formal schooling. This was largely due to the fact that naturally I would be exposing myself to additional germs. However, this would mean leaving Sawyer out of school for an extra year, which didn't feel right to either of us.

We met Carla Morano after looking at several preschools that didn't feel like the right fit. Of course we had high expectations and probably unrealistic ones too, but we are first-time parents and so goes the territory. From the very beginning, Carla just pulled us right into her heart and made our experience an easy one. She knew what our family had been through, what we were going through and wanted to be part of our healing. Unfortunately as we were getting a late start, all of her classes were filled. With blessings from God, she told us that she had one spot that she would like to try for Sawyer. It was a reach because Sawyer would be a year-and-a-half younger than the kids in the class, but nonetheless she decided she would make it work.

I would like to say that the year was a breeze, but there was a lot of adjusting and learning on many levels. The group of teachers at Jack and Jill Preschool all helped Sawyer integrate into his new environment; it was truly amazing. As I have said before, I believe that God puts elements into our lives so we don't have to suffer and this is what we must embrace. This was a learning experience for Sawyer, Tad and me, as well as the teachers at Jack and Jill. They all embraced our family on our road to health.

It wouldn't be long after we were feeling very settled and calm before another storm would rock our boat. After a very long day at Dana-Farber and a number of appointments I was told that I would not biologically mother any more children. The day this word was official I was by myself driving home from Boston filled with many tears and misunderstood dreams. I just wanted to go fall into Tad's arms, but as it stood I had to put on my mom hat and go to Sawyer's parent-teacher conference. I thought, *Of all days, this is going to be a rough one.*

The greatest part of this story is that none of us know what role we will play in another's life. You could be the moment that changes someone's entire life or just be the divine support someone needs to get through a difficult moment. Barbara Ward had no idea what she was about to encounter that day and neither did I. I sat down across from "Mrs. Ward" as she began to explain how they formulate progress during the year. It wasn't far into the assessment that I broke down into tears thinking this would be my only child to have an "assessment." It is funny when we look back at our reaction to things in life, but this was a tough moment that I knew would be difficult to sit through.

I was doing everything within my power to hold back the tears, but that only made it worse. As I looked across the table through my blurry eyes, Mrs. Ward was getting up from her chair. I wasn't sure if she was going to walk out of the room to give me a moment, but to my surprise she stood up and asked if she could give me a hug. It was a moment that I will never forget, and one that I embraced with true gratitude. After what felt like a hug from "momma bear" we sat down and talked about my day. Mrs. Ward listened intently with compassion and love. She didn't offer much advice, almost like she knew that she just needed to take words from me so that I could heal. She handed me Sawyer's progress report just so I had a copy and gave me another hug. It was that day I knew how lucky our whole family was to be guided to Jack and Jill Preschool and their angelic teaching staff.

As Sawyer was starting his new normal, I thought it was time for me to embark on an adventure so I started teaching a couple of yoga classes. One night after teaching I came home and felt tears prepare for their grand entrance. As soon as I saw Tad, I immediately burst out crying and tears spilled over without any control. After a few moments of hard crying, Tad commented that I probably released something during yoga class. Did I ever. So I cried some more as he shared some amazing words of wisdom. I had taught a class themed with life purpose and it was after class when my own message really knocked me off my feet. Again why yoga is so amazing, you are always a student and a teacher.

Questioning where to go from here, I began to doubt when I would hear and receive guidance. What to make of my purpose now that I had a "new normal." Tad reminded me of who I am today, "A person who loves, a woman with inspiration, courage, and gratitude, a mother, a wife, a friend" … did he need to go further? He continued, "All by leading by example you have taught Sawyer to be such a special boy, who will grow into a connected, loving man." These were the important things in life that I forgot in a clouded moment. Just by knowing this truth I would be given the answer at the most divine time a belief that is so rooted in my soul that I should have said it to myself. However, when we try to go against the flow of divinity, I have seen that this is when we suffer the most.

I continued to reflect on my journey since October 6th and I thought about all the things I have learned. I've thought of all the serendipity of people who have come into my life for the perfect line or just to offer strength. I am so grateful to all and so grateful for love. Most of all, I am blessed that I am no longer fearing the worst but am living with all the possibilities that will cross my path over the years to come. I may not always have chosen the route to surrender the first time around, but it only took a short moment of suffering, an emotional release, and then I would listen to the guidance that made life feel alive.

CHAPTER 29
SAMSARA, THE EVER-CHANGING YEAR WHEEL

OCTOBER 15, 2012

It was one year ago yesterday that I walked through the doors of Dana-Farber to embark on a journey that would forever change my life. I had no idea what to expect, and fear was probably spilling out of every cell of my body. Looking back I cannot believe it has been a full year. When you experience a certain level of shock, your body seems to evade time and space.

It was a time that was all so unclear and filled with much confusion, but somehow I was able to make some pieces come together. Even though I was so unsure, looking back I was blessed with all the tools I had spent the last five years working hard to discover. I found the space in my soul to implement these ideas and help merge my soul with my heart and mind.

I don't think I realized what a sad memory it was to leave Chicago without saying good-bye to so many friends I met through the yoga community until well after the transplant. Life seemed to move in fast forward, taking with it so many things that didn't receive my attention.

I remembered Tad telling me about the morning I left. He woke to Sawyer screaming, "Where is my mommy?" This thought still hurts on so many levels that I choke down the tears. I believe we are working with God, using his guidance to become better and to better those around us. However, when God calls you home, it is your time. With that being said, it is a strong fear to think that you will not have the opportunity to watch your child grow up.

It was these thoughts that I had to ward off in the discovery phase of my journey to make clear decisions. I had a strong gut feeling that there was a purpose stemming from all the things I was about to face. I remember with confidence a feeling that was so surreal, an emotion of health that was being shadowed by fear. It just makes you realize how much fear can affect you. I was committed to making sure that each decision I made was not out of panic but made in my best interest out of love.

When we first met as the Loveolution group to set some ground rules, which was basically statistics and symptoms, I felt such a high level of fear. I didn't have one symptom, so I didn't want or need to hear statistics that are so difficult to truly determine and can be driven by the statistician concluding them. I thought this would not only cloud my decision, it just seemed to create more fear.

My meeting with Dr. Steck in Chicago was so comforting, and her nurturing way made me feel safe. It is amazing how one's demeanor can affect another's during a challenge. It was a difficult choice to leave Chicago, but there was a chance that Shad would be a bone-marrow match, which is considered today to be a "cure."

Looking back I remember my first appointment with Dr. Woods, which definitely did not start out on the right foot. Within minutes I fell to tears. She was very factual, and in her defense she didn't know what she was walking into when she came to the appointment. It was late in the day and I was a ball of anxiety, breathing moment to moment. In one minute I was strong and filled with courage, and the next I would fall apart; it was like a tennis match. She got a very difficult moment and it became clear that she was no-nonsense.

As we got to know each other over the passing months, I saw a very different side of her. She is there to save lives, and in her field I am sure there is some need to place aside your emotions so you can present the best options for patients.

When I finally got it together, with my mother's intervention, I told her what I wanted: no symptoms, no statistics, just options. At that time there was a pediatric regimen that was working well, and from there a bone-marrow transplant. I wanted to take one step at a time, but it really was an easy choice after the research I did in Chicago.

Treatment started right away, so there was no time to really over-think anything. There were many tears cried along the road to my decision and many cried following. During the moments that I felt encased in love I could hear God's voice guiding me on the road to knowing I was well. There was a moment when I realized my mother was watching her baby go through this mountain of a challenge. It was in that moment that I had to force myself to surrender, as this thought was almost unbearable.

I made a choice and needed to move forward, so that is what I did. I believed I was well, I believed all the reminders I created around me, and in the most difficult moments I willed myself to put forward my best "fake it until you make it." I used a technique that Deepak Chopra teaches quite often. You replace things that are fearful with things that are more "butterflies and rainbows." Hey, I love butterflies, and I was at the point of trying everything to get my mind into a better space.

I called the chemo an elixir of love. All the nurses loved it because under such circumstances it is so much better to be positive. Every nurse went along with my requests and even added her own twist to create a healing environment.

I had vision boards all over my room and had friends send all kinds of spiritual reminders. I was in remission in two weeks. *I was and will forever be grateful,* and then I got a second chance upon finding out my brother was a perfect match.

The bone-marrow transplant was definitely more difficult than I thought it would be. However, it was really just part of the process. Shad produced almost 60 percent more cells than you need and I got them all. It was a gift and one that I will never forget. Shad saved my life; he gave me a gift that no one can ever top. He gave me a second chance.

With this I will honor God, my heart, and life as a whole instead of segmented visions. I have learned that you do not need to sugarcoat anything in life. Being honest with love is always the fastest way to evolve. Telling a white lie is just deciding upon a lie you believe is okay to tell. It is so difficult and trying at times to be honest, but it does not need to be forwarded by brutally; it can stand alone in love.

Shad and I have never truly understood each other on many levels. However, the one thing we will always have is love. Shad is my biological brother; he is my blood and part of my soul. I love him unconditionally. Our relationship may be very different from the typical kinship, but this is where we must start separating from making different wrong. I believe we will always have our own special relationship. I would do anything in this world for him, and I know he feels the same—his actions certainly proved this without question.

When we found out he was a match, he was not surprised at all. I was shocked. I just did not think he was going to be a match; the percentages are not in anyone's favor. Dr. Sieffer told us that he had a recent patient with nine siblings and not one of them was even close to a match. It is down to such a science that sometimes people have difficulty finding a match out of the entire registry of donors.

When I got home from almost six weeks in the hospital, I moved very slowly and spent a lot of time sleeping. There were many books, Internet sites, blogs, and crazy reality shows that entertained me. However, my family and friends were the most important. Whether a phone call or short visit, it was just enough to remind me that I wasn't part of the walls in my parents' house. When you are confined to a space for a long period, you would laugh at some of the things you start to think and do!

While celebrating such a wonderful mark, last night we officially celebrated by walking in a "Light the Night" event sponsored by The Leukemia & Lymphoma Society. I didn't really share or promote the walk for a number of reasons. First, I had never heard of "light the night," so I wasn't really sure what it was all about. Tad had explained it to me, but for some reason I never quite wanted to embraced it. There may have been part of me that emotionally wasn't ready to go to a big event like this.

Sawyer had just started school, and I was slowly making my way out into the community. I decided to continue my education, taking a class in bodywork with the hopes to enhance my skills as a yoga teacher. Then there was the idea of raising money.

Money can be such a weird thing. I look at it as a form of energy, and just like everything else, if it holds a negative space for you, you will find it difficult to draw it to your life. On the opposite side if you don't fear lack and have positive thoughts around it, you will attract more of it. But after all these excuses, I think the biggest reason was that I still had some fear tucked far away, layers deep that didn't want to celebrate early. I was dealing with the aftereffect of the "what if." It is a difficult phase of healing and one I knew without question I would surpass, but this came with time and wisdom.

I was blessed to have gotten through this journey without too many scratches. I can't even imagine trying to heal with a number of external worries such as money. However, in the end those were all silly things to worry about, and I do regret that I didn't reach out to my family as I think many would have come to walk.

We parked the car and were amazed to see the number of walkers in the rain. There was a period of about twenty minutes where it just down poured. It was like God opened up the skies and sent healing to all of us, it felt very refreshing.

The rain was fun when we used to play in it, but now we run from it. But I was grateful that my dad had the biggest umbrellas in the place, with all five of us huddled under it to seek some refuge from the pouring rain and winds.

After the rains settled to a whisper, we got in line to register: there were three different shirts: "I walk in memory of a lost one"; "I walk because someone's life depends on it"; and "I walk because MY life depends on it." Each shirt was marked with a different balloon color. White was the survivor, red was the walker for a loved one who needs support, and yellow was a loved one lost. As I put the survivor shirt on I burst into tears, and I think I scared my parents half to death. In line I could feel them welling in my throat and I did everything I could to push the tears down. However, this was too big an emotion to save for later. It was happening. I could not control the emotion that was pouring out of me. It was definitely a long, intense cry, with snot and heaving sounds, but I couldn't control it. And then once my family was surrounding and hugging me, I felt safe and loved. I did this with the help of many, and all those walking at this event had too.

They brought the survivors onstage and shared a few stories, and it was really inspiring. Then we started our walk through a neighborhood in Cranston, Rhode Island.

All the houses were brightly lit, and we carried our balloons that were lit from the inside designating what we represented in our walking. It was beautiful, and there are no words to describe watching Sawyer carry his red balloon. It truly lit up the night. As we walked there was a path lit for us; some houses were decorated, and some residents were even outside cheering us all on during the walk. We walked, laughed, and shared stories of the past year.

Of course Sawyer was the center of much laughter, as usual. He looked me in the eye last week and said, "Mommy, I knew you wouldn't let me down." I am not sure what that meant, but I have my ideas. There has been a great deal of laughter since I have been out of the hospital. My mom is a mom and worries about everything. She would make a Cabbage Patch doll wear a mask if she thought there was some way I could catch an infection from it. For this I am grateful, and Light the Night was a great start. I felt the oneness and love all concentrated in one event. It was such beautiful experience to enjoy with my family.

As we got toward the end of the walk, you could hear the cheers and clapping; the entire finish line was full of amazing people supporting those who walked. Again tears came to my eyes because one woman was from Tad's company, and her husband has been going through this for two years with many challenges. He smiled and laughed as he shared with me (because we had some of the same nurses) his funny stories. When I asked what floor he was admitted to at Brigham and Women's, he said, "Four, six, eight, nine, ten, and eleven," and we just laughed. His inspiration and dedication to life was so graceful that it reminded me to always embrace life to the fullest.

People are amazing, especially when they get together in numbers to support and love. However, it is the time when it is quiet and you are alone that you still need to find that love and inspiration within yourself that is the blessing. I have realized that it truly all comes from within—whether you are alone, with family, or at a big event it is love without judgment and fearless faith that will help you walk the steps of life as your story is told.

CHAPTER 30
PEACE

> If we have no peace it is because we have forgotten we belong to each other.
> ~Mother Teresa

OCTOBER 22, 2012

Spending such a great amount of time in your home, you begin to think about things on a deeper level. You tend to look at the intricacies of many things that seem so simple. Peace is a word that seems so simple but harbors many emotions. When you really think what the word means and how it resonates in your soul, it may take you somewhere different.

In moments of peace, no matter where this is, have you ever thought about what it would feel like to have matched peace on the inside and the outside?

I have questioned the emotion of peace before I even knew exactly what I was questioning. During my search for understanding such depth, I learned that there are many ways to express peace, feel peace, share peace. In addition, there are many ways to speak peace—for example, *paz*, *shanty*, *vrede*, *paix*, and *shalom*—each having an innate reaction for each of us. However, within each language you can feel the beauty, just as it was your native understanding.

While going through treatment, I met another understanding of peace that I have consciously embraced. I have encircled myself with every breath, trying to keep peace in my thoughts and actions as much as possible. The reality is that in learning there have been many moments that I watched peace slip out of my grasp, and the trade-off was pure suffering.

During my journey I set an intention to simplify most things in life to make more space for peace. I knew that understanding peace would be a major part of the experience because if you don't have peace, how do you have love? They really go hand in hand.

One night I was watching Sawyer sleep and I saw such peace in his soul. When he first woke up that morning, he looked at Tad and me and said, "I love my family." I saw such love and peace in his eyes and then it began, the crazy energy that zips through every child's body, their desire for adventure and quest to learn, working to expand their world.

This is when we started the "family hug," which now is a tradition of love. Anytime a family member needs love, we all go in for the family hug. It has been fun to develop ways to support Sawyer as he learns and expands his emotions. It has been helpful for all of us because, once again, as adults we stop providing a platform to express emotion. We are making sure Sawyer talks about how he feels, especially when he is confused about an experience. However, even with his continued excitement, and some misbehaving, I consistently see peace in the eye of his storm. I often wonder, if you look into the eyes of others, would find this sweet spot of peace? It is easy to spot in the eye of a child, but adults may have it hidden layers deep.

Our eyes are just one of the many senses that hold space for expression. Just with one glance Sawyer will know if I am looking for better behavior or if I am pleased with his actions. It is amazing when you really think about how much you can speak with your eyes. As it is beautiful to use your body as a language, it is even more beautiful when we can tell a story with just one glance. With this understanding, I wanted to learn more about peace and the culture that supports it.

About four years ago, I came across a children's book titled *What Does Peace Feel Like?* by Vladimir Radunsky. It was such an intriguing title I couldn't pass it up. It is based on the foundation of peace through the eyes of a child. It is an archive of children's expressions and how they perceive peace in their hearts. The author starts by bringing attention to the beauty of the spoken word in so many languages, which is simply amazing.

He asks, "Did you ever close your eyes and try to imagine peace?" I have imagined peace but have never created an image of peace. I had never really gone beyond the stillness after war, the healing between two parties, etc. As I read on I realized the direction he was going and took a moment to let go of any preconceived ideas so I could fully open my heart to learn.

I began to read the children's answers, which were so amazing and simple that it brought tears to my eyes. If only children could run the country, things would probably go so much smoother. Their idea of peace was so uninhibited, filled with pureness.

That night before bed I set out to imagine *peace*. I asked myself what peace felt, looked, sounded, and tasted like. A myriad of feelings swept over me. It felt warm, colorful, sweet, and so loving. It felt like no matter what you were so safe, and every problem in the world could be solved with an easy solution. It was definitely an amazing feeling and I got it: all the beautiful words I have ever used in yoga classes, and the words writers use to express thoughts of love start with loving yourself and then expressing this beautiful energy outward.

Imagine a day where everything you do is in peace, no matter what the action of the person at the drive-through of the coffee shop, your response is peace. At work, a coworker who may not care for you, you enjoy more because you aren't trying to judge her or his actions or surrender to your own insecurities. Everything is exactly as it should be. There is no need to fit a label, or rise to someone else's expectations. Your love and confidence with your desire to be happy is selfless, not selfish. Love for self, peace, and happiness: they all follow each other like a train through the hills of Tuscany, with the option for a little wine to brighten the color!

As I nestled deeper into bed and thought about the things that have brought me peace, I quickly realized how long the list was. In our moments of frustration and anger, we may simply forget how may moments we have of peace. It just may be that we have a new understanding of peace: It does not mean to be in a place void of noise. It does not mean that our life does not face challenge or trouble. It does not mean that you choose the wrong direction and regret your reaction. It negates the pressure of a standard, but peace means being in the midst of all these experiences and still being connected and calm in your heart.

I wrote in hollysloveolution,

"If you only read the books that everyone else is reading, you can only think what everyone else is thinking" (Haruki Murakami).

*

I believe strongly that at some point in life we must slow down and listen for guidance from God, Source, whatever your higher power. It may come in the form of a teacher, it may be a book given to you by a friend, and it may be a statement from a stranger, but listen. It is always so exciting when the perfect ideas come to you from the most unexpected source and in your gut it feels so right.

During the Loveolution, it has been commonplace to see the most perfect sign or have the perfect book slide right into my hand or be recommended at the most divine time. I always listen to my intention before I suggest a book because not only is it important to stay on your own journey. In the words of Edmund Wilson, "No two persons ever read the same book."

This becomes a great metaphor for life as we may see the same the same thing but have a different experience, a different reaction, or a different lesson. This is where God's guidance directs us to our path of evolution. This is where we have to look outside "the box" and remember the pureness that encompassed us as children.

I have read a lot of books that have advanced my spiritual foundation. Each has taken me deeper on the journey, each serving its own purpose for knowledge, growth, and validation. One of my many favorites is called *Dying to Be Me : My Journey from Cancer, to Near Death, to True Healing* by Anita Moorjani. Anita developed an advanced-stage cancer and tells a thrilling story of her experience with a miraculous healing. You cannot help but feel the connection to her story, learning and wisdom shared on a different level. It goes beyond a book that you don't want to put down; if you are ready for the wisdom, it is there to be shared. When Anita found herself in a coma, she had detailed experiences of death that will have forever changed her life. Upon awakening she was healed, and doctors were baffled by this unexplainable event.

The interesting thing is that I have read many books about such events, but it becomes clearer it isn't as unexplainable as we think. The power of our mind goes far beyond any "hocus pocus" some people may refer to out of fear. The unexplainable tends to be a difficult position for many to digest. However, "miracles" have been documented for thousands of years and may bring us a step closer to understanding our ability to heal. As we only use about 15 percent of our brain, we know the rest remains in a world with many questions.

After Anita published her book, she had such wild success that Hay House Publishing asked her to do an online course. I signed up and listened intently to her experiences and explanation for how we are all one. She did several exercises, and one particular exercise was designed to discover self-love.

I have done similar exercises, but this one really got right down to the point.

*

Exercise

Sit down in a quiet place with a pad and pen. Write down all the things you don't like about yourself. Maybe things you have done or something about your personality; it may be simple or more challenging, but write it down. Now write down all the things you love about yourself, everything from external to internal. Look at the two lists, and you will have your answer of love for self.

Be honest with this exercise because I believe this is the knowledge that will give you the power to understand yourself, deepening your relationship with intuition, healing, and life prosperity. In addition, it will help you become more in love and at peace with your soul. Each time I have done this exercise I have noticed that I have worked through things that I believed I didn't like and have turned the "like" list to a "love" list. I will tell you it was tough to be thoughtfully honest, but there was such a shift, and the release created a space that felt so much lighter.

We all have all have relationships in life—husbands, wives, partners, friends, animals—but if we do not have love for ourselves (which is just our ego trying to cause suffering), then we cannot truly extend love to another. The love you feel when you first meet someone is the reflection of your internal love. If not, then it is just lust. I am not saying lust is bad, but truth and honesty is just so much better. Cut away all the fat that you don't need in life, but remember that some fat is good. It's a difficult balance to maintain. In the words of Joel Osteen,

"Shake it off. Don't stay where you are tolerated, go where you are celebrated."

The more ways we can be honest with ourselves and move away from negative situations and toxic relationships, the more we can stop creating experiences that cause suffering. The more ways we can truly identify areas where are insecurities hide deep inside, the more space we will have to love self and all those around us, with peace and complete happiness in our corner. It is the elements from strong peace and love that open the door to simple forgiveness. The beautiful part of forgiveness is that you do not need confirmation from anyone, you only need identify that you have opened your heart to this clearing action.

CHAPTER 31
MOUNTAIN CLIMBER

"Those who have failed to work toward their truth have missed the purpose of living" ~Sivananda

OCTOBER 26, 2012

There are many metaphors that I could use to match up to my experiences throughout the past two years that would give a different perspective or learning handle. However, one of the better metaphors I have thought of is that of a roller coaster. It starts with that feeling in your belly when you see the sites of this huge coaster, making its way in every direction and sometimes doing it all at the same time. However, more then the anticipation of this wild ride is the level of intensity created by your thoughts especially if this is your first time.

I can remember the first time I rode Space Mountain at Disney World's Magic Kingdom. It was a one-of-a-kind coaster at that time and was creating such a buzz that people came from all over making the wait time hours. It was so intense that there were warnings placed along the walkway as you headed to the platform, warning you about the potential side effects, cautioning those with heart conditions, etc.

As you made your way to the platform you see all those who have just taken the ride of their life. Their hair and eyes look as crazy as their faces, but everyone was laughing and sharing their experience with family/friends; the buzz was contagious.

Suddenly you're seated and after all the buildup of fear and anticipation, you feel the harness come down over your shoulders. You realize you have no choice but to trust that you will be okay. From a metaphorical perspective, all those behind you are there to support you through this wild adventure, through the ups and downs, highs and lows. Each individual supporting you in his or her own way, which makes it all the sweeter, as it is coming from love, not obligation.

You see the light turn from red to green and off you go, the journey of your lifetime. This is really one of the greatest metaphors for the past two years. There have been very difficult times where I let myself get beat down, there have been a great deal of moments with stillness and quiet. I have cried many tears of emotional distress from years before, and mostly have dealt with ego and fear.

Bottom line: You cannot have faith if you have fear and you cannot love others if you don't love yourself first. Most importantly, if you let your ego run the show, allow your internal dialogue to be negative and filled with defeat, then this is where you will stay. However, if you believe in the unbelievable and let your imagination take you high into the sky, you will live the true life that you desire.

I realize we are all human; we will all have days that are challenging. Some of the challenges we have created ourselves, and some have been handed to us for growth and learning. It is definitely a challenge to live with kindness and love all the time. For some it just takes one little thing that allows the ego to tell you how bad things are or how unlucky you are. "When are you going to get a break?" But it is there for the taking.

As I reflected upon how many similarities passed between the Loveolution and The Space Mountain Coaster, I decided I wanted to put it down on paper because it always amazes me what jumps out at you when you read your journal a day or two later. It is like wisdom is just staring you right in the face. That day I wrote in hollysloveolution:

*

> Life is a blessing. Those who have extreme challenges are having a lifetime full of evolution, or I should say the opportunity to evolve. I share these words with you as I have lived them and still do as I work through my own judgments, as I work through my fears and uncertainties, to clear through to the beautiful thing called life.
>
> I have learned that loving yourself is the key because it does

not matter at the end of the day what anyone thinks or says, as you have your own heart to share and your own choices to make.

Earlier in my coaster ride I asked God daily for affirmations that I was going to make it through this experience, especially prior to my bone-marrow transplant. I had to keep my head clear and believe that whatever my true journey was would unfold. But I still wanted affirmations, signs that I was on the right track. I wanted to believe that this eight-hundred-ton thought of fear would go away. However, bit-by-bit, I have chipped away at the fear, while it pushed back. It was not a seamless excursion; it was at many times blood, sweat, and tears.

One afternoon I walked into my garage and found one-third of a butterfly wing. I smiled as I remembered from my *Animal Speaks* book that butterflies are a sign of rebirth, which is exactly what I believed this journey represented for me.

As I continually saw butterflies everywhere (I realized it was summer, but I saw butterflies in the most unlikely of places and one day one even rested on my shoulder). I couldn't help but think of a quote: "Happiness is like a butterfly. The more you chase it, the more it eludes you. But if you turn your attention to other things, it comes and sits softly on your shoulder" (Henry David Thoreau).

Over the next week I was astonished when I found one-third of the same wing in my backyard, and another one-third of the wing in my front yard, all in the same day. When I put them all together they made a beautiful butterfly wing filled with colors of zeal. I have saved it as an amazing memory that God is always ready to send you a message of comfort if you ask; there are no reason to suffer. Once we truly believe there is no reason to suffer, no reason to let fear be in the driver's seat, we take control of how we react to the roller-coaster ride and actually feel excitement.

After the transplant I could feel the strength in every message and I could feel my physical body getting stronger. I would make small trips out, and with each trip my internal courage would widen. I had to wear a mask and gloves; I was certainly a curiosity stare. However, I was changing more than I already had, and it felt so peaceful and divine.

At first I would notice the stares. Some were worried I had

something to share with them and others were just curious—and let me tell you, you could feel the difference between those that were curious and those that were judgmental.

However, the best story was recent. I was sick of being in the house, and we all went for a ride to Best Buy so Tad could log some "man hours." Oh yes, as a man Tad could stay in Best Buy for hours, days, and maybe a year if I let him. However, I needed a new phone so there was no delay getting out the door to a secret man town.

I was entertaining Sawyer as we were running through the store laughing as he chased me up and down the aisles, hoping to catch me. As I began to head for the door because I knew it was time to leave, this woman turns around (now mind you I would not run up on someone while wearing a mask; we were plenty far away). She screams and throws her hands in the air, yelling, "Oh my God! Get away from me!" She runs back inside Best Buy as Sawyer and I stand by the door waiting for Tad, who missed the whole show, but it was funny telling it over as I watched her pace the registers until we left. It was hilarious!

With such a simple thing as wearing a mask, I have experienced judgment at its finest, and I remember where it started: when we were in our insecure eighth-grade bodies and just learned to keep going until some experience began to soften our sense of judgment. Then an extreme experience made it unacceptable when the judgment was unkind or mean. There is a big difference between judgment and curiosity.

I have had people ask me why I am wearing a mask, which has started some very kind and loving conversations. The best was one Sunday afternoon. We went shopping, and to this mother's horror, her three-year-old son nonchalantly asked, "Miss, why do you have a mask on?" Oh, the mom's face and the question were so beautiful.

Tad stepped in as the mother was apologizing all over herself, and he said, "Son, I am so proud that you so nicely asked my wife why she is wearing a mask." He went on to tell him a very simplified version, and we all walked away from a strong lesson.

Judgment is a tricky thing because we learn through others' judgments. As it is something we have discussed in a number of directions, it is really just about keeping your thoughts and words in check. There is a book I read and have just taken off the shelf to reread called *Above All, Be Kind: Raising a Humane Child in Challenging Times* by Zoe Weil. It was amazing and just filled my heart with such pure love and light. I affirm to myself each morning while Sawyer watches his morning *Word World*. I love myself, and no matter what I do I am doing the best I can each day with loving-kindness.

A little exercise that I started in my journal was to write down all my negative inner dialogue and/or judgment. I did it for a week without looking back at it. The following week I would access these thoughts and found that most, if not all, were ego based, which I tossed away, clearing another sheet for me to write in love.

I began to notice that all the thoughts were somehow connected to deep inner fear or insecurities that I still have not embraced. Once I had this realization I let it go, surrendering it to God.

*

It was many years after my first ride on the great Space Mountain, but after college I went to Disney World with a friend. We got in line for Space Mountain and made our way up to the front, got in, and took a breath as the harnesses made its way over our shoulders. Then the green light flashed, and I will never forget how much fun I had. The ride once filled with fear was replaced with pure joy.

CHAPTER 32
A SUNSET OF HISTORY

> Earth Mother, you who are called by so many names. May all remember we are cells in your body and dance together.
> ~Star Hawk

OCTOBER 31, 2012

The holidays are always a mark of excitement, filled with rich tradition and cultural exchanges. As a family we always take time to learn about the different cultures and the history that has evolved this special day. We instill in Sawyer the importance of the history of each holiday, the traditions and growth. Last night we celebrated All Hallow's Eve and took Sawyer trick or treating at my parents' condo complex. Halloween is a holiday that is so rich in history, but many only know it for the "trick or treat" tradition.

Hundreds of years ago, every October 31 was a major celebration of ending the old things in our life (embracing a type of death) and opening up and manifesting a rebirth. The witch's New Year is called Samhain. Sunset on Samhain is the beginning of the Celtic New Year. The old year has passed, the harvest has been gathered, cattle and sheep have been brought in from the fields, and the leaves have fallen from the trees. The earth slowly begins to die around us.

This is a good time for us to look at wrapping up the old and preparing for the new in our lives. Think about the things you did in the last twelve months. Have you left anything unresolved? If so, now is the time to wrap it up. Once you've gotten all that unfinished stuff cleared away and out of your life, then you can begin looking toward the next year.

Samhain is still practiced today by many in a celebratory tradition that asks you to magnify the past year of your life. (Metaphorically a cycle of death and rebirth.) If this is your first time doing this, you may have things from several years past, so don't limit yourself to just this year. This is not about setting a goal, which is typically what many think. This is about acknowledging in a very loving way the things that no longer serve you, as you have changed due to the past years experiences, lessons, and newfound wisdom.

We look upon this time as an opportunity to let go (death) of all things and put yourself in a mindset to move forward without holding anything. The most important thing to remember is that you do not need permission from another person to clear something from your life as long your heart and intention are pure. Oftentimes there can be emotional pain that remains, and those again are emotions that you need to identify to set them free.

A BREATHING TECHNIQUE

I use this often to visualize release.

Make a list of the things in your life that you would like to let go or surrender. Be honest and loving as you will either burn or throw away this list, so it is only for your eyes.

To begin, start with focusing on your breath: Lie on the floor or sit, starting with big belly breaths. You can place your palms on your belly so you can direct the breath, and over time you will be able to direct the breath towards your back body, which is where the majority of your lung capacity takes space. While you are drawing breath to your belly, press into your hands so you can feel the strength of your lungs. You will be amazed at how much breath you can actually bring into your body. After several deep breaths, allow the breath to return to a more natural state of balance (inhalation being the same as the exhalation).

At this time begin to imagine your breath coming into your body through your feet in a light color (or white), traveling all the way up your body nice and slow. Once it gets to your mouth, allow the exhale to be peaceful, but the color on the exhale is gray or black this is a representation of all the things we want to release from our physical mind/body. You continue to draw the breath in through your feet as you hold the thought of the challenge, and on the exhale let it go. Eventually the breath will become circular, and when you have released, each exhale will be just as white as when it entered your body. Some people like to use the breath as a vacuum cleaner. This is another visual technique where you use your breath to vacuum up all the ideas that are not serving you and are blocking your ability to evolve.

The last and most important part of this exercise, now that we have let go, is to focus on the things we want to *"rebirth"* into our lives. I have since learned a lot about manifesting. I am always humbled to learn from so many others who have mastered the craft of manifesting. I always thought it was as simple as a corkboard and a few cutouts of things you *"want"* in your life. This isn't wrong as there is intention set and there are many ways to manifest. Therefore, there is no right or wrong, just evolution.

As life will never be the same, I have learned that with all things I look and feel differently about how they present in my life. So this year I also dressed up to share in the Halloween fun, and it was just like being a kid again. I almost forgot how much fun it is to dress up and play a role. I was a good witch, and Sawyer was the Green Lantern, and together we saved Webster Lake from anyone having extra candy.

I was pretending to play the part of a fantasy witch in make-believe land; Sawyer is there all the time, so I figured why not for a night? People were very surprised that I dressed up, but had many compliments for our duo and the show Sawyer put on as he yelled, "Green Lantern to the rescue!" I was his sidekick, the good witch to help with anyone coming from the side or behind.

It was so much fun to be part of this fantasy world and the special night of Halloween. Last year I lay in a hospital bed watching videos of Sawyer and Tad going house to house.

At one point I stopped and just watched Sawyer. Through his mask I could see his intense eyes, which told a story of fun and love. He knows it's just a costume but had so much fun pretending to be a superhero.

Last night he was my teacher, reminding me that we all need to have fun, not just when we are children. Our imagination doesn't just go away when we turn a certain age. If anything it could be a tool that propels us into so many adventures.

We are all too busy to have "fun." Sometimes it seems life is too busy to just laugh. When was the last time you belly laughed? Our children do it every day—do we? It is so fun to be silly and bask in that light, even if only for a moment a day.

On my way home I drove alone, quietly sitting in silence as I thought about the end of the night. Sawyer showed me that fun is a must, which I quickly forgot as soon as we started the business of the holidays. Some adults don't enjoy the holidays, or some aspects of them. I usually hear from many that, "I have to make a turkey"—which would be mind blowing … thank God for Tad!—"get presents, a tree, etc. The list is endless." But all these to-dos really can be a lot of fun, so we should make the extra effort to turn it around when it begins to feel like an obligation.

I think there has been a magic spell put on adults that makes the entire holiday season seem like a job: a checklist needs to be done by a certain date, parties we must attend, dinners to host, presents to wrap. So as Sawyer was a superhero last night, he reminded us all that it can be simple, and it is just about finding your inner imagination.

We have a lot to celebrate this year. Last year Thanksgiving took place in a hospital room as I ate Sawyer's leftover turkey like I had never seen meat before. Sawyer lay in bed with me and cuddled, somehow seeming to ignore all the lines and beeping machines all around me. Tad was filled with emotion seeing this because we all believed it was going to be a good outcome, but only God has that plan laid out.

Today I am going to live each day as the best day ever or doing the best. I am sure there will be some rewiring of the brain here as the adult spell was cast and I too have treated the past several holiday seasons like a part-time job, losing the real identity of the holidays, which is love and family.

A few years ago I ran around like a crazy person because I wanted Sawyer to have the best Christmas. He enjoyed the wrapping paper, but he didn't get the concept; he was one! What a lesson for me.

There are amazing reminders and signs all around us to slow down and feel/enjoy the moments of the holiday or any day for that matter. During any hustle and bustle just stop and watch your breath. See what it feels like as the buzz continues to stay energetically moving by, but you stop just for a moment as a reminder to slow, watch, listen, and learn.

May we all enjoy every holiday together, with well wishes of love and light!

CHAPTER 33
THE STORM

> Every storm runs, runs out of rain, just like every dark night turns into day. Every heartache will fade away, just like every storm runs, runs out of rain.
> ~Gary Allan, "Every Storm (Runs out of Rain)"

NOVEMBER 30, 2012

Music has been the center of our hearts since the dawn of time. Even if you do not have a musical bone in your body, it doesn't stop one from singing in the shower or car, singing like no one is watching. Music makes you feel good; it makes you want to dance without insecurity, linking you to the seat of your soul.

Additionally, music is a vibration that fast tracks the connection to your soul. Music can make you laugh, cry, and contemplate many things in life just depending on what the artist is pouring out of his or her own soul. Then when we know any back-story to a specific song, it just gives it increased power.

We learn so much from the lyrics presented in music, the artist telling a story so deep that he or she hides it in a collage of metaphors. Sometimes musicians will disguise their journey in words that are wrapped in a tune so catchy that we miss the entire message. Either way, it is truly amazing how music transcends our subconscious and is a direct connection to our soul.

For centuries yogis have chanted and drummed to their own tune with tools like a singing bowl, drums, and even their own voices. Many yoga classes will apply a chant at some point during class. Usually it is the very popular symbol "OM," which many know represents home or universe.

However, when chanting with "OM," many are so mystified by the vibration or sensation that they overlook the symbolic meaning. In fact, symbols have always been misunderstood, but this very popular symbol may be one whose meaning is so simple yet perhaps confusing.

Just as an example, the beautiful symbol above is one that has become a common reflection of yoga. The syllable OM is actually represented as a sound in the universe. Whatsoever has existed, whatsoever exists, and whatsoever shall exist hereafter is OM. This is all captured in the text from the Mandukya Upanishad, which was written somewhere between 800 and 500 BC.

Understanding the breakdown of OM on a philosophical level can be quite confusing so I am going to keep it simple, as I can.

"The Self, which is one with OM, has three aspects, and beyond these three, different from them and almost impossible to define is—the fourth."

As this definition seems to spin us in a circle, we need to just sit with it. In the book, "Proof of Heaven" by Eben Alexandra, he speaks about "OM" as the only explanation for what he felt. There were no words that could explain the intensity of the vibration that elicited two letters. This is a man who is a Neurosurgeon, not a yoga teacher.

Even if you don't quite understand these definitions, the beauty felt as it is chanted, the vibration throughout your body may be a start. However, just as with music, understanding the message will allow you to go deeper into the rhythm.

Everything that surrounds us has an aspect of the divine, just as we do ourselves. The chanting of the sound OM reminds us of those connections to the divine and to each other. But OM also represents the states of human consciousness. The Mandukya talks of three states of consciousness—plus an indescribable fourth.

The first state of consciousness, known as Vaishvanara, is waking state, which is focused outward to material objects. The waking state is represented in the symbol by the lower curve (the bottom of the "3"). The second state of consciousness, Taijasa, is dreaming sleep or the mental nature, which is focused inward to only the thoughts in the mind. The curl coming out of the center of the "3" represents the dreaming state. The third state of consciousness, Prajna, is dreamless sleep or deep meditation. As stated in Mandukya Upanishad, "The veil of unconsciousness envelops his or her thought and knowledge, and the subtle impressions of his mind apparently vanish." The dreamless state is represented by the top curve (the upper part of the "3").

The fourth state of consciousness, known as Turiya, is the hardest to describe—in fact, the text calls it "indescribable." But perhaps the best attempt to describe it is as follows: "It is pure unitary consciousness, wherein awareness of the world and of multiplicity is completely obliterated. It is ineffable peace. It is the supreme good. It is one without a second. It is the Self. This Self, beyond all words, is the syllable OM."

~The Yoga Community

As this may sound confusing, OM is a sound and a symbol that is rich in meaning and depth. It represents the divine in each of us, as well as our interconnectivity. It reminds us that we have the ability to move past our physical and mental states of consciousness and connect with the divine, in others and ourselves.

This is the beauty of music, whether it be chanting, following fish, alternative, hip-hop, or country; all genres touch a special spot in each person's soul. That space can turn your mood on a dime, bring tears to your eyes, or melt your decisions within minutes. This should lead us to understand that music, its sound dimension, can take us to many places beyond the physical.

I embrace all genres of music, but there are several artists I really connect with as they have shared their great tragedy in the hopes of helping others grow.

Gary Allan is a country rocker who does what he wants and doesn't care what anyone thinks, so his persona tells us. His concerts are extremely intimate and amazing, and he pours his heart out and rocks all in one moment in time.

When I was pregnant with Sawyer, Tad and I took a baby moon to the Dells in Wisconsin to see Gary Allan. As I was singing and connecting to the music, I could feel Sawyer moving around like he too was having his own private experience. Tad and I were so happy that Sawyer could hear him rock before he was born as it will be years before he can go to a live concert. Sawyer also got to chant with the likes of Krishna Das, and once again, he moved in perfect rhythm to the vibration. My friend Sharon was witness as she felt him moving in turn to each beat that was felt in unity.

Many of us have had a memory at a concert that was filled with an epic memory. One night, while Elise was staying with us, we got last minute tickets to a Gary Allan concert. It was an amazing night filled with one too many beers and a great deal of singing. Tad was the designated driver, and he smiled as he watched Elise and me dance to every note and swing into each other as we sang along from the front row. It was so much fun. Actually, fun isn't a good enough word, but the next morning there were two mommies both with hangovers. That was a first and last but so worth the memory.

It is a mystery to me why one would like a certain genre over another. However, for me country music has such a deep story and is always filled with life lessons. Allan is an artist who not only has many amazing songs, but lyrics that are measured with great love and hope. Allan wrote, "Best I Ever Had" after his wife took her life. It is difficult to understand where one must be to go so far, but in trying to understand we must have empathy and know that everyone is doing his or her best.

The beauty that comes from an artist like Gary Allan is that he is real and wears his heart on his sleeve. He shares his real life with fans, which creates power with his lyrics. I am not sure when this letter was written, but sometime after he lost his wife he wrote an intimate letter to his fans about his wife and family. She apparently had vicious migraines and nothing alternative or allopathic helped. It led to a deep depression, and then she took her life when he was just rooms away. I can't imagine going through something like that on either side. I just listen to his words, as music is meant to inspire or guide us, which is what he has done.

It is a difficult time to process something after it is over or when you are in the final stages. The haunting fear that will never go away … the what-ifs. This is why I shared this story. I admire the strength and courage of anyone who lives in the public eye to share such a difficult life challenge with the intention to help others through his or her expression of healing.

This year unpacking Christmas ornaments, all I could think of was "what if" I wasn't there. Tad and Sawyer would have been opening ornaments from my childhood, from our wedding, our first home—and how would they have felt? So as I am processing how to shed this fear and tackle yet another hurdle to continue on a path of gratitude, I look to others who have done what I think the impossible. Learning from many artists, in many genres, has given me direction when I have felt lost. I have turned to music in the deep hours of the night when I have felt paralyzed with fear. Whatever the music, it seemed to pull me out of whatever held me prisoner in the moment, like a rhythmic yellow brick road. However, I felt the courage to look behind the black curtain. There was nothing there but my own reflections and creations of fear. This was a defining moment of my personal empowerment.

As I reminisced about concerts, I thought about the lyrics to "Best I Ever Had," trying to understand the intricacies of the message Allan was releasing with his brilliant guitar work. I immediately realized that my heart was filled with love, as Tad is the best I have ever had. He has been the most amazing husband anyone could ever ask for. He has looked deep into my soul and through my eyes to see all my beauty when I felt I reflected tired eyes. He held me up with his words, with his actions, and with his love. He is love and we are love, grateful for each other.

The night of the transfusion he held my hand and said, "This is the beginning of our new life. Just think how lucky you are that your brother saved your life." There will never be words for that, but it is a miracle. Shad and I are connected forever in many ways, and I have such a deep gratitude and love for him. I will never truly be able to explain the gratitude and gift that makes this Christmas so much more special this year. However, it is based on love that goes without saying.

To my best husband, my best friend, my best lover, he never wavered. The first night we got the news we cried together, but after that something shifted inside him, and he knew I was going to make it. When I wavered and spent a night in a place of doubt, his smile and gentle touch made me believe too.

He shared hard words when I needed to hear them and took significant amounts of stress off my shoulders for all the hats he wore during this time. A thank-you will never be enough, but a lifetime of love may just crack the surface!

Which leads us to the present, probably due to the holidays; there have been some difficult days. I want my life back, and I have realized that it will never be what it was, it is and will continue to be so much better. This gift, the Loveolution, has taught me to love myself.

Tad, my family, and friends circled me to help me heal in so many ways. Some were extremely unexpected and some were shocking. People deal with illness in different ways and some just can't handle it at all. But I have learned that everyone does the best he or she can and that must be respected. However, when you look back, the perfect people divinely supported all of us.

As I am learning to celebrate my health and bask in the gratitude of new life, I have to remember that I am also doing the best I can after such a shock. It may take some time to patch me up inside because fear is something along with your ego that doesn't want to go away. I have worked hard to find ways, many ways to let truth and spirit be a constant in my life.

I am a very different person now and look forward to the many blessings that happen every day. There is always validation to my healing and life. As we were unpacking our ornaments and I shared I was having a tough time, working so hard to choke down the tears. I sat down for a moment to look at our work. Sawyer's ornaments were all in one section of the tree front and center about three feet high. I took a few breaths and looked down to see a penny sitting in the middle of the floor when I am positive it was not there before. I have a thing with pennies and feathers. For me, they represent a sign that life is beautiful; divinely the way it should be. I smiled to myself and felt my emotions of fear slip away.

Allan has a new single that has just blessed the charts, called "Every Storm (Runs out of Rain)," and although the rain was magical, I have had moments when I have been pushed around too much. This storm needs to move out to sea or up to the heavens, so it may return as love and continued blessings that set us all free.

> "Music is a moral law. It gives soul to the universe, wings to the mind, flight to the imagination, and charm and gaiety to life" ~Plato

CHAPTER 34
THE NEW, NEW YEAR

> How can you follow the course of your life if you do not let it flow?   ~Lao-Tzu

JANUARY 6, 2013

This morning Sawyer and I were looking into the front yard watching the rain and wind dance together in perfect harmony. It was a beautiful day and watching the rain clean and clear away all that was no longer serving the landscape was such an amazing process. A cleansing process that was trusted and true making way for new growth, new starts, and new life. Similarly, like a seed opens in the dark and trusts its true process to rise toward the sun, we also have that innate guidance and wisdom. The question becomes, do we choose to use it?

We all have our beliefs—spiritual, philosophical, and religious—and we can all learn a great deal from each other. We can do this without compromising our belief system, but at the same time kindly respecting another's and maybe even shifting slightly within ourselves. This makes the journey to connectedness filled with love and kindness a much easier process.

Each day presents another opportunity of awakening and awareness, a chance for one's compassion and understanding, which takes us to the beginning breath of our truth. The starting places where decisions become easy, as they have already been made to serve you. A divine space that is filled with kindness and love, instead of confusion and fury.

During treatment I had so many experiences that softened my heart and soul. I realized that it is so important to *slow down and listen* to the flow that our higher power shares within each and every one of us. As we evolve, the truth is there to guide us it is as through "the best of times and the worst of times."

However, it is usually experiences when we see wisdom residing inherently within hardship, that we have the most growth. We learn to listen to the inner guidance and choose to stop suffering on so many levels, applying forgiveness, love, and understanding as just a few options. Once you peel back a layer, it is important to set it free, as there is no guilt just a new understanding of who you are. If you are a person who holds on to "everything" then let some things go that you don't need because the memory will always be there, but it may no longer be who you are today. Allow yourself to move forward and embrace freedom.

> "If it weren't for the rocks in its bed, the stream would have no song" (Carl Perkins).

Listening to this inner voice connects us to love on a whole new level. As an energy, as a thought, as a concept, and the list goes on and on. Love is the bottom line. It teaches us how to continually trust and live life without attachment. During the holidays, such a special time of year, we give not because it is an expectation but because it is of love. We give because we want to bring joy to others, not because we want recognition. Our inner truth guides us to do for others without any recognition in the truest form.

This is a difficult concept because we can spend a lifetime trying to make sure things are even, and oftentimes it seems they are not. However, that is just for the human eye to see and right around the corner is the balance, making us whole. We all need to practice listening and connecting to our intuition, which helps us see this harmony. At the same time, we will emerge and peel back layers to our soul instead of judging and trying to determine the control of the divine flow.

I have realized that the answers to many of my questions have been right in front of me for a long time. However, it took a series of events to make me realize that I needed to flow while I created, practicing what many yogis call nonattachment. "Let go and let God," as one saying goes. Trust that everything is of free will to go in the direction that is most beneficial for the overall landscape and for the greatest good of those who are connected to this landscape of life.

Just an example of an amazing tool, the idea of manifesting, which has been around for a very long time, is such a wonderful gift. Authors such as; Wayne Dyer, Katie Byron, and Eckhart Tolle (just to name a few) have played a significant role in teaching us how to bring manifestations into our lives. Ideas such as moving beyond just believing, taking it to an emotional level and acting as if it has already happened are keys to the success of manifesting. The particular words you use to manifest and the words other people use become strong vibrations and they are set in motion. This is where the process really begins, saying these words out loud. Believe what you are saying or say them until you do believe because this leads to the real magic—*imagine*! These are the ways we bring it full circle. As many before us have said, it just isn't the words, it is the emotion and imagination we put behind these words that creates the journey.

I believe one of the most important aspects of manifesting, going past the emotional and imagination, is *trust and faith*. Trust that each and every idea is for the greater good for you and those in your life. If it is not for the greater good, then the motion stops or changes. Some take this as a sign that it doesn't work for them, but in reality this is the universe helping you make a good decision (this is where listening, as difficult as it may be sometimes, is so important). Many times it happens that the same situation will come up again and again, a repeat for you to get a second chance to make the right choice. This is an opportunity to ask yourself if the path you are on is turning too muddy as you realize you are walking upstream.

This can oftentimes be very difficult to identify and an important time to slow, breath, listen, and feel, combining facts, faith, emotion, love, and intuition. Usually the answer becomes clear, and if not, then you are just not ready to know.

Think of how many things in your life right now could serve you better if you kindly set them free? Just as an example, many focus on weight goals. For some, this is such a difficult goal and a struggle that creates extreme levels of stress. Should we be going the opposite direction? Ask yourself some very difficult questions. Is it torture to go to the gym? Do I feel comfortable there? If I had a partner, would I feel better and more motivated? Am I afraid to fail? You can see that there are many, many options, so maybe it is time to look outside the box as a gift to yourself. You don't have to roll the way others think is the best way as this is just a suggestion ... there are lots of ways, and it is okay to take the path that looks a lot different; no need to try to measure up. Ask for guidance and you will be amazed what shows up for you.

Evolving is a gift, surrounded by a number of successful tools. We should acknowledge these gifts as an altogether new way of living. The greatest of the blessings is that we continue to learn and apply free will. We get to choose to listen and see what we may never have seen before, or we get to cling to the landscape, not wanting to let go.

It is a challenge, as clinging to what we know feels safe and hearing intuition takes time, trust, and faith. But before you know it, another teacher has just divinely brought a new gift of learning so we may continue to grow and evolve. Once you learn the truth, it can't be "unlearned." We can only move forward or sideways. Take a leap of faith, shed a layer of you and enjoy your truth!

With all that said, evolution, unlike many other aspects of life, does not evolve in a linear fashion. There is no telling when and how one will evolve, what experience will push him or her to the front of the room to be the teacher. Sometimes the problem is that everyone wants to be the teacher and no one wants to be the student. However, I was ready to listen and learn ... I was looking over the past year with many unanswered questions, but life was moving forward and I was going with it.

Reading a book like *The Power of Intention* may be a starting point on your journey or a great reminder of the tools you have at your disposal. Either way, we all need to go back to the basics to evolve on our journey, especially when we feel stuck. This book helps create/develop your inner imagination and offers tools for manifesting your reality. It ultimately helps you see where your words play a large role in what makes up your reality. It shares many ideas of how to bring peace to your life, while you are creating the journey you truly want. One of my favorites is his guide to "Making Your Intention Your Reality"

1. **Move away from hoping, wishing, praying, and begging for the right person to show up in your life.** Through this past year I have journeyed with God, listening and I believe what I want to see in my reality. I have done it without fear and replaced it with trust. (I have my moments that are challenging, as I am always a student.)

2. **Conceptualize the person you want to be and detach from any false outcomes.** Many old habits that we learn when we are young or older may be hard to break, so continue to conceptualize the person you want to be as you can change. Each breath offers an opportunity to change, and the old habits will eventually fade away. There isn't a song called "Old Habits Die Hard" by Dave Stewart for nothing. It takes work and dedication! However, this work doesn't mean letting go of who you really are, it means finding the true you and surrendering to the parts of you that are no longer serving you. In addition, look to every person who has ever been in your life, as they have been sent to teach you a lesson on your journey. I wrote a list of those that are no longer in my life and after really looking at it ... I could see all the blessings and lessons learned. You never know when a person will jump back in ... will you open the door?

3. **Act upon the inner picture and take the path of least resistance.** Following your intuition and listening to God is such an important part of life. It makes life so much easier, when we do this. If something seems really difficult and you keep coming back to the same circle, then it is time to find a new route on the GPS. Ways to practice connecting to this space is by just sitting in a room with complete silence. Let your ego thoughts pass by almost as you are a watcher. Then let yourself go deeper; this is the voice of intuition. You will get to know it better and better as you develop a relationship, so you won't confuse it for your ego.

4. **Practice patience.** There is no question that this is one of the most difficult actions to practice. Patience and peace come together, but the question is really how do you practice patience. I have thought about this quite a bit and realized that you have to literally practice. There are opportunities every day to be patient with someone else's choice of action. Again, all you have is your reaction, so patience for yourself and for the other will make things much smoother.

5. **Always remain in a state of gratitude.** This is challenging because we don't even have extra time to breathe full breaths. Being honest with yourself, how often do you sit down and think about the things that you have to be grateful for in your life? Writing them down

is always a great idea, but you don't even need to go that far. What about in the shower? Or turn the radio off in the car, or shut your cell phone off for an hour. There really are a lot more opportunities to meditate imagination and think about the intentions you want to bring to your journey. We all have a lot to be grateful for in life.

This is a great list that has been taught by many over the years. I believe in my heart that now it is time to take this work and move it forward, listening for the next piece that helps complete the puzzle.

CHAPTER 35
BEAUTIFUL MISTAKE

JANUARY 24, 2013

There are so many interesting elements of studying a five-thousand-year-old tradition and how it impacts your soul. It seems each day; yoga offers a new reflection of living a better life and evolving to a greater inner truth.

There are so many aspects to recognize and learn from the healing of your heart, your physical body, to understanding the tools that will help you most. This tradition was spoken about in the Bible. All the great sages (such as Gandhi) and saints have been able to love and perform duty or service because of their lack of egotism and knowledge of yoga.

A mind that is calm can do the most intense work for long periods of time without fatigue. It doesn't become diverted by external distractions or inner disturbances. It remains focused on the work in hand.

Many of us at some point or another waste our energy on useless, petty, egotistical arguments, or heated discussions about nothing. Although I believe it is great to debate, how often is it kept within the realms of respect and kindness? It actually furthers a stronger divide that says my way is right and yours is wrong.

During these types of interactions, little or no power goes toward the work that needs to be done. Without this diversion there would be one fewer opportunity for each soul to evolve. In reality there would be no room to learn our lessons and make our beautiful mistakes.

Mahatma Gandhi clearly reflected his evolution by his actions, making his spirit known. His work and the work of many others have taught us to love ourselves, have strength in forgiveness, and seek unconditional truth.

They have inspired us by leaving us the tools to keep a clear head, even though it may take years to really learn how to use them.

One thing I have learned is that sometimes a discussion is important to have, but it is the energy, the spoken words, and the love we give to it that gets us to the bottom of truth and understanding. Gandhi stated, "An eye for an eye only makes the whole world blind." Sometimes it is important to pick life's battles and possibly move on, and as each situation is different, this is where we gain our knowledge and wisdom.

Gandhi has been a great inspiration for many of us, being a light of action and ideas. There were many things that surprised me, such as his approach to war, friendship, and love. It wasn't at all what I expected, but most of it was the insane beauty in his wisdom. There is so much to be learned from one man, but I would say in a nutshell he believed everybody should do his or her part to spread love and peace even during the most difficult of times.

Many years ago when I first started practicing yoga, I, along with many, thought that the asana (poses) were yogic. I believed it meant you were strong in mind and body. However, from being a yoga teacher, I know it goes far beyond the asana, which many think is the full circle of yoga. The full circle of yoga is connected to all the wisdom that has come from many before us to help guide us to evolve. Much of everything else is just your ego trying to dirty the water.

While going through yoga teacher training, I was blessed to have an amazing teacher. We became very close, and over the years she has shown me mostly with her kindness and love what yoga represents.

One thing I always remember her saying is, "When you take this training you become a yoga teacher, not a yoga instructor." It doesn't matter where you teach, but you teach a tradition that has gone back five thousand years. "You are always a student and a teacher, never one without the other." I have always remembered that as I have taught each and every class. Within each class the teachings silently lined the outer layer of my heart and continued toward the center to this very day.

Teaching this practice is priceless because many times class becomes your own personal course of therapy, even though you are there to serve the students. You feel the circle of support that begins each class. When you walk to the front of the room to begin, there may be eighteen separate mats, each with its own yogi, each with his or her own problems, concerns, and questions.

Somehow through the process of class we all become one, energetically sharing the answers innately with one another. I can't explain it. Even as I write it, it does sound a bit hokey, but it's true. Any teacher will share with you the closeness and love that circularly envelopes the room, shifting the mood and emotion of everyone in class. It is truly magical, a magic that a mystic once said could span across many seas and still have the wisdom to redirect yet another.

One specific part of the practice that I love is the beautiful language of yoga, Sanskrit. Not only because of its beauty when spoken but also because of the mystery that still remains at the hands of time. Today, Sanskrit is one of the oldest languages still in existence. In class I use the English first and then translate to Sanskrit so students can begin to recognize the poses by their true name.

About three years ago a friend and I went to a Sanskrit workshop in Chicago. The class was so amazing because it went far beyond just the teachings of poses. This scholarly yogi taught us so much about how the language breaks down and its historical roots. It is just so beautiful, the more you learn the more you want to envision a conversation and the energetic vibration that left each word hanging from your tongue.

I have always wanted to get a Sanskrit tattoo but haven't yet decided, as there are so many beautiful words with extremely deep meanings. Yesterday I was doing some reading of symbolic Sanskrit and came across the most beautiful symbol, which means "beautiful mistake." As I said, each word has its meaning but then could be taken to a much deeper context as Sanskrit was a spoken language before written. It then came up again on a TV series, which I took to be a sign of the importance of the mistakes we make.

"Beautiful mistake" is simple yet complex. It means that each mistake, each lesson, is so important to redirect you back onto a path of beauty. When your ego, inner dialogue, becomes so negative that you drop off course, a "beautiful" mistake seems to take you to your knees. Then gives you the courage to slowly stand back up and make sense of the gift that was just handed to you. When we look into our past, there are only beautiful mistakes that have kept you on your path of truth.

Many think it is wrong to look back, that we should only stay in the present moment to guide our look forward. However, all our memories, mistakes, and successes have made us who we are today, in this present moment.

Tomorrow will be another day, a day to embrace as many beautiful mistakes to your list of life experiences, which will propel you forward in your learning. This could be simple or complex—such as the courage to change jobs, or the day to "let go and let God." I have had many beautiful mistakes, for which I will always be grateful. They have allowed me to see when I just couldn't get past. They have allowed me to evolve to my truth, leaving behind all that is no longer serving me to reach my highest potential.

One day while looking to organize all the boxes that Tad packed up when we left Chicago, I came across some old poems and writings. I smiled as I saw the old resolutions that I committed to years before and was amazed by the power of the intentions, the power a spoken word holds as you set it free into the world. It just encapsulates me, as if this were the first time someone shared this "secret."

The writing went without a title, but as I read it I remembered the intention in my heart was to have a deeper connection to and understanding of "oneness." I feel that through these words, my prayer, my call to understand has been answered.

"Untitled"
by Holly Peckskamp

My heart lives to inspire others and stays opened to be inspired by others.
I find joy in each movement of my physical and spiritual body.
I love and honor myself working each day to leave judgment reserved for history.
I see the best in everyone and when I don't, I know I need a restart.
I shed tears of gratitude every day for all you have given me.
I ask you to lead us, evolving us from untruth to truth and darkness to light, only sharing as much as we can handle in that moment.
Much love and light—OM Shanti, Shanti, Shanti

CHAPTER 36
RIVER WATCHER

> What makes a river so restful to people is that it doesn't have any doubt or fear—it is sure to get where it is going, and it doesn't want to go anywhere else. ~Hal Boyle

FEBRUARY 6, 2013

I have always had a fascination with rivers and the way the water naturally flows with such power from its source. The sounds, the beauty of the water moving is enough to stir some natural force within our deeper soul. A river's strength is enough to create new paths without worry or fear. Through Mother Nature's guise, the river is her way to balance out the lands and provide Source for people in so many ways, spiritually and physically.

As we move through life and co create with the universe or Source, we have many symbols and references to help guide us to our deeper intuition, which exposes our truth to us, a pure map to our personal evolution. Many of us ignore this internal direction, but over time you can't help but hear its power direct you with such force.

We all ponder what we are here to do, what our life purpose is, or what direction is taking us closer to it. It oftentimes becomes one of the more difficult challenges as our inner heart is clear, but the outside influences may take us years out of our way. On top of external influences you may experience, society also has its role defining what is "success" and what is "ordinary." It is hard to really determine how many outside ideas direct your evolution. It is often when we retreat to nature or solitude that we realize how much influence there really is daily.

Working with moms as a birth doula, I have heard, "I am just a mom" when they talk about their "job." Just a mom? Raising future generations to be kind and full of love is such a difficult job as it is not taught but observed.

When children are young they are so connected to their truth, to their heart, and it becomes clear that the people in their life will be the first to offer influence, which begins to shape them. However, if we guide them to stay connected to this truth of who they are, who they want to be, and how to continue to evolve and awaken as they knew when they came here, things somehow turn out great. You have a healthy, happy adult who is excited to live life.

The quote that started this chapter is a breathtaking reminder that we have to listen to our inner intention and intuition so we can stay on track with the gifts we have to help others and ourselves.

We can be the power or source the river needs to flow. If we live in fear and constant doubt, the river will overflow and offer limited supply. If we listen to our inner tune and trust with intense love, the river will flow at a divine pace, directing us to the opportunities to learn and evolve. With this we must have patience, which is a challenge for us all.

May we ride the river, instead of grasping for the shore!

CHAPTER 37
BREATH OF CHANGE

> The glassblower knows: while in the heat of the beginning, any shape is possible. Once hardened, the only way to change is to break.
> ~Author Unknown

MARCH 28, 2013

When I met Tad, I knew my heart had just met my future, all my dreams of a partner in one hello. I just knew this to be true, and no matter what anyone shared regarding moving too fast I just brushed them off as good intentions. My heart was screaming to me and so it was done, but just like everything else we both had scars on our heart. We had both experienced a failed marriage and other experiences that left us both a little hesitant to trust this love that seemed already understood.

I can't tell you enough how this has been a beautiful journey with many ups and downs, but there was not one lesson too small to not inspire gratitude. I have learned to love, forgive, and embrace the shore with all its beauty because I have learned the oceans have many moods.

I have faced the greatest fear I know, which is death, and erased the fear from my life. I haven't quite figured out how to erase all the triggers that can bring back such a wasteful emotion, but I'm working on it.

I believe our physical vessel carries our soul, so when it is our time to go home we hear God's call. To my point, I believe there is no death, as your soul cannot die. Realizing this truth has set me free from so much fear and worry. However, even with this belief I still have moments of weakness, which shows you how strong this fear—and fear alone—can really impact one's outlook.

I have shared a lot of my experiences through my blog over the past year, but there is a lot I have left out as I am still trying to process it. I consider myself blessed in so many ways, and this is something I cannot say enough.

I never dreamed facing my mortality would be a gift that would allow my inner light to shine so strong. Its lesson has proven that holding on to the past to define yourself is a waste of sweet time.

We should listen to the inner voice of God to guide us to live in the present moment. Within each breath there is an inhale and an exhale, each being an opportunity to invite and shed. Let go of the things that cripple you because this shows you still have not embraced the lesson.

I just read a book about self-love. One of the chapters was about a mermaid who fell in love with a human and was brokenhearted that they could not share their life together. She felt this cruel and unfair, but the lesson missed was that we cannot always go where others go. He could not live in the depths of the ocean, and she could not live on the shore. I have learned that because of this experience, my life has changed quite a bit, and as we all have a zero to ten scale for the challenges in life, mine is vastly different than it ever used to be. I am brave and can go alone where I could not before, and for this lesson alone I am grateful.

In yoga class I was teaching tree pose, and again, I felt a sense of gratitude, as I know that a tree reaches but never holds. I am slowly making my way back out into the world the same person, with many new experiences. This experience has opened a new door for life, a new voice of love, and an inner sense of guidance that will forever direct with God's work. Thank you all for supporting me by letting me go where I needed to go.

THE CHALLENGE OF PRACTICING NONATTACHMENT

Ask the waves, ask the leaves, ask the wind, but remember you are one and you too hold the answer.

After I graduated from college, around five o'clock on Sundays I would begin to get that feeling in my stomach, waiting for the week that was about to begin. How was this week going to be? Would I be stronger, more successful? Would I be heading toward my life purpose? Sunday had become the night I started to call "Sunday stand down" because I was working toward moving away from being connected to days of the week, as they held me prisoner at my own cost. I created a "routine" that usually followed the days of the week. I think we all do to a certain degree.

At different points in life, time has each served as a milestone, for lack of a better word. However, there is no pace or time for inner learning.

In high school, Friday night was the big football game, and with no responsibility came pure fun, living in the present moment like we have never known.

In college, it was a free-for-all. Depending on how you chose classes, you may only have gone to school two days a week. It was a time filled with complete freedom, bad choices, which led to lessons learned.

After college was when the bubble broke and life really began— the Monday through Friday workweek, and then the weekend—the two separated, creating yet another boundary to overcome. On Sunday night we all knew we had to ramp back up for a week of work.

Sometimes a group of us would make it a point to go out on Sunday to break the cycle, allowing Sunday to be the big night out … but it still felt weird, and we all knew we had to get up in the morning. In my mind this just set the scene for lessons to overcome and release.

Over the years our family has had so many blessings. I met Tad, we moved to the Midwest, and I got to experience a whole different life. I connected to my truest life and was blessed with a beautiful son. After Sawyer was born I stayed home, so I went from Monday to Friday to "What day is it?" I always knew Sunday meant less help. Sunday in the military meant it was a light duty day for everyone … and then Monday was "game on."

What it all comes down to as I look around at how blessed my life is (even through moments of pity), I realize the days of the week will always flow Sunday through Saturday. I am not sure who made this up or who decided on the calendar, but this is another example of how a boundary can create very deep emotions. What we learn comes when we need it, no matter what day or hour, how old or young, no matter how many times we have to start over or have to learn the same lesson. We fall down as many times as we need to, and then we get up whether it is Sunday or Friday. We misunderstand the truth that utters it choir all around us until we finally let go. We realize that slowly we will let go of the week, which only takes our attention away from evolving.

It is official when the days of the week do not matter any longer, and we are just living to embrace each day. Enjoy each interaction, make the most of the beauty that the day will offer, and remain blessed.

The yogis believe that we are assigned a specific number of breaths the day we are born. So why would you rush your breath? Take each one slowly, cherished with love and filled with life. Take each day, each moment slow, and cherish it with love.

"When you realize nothing is lacking, the whole world belongs to you"
~Lao Tzu

CHAPTER 38
SURVIVING SURVIVORSHIP

>Your fear is 100% dependent on you for its survival.
>~Steve Maraboli, Life, the Truth, and Being Free

JUNE 4, 2013

These words could not ring any louder as I move further past a moment in time that took my life on the greatest excursion without a hint of warning. June is survivorship month, and being at Dana-Farber has taken on a whole new life, with much celebrating. I am almost expecting a parade at a place that is usually filled with much challenge and stress.

People buzzed around, not stopping for a moment to look past their iPhone as no one wanted to be there a minute longer than needed. Most people pretended not to see each other, because if they did it may confirm their worst fears. There is the rare occasion where you or someone takes the opportunity to reach out to another and love is shared. Courage is shared and wisdom that guides the very journey you step each day is open to the unexpected.

As I sit here today, in the Blum resource room, I realize that years ago many did not have all the external support services cheering them on to know they are healed. They did not have resources to help those who didn't know where to turn, except to suffer alone with fear. When I walk through the hallways and see a young person, or anyone for that matter, wearing a mask and gloves, I know he or she is going through one of life's greatest challenges. I can't help but go back to my personal journey of healing.

The desire to speak with my eyes, to will each person to health becomes more than a need, almost mirroring the energy of obligation. Of course this comes from a form of my ego wanting this out of love. Again I am grateful to find comfort in understanding that we each have our own journey to enlightenment. This is something I have learned to trust, but as you can see, it is still a challenge. So I shine my reflection on them and share a loving intention of healing. As I see their reflection of hope and health, I wonder what their journey is like. What are they learning? What gifts are they opening?

Until today I had never utilized the support center because I didn't know it existed. Now I sit in amazement, looking at all the resources that I know would make a great difference for patients and their supporters. As I sat silently gazing the room, I felt a soft tap on my shoulder. When I turned I was greeted by a genuine smile that was an immediate escape to heaven. It was as if I had been transported from hospital to Loveolution Land! A fresh breath of air, the support streaming through like a wave in the omnipresent ocean, I smiled softly.

He was the manager of the resource room, and right away I knew there was no better person for the job. His heart was on his sleeve, and he had a very gentle way. He was so proud to walk me around the room, identifying the programs, workshops, and services they offered. He asked me what brought me to the center and with a long breath my heart followed his. After listening to the shortest detailed version of my journey he smiled, eyes wide. He reached his hand to mine and said, "Holly, the only thing that would make this story better would be if Julia Roberts was young enough to play you." My heart melted as it is always wonderful to accept a compliment, especially one as good as this.

It confirmed my thoughts once again how just a small gesture of kindness can immediately change your pace, your day, or your outlook. It would be that comment that would get me through a more challenging day. This is why we must have gratitude for even the smallest gesture of kindness, as it may be the rainbow that takes us to the other side of a difficult day.

After we talked, I went over to look at the books that stood tall on the shelves. My eye immediately fell upon one book; "surviving survivorship." I can still feel the visceral reaction that took me back two years to October 6. It brought forward the memory of just one single phone call and how so many things changed in my life. What a gift I was given, but at the time this gift and my greatest fear in life was all raveled in one moment.

I ran my finger over the stitching that spelled "survivorship" and concluded that I have survived. I feel stronger with each breath and now know I am ready to share the wisdom that others shared with me, the wisdom that grew with each passing day, the hearts that helped me heal, the love that engulfed me; I am ready to move forward. Knowing exactly how to move forward with all the emotions that sat aside while I focused on healing is now a new challenge.

This journey has taught me to embrace each day with a new outlook, a different perspective on living in the present. I have been blessed with the wisdom that I may have spent a lifetime trying to evolve to learn. I have opened my heart and shared my journey through a blog. I shared my learning lessons and challenges all while watching my greatest insecurities and emotions rise to the surface. Now it is time to move forward past survivorship, reflecting on how to share this journey. Having the courage to share such an amazing experience without reliving the emotions that have become part of my wisdom.

I have learned to live, forgive, and love, moving past being a survivor. Living as a survivor is living each day with one foot in the past. Many will feel this controversial because overcoming such a life challenge should award you the acknowledgment for life. However, I personally struggled in the space of "survivorship." We all are survivors each day we live, all embracing our own personal challenges. Although some are more difficult than others, it is clear to me that the wisdom falls in the divinity that comes with such struggle; this is what creates our growth.

As much as I acknowledge those who have gone through the deepest experiences, looking the ideal of death and truth square in the eye, I now believe that surviving is a phase we need to move past. In the dictionary, surviving is defined as enduring or living through adversity. It is also stated as remaining healthy, happy, and/or unaffected in spite of an occurrence. This occurrence could be a life threatening illness, a divorce, loss, and/or financial distress. Moving beyond surviving means taking the next step and embracing the experience, all the emotions and wisdom, moving forward with your new, beautiful life. This may contain a period of discovering your "new normal" because so much may have shifted during the challenge. However, this new change, this new normal, is what surrenders us to evolve (even if we sometimes don't want to).

I look at my parents' new neighbor, who was diagnosed with A.L.L. some thirty years ago, only to be told he had a 5 percent chance to live. Is he a survivor or an inspiration? He is my hero because he willed himself past what others thought and embraced his truth of life. He now is an older man, with a jolly laugh, and he lives each day with pizzazz in his step.

To all those who have survived an "occurrence," may your new wisdom carry your face to the wind while your feet will always remember life's most challenging experiences.

I wrote in hollysloveolution@wordpress.com with great excitement:

"Personal empowerment."

*

Yesterday marked an amazing day for quite a few reasons definitely worth celebrating. I set new intentions and hopes for my thirty-seventh year of life, which was extremely exciting. I also had some major awakenings of personal empowerment that without the past two years I would never have achieved. "They" say, "God only gives you what you can handle"—this may be true, but in the difficult moments of life we do not always see that light. We may have flashes of clarity, but doubt and fear may cloud the sky.

I spent a period of time yesterday journaling and writing my "greatest hits," and while I was writing it all came together. Like all the little pieces of a puzzle, they came together all at once and it was a beautiful sight. I found my personal empowerment and it almost surprised me.

You always have goals and hopes, and layers to peel. It is truly such an amazing tradition that keeps moving you along the flow of the river with you deciding if you are going to cling to the shore or just enjoy the current ... maybe both?

Acknowledging my own personal empowerment was such a great moment, as it came when least expected. I was poolside, reading an article about imagination, while I watched my dad and Sawyer swim with great joy. Watching Sawyer take these first steps of trust, swimming without his vest, realizing his great power may have been the catalyst. Or maybe it was the article.

Either way, it all connected perfectly, reaching layers deep and miles wide. Once you meet the entire scope, you fall into love. It encased your imagination with pure forgiveness where you give yourself permission to be your heart and expand on your connection to God's soul, as we are one. I can't describe the emotion other than it being so pure, solid, and malleable all at the same time, as to allow for positive change going forward.

I sat there with a smile on my face. I remembered years before a friend asking me if I really wanted to move back to the Boston area after Tad got a job in Providence. I realized as I was dragging my feet that I did not want to move back for any reason other than my own insecurity. When we moved to Chicago, I had a blank sheet of paper that I filled with my hopes and dreams, evolving to my true self, not what someone thought I was or should be. It was seeds I had planted when I was young, seeing slight glimpses of who I truly was in my heart. Moving back to where I grew up made me feel that I would not be welcomed as who I have become, that I would just be remembered by who people thought I was.

Over time these seeds blossomed divinely as they needed, each seed presenting me with information when I was ready that would help me evolve to who I am today. I am a mother, a yoga teacher, a birth doula, and an educator, but most importantly I am a student of my own evolution, one with God. This was a moment in time where my life externally matched my internal heart, desires, and dreams. Shortly after this realization came the greatest challenges I have ever experienced in life, which was filled with so many learning lessons. Once again, as it was divinely designed, each stone was placed perfectly for my next step, supporting me as I caught up with understanding and love, and resolving fear and anger.

The day I began writing *Always A Loveolution*, I realized just how many layers deep, how many old and new fears and anger existed. In addition, there was the conflict of forgiveness and self-love. It is there to meet you when you are ready, like a prepaid ticket for a trip.

Some days the writing just leapt off my fingers, and some days I scratched my head as I was learning at the very same time as I was writing. All the while, some things and experiences are difficult to put to paper, finding the right words, the right emotion to truly share this experience was very difficult at times. In my final stage of writing, I have unveiled a new realization that I do not have to defend who I am or my experiences like I often have in the past.

Now I look around me and see those who have supported me with love and embraced my heart. They have shared their thoughts and guidance like a loving idea instead of an imbalance of power, making their opinion more than a suggestion. I have lovingly blocked or ended those relationships that unintentionally tried to pollute my imagination, even though the intention may not have been to do so. This was very difficult because it was first identifying the relationships, which often brought sadness. This was another simple but hard lesson in understanding freedom, never allowing ourselves to "attach" to any relationship.

Back to my poolside read, I want to share the article that sparked all the pieces of my puzzle coming together divinely in a perfect fit. It was probably a number of events that divinely unfolded, but it was at this moment that personal empowerment became real. I gave myself permission to be. I am not coming from the perspective of "take it or leave it." I am coming from who I am today and the idea that I hope to continue to evolve toward a loving being. During this process I will not defend myself; I have realized this is such a waste of energy because we are all different; this does not make it right or wrong, just different. If someone else misreads my honesty, I know my intention comes from love, so there is nothing to defend. Really, I cannot share how freeing this is as once again love is the answer.

I have become one who walks a thin line when it comes to "rules." Rules can be healthy, but with a short slip they can turn into an impassable boundary. This article, however, identified great rules that empowered one's imagination.

Dr. Wayne Dyer (wrote articles titled "The Power of Imagination" and "The Power of Intention," which are both great resources) stated four rules that help you harness your imaginations, the power to manifest all your truths and desires. It starts by stating that one must unlearn the ways you have been misusing your imagination, creating limitations. Instead, you must live from the "I am God awareness," which refers to the changeless spirit that is one with Source. It is important to remember that you have a great deal of power in your imagination, and it is yours to be as you desire.

Rule #1: Never place into your imagination any thought that you would not want to materialize. Be conscious with your thoughts and be kind to yourself.

Rule #2: Never allow your imagination to be contaminated with ideas about how your life used to be. The past is the past and the door should remain open as each of these experiences have brought forth wisdom; however, when we live with one foot in the past, we can never truly move forward. Giving up the journey is evolving.

Rule #3: Your imagination is yours and yours alone. It is a vast, boundary-less realm within you that no one else has access to. It is usually with good intentions, but many people try to imprint upon your imaginative wall (similarly to your heart wall) their thoughts on how you should live. These viewpoints usually involve their own self-interest, affirming their own ideas of right or wrong.

As a society we have forgotten how to listen and just offer support. Many conversations are marked with individuals who are already planning their next move instead of just listening. Take a moment in your day to just bring consciousness to your listening; it is much more difficult than you may think.

The ego interferes by trying to fix it or show you the better way when really there is no better way, just God's way. Dr. Dyer uses an example in his article about life coaches. "And so it is with most well-meaning, self-appointed life coaches who tell you how you should be thinking about your future. Often they're trying to fulfill their wishes of needing to feel superior by advising others." I believe fully God sends us guidance, which comes in many forms. However, it is important to listen, as it is up to you to learn to decipher between the mortal mind and God mind to know if this guidance is for you.

I have learned the hard way that when something gets too difficult, we have fallen off our path. It is our job to harness a way to listen to others and ourselves. As a yoga teacher I have definitely felt that fine line as students have asked questions about the path. I always try to stick with factual evidence, but when I move toward my own belief system, I clearly outline that is my belief, from my experiences making it a belief; there is neither right nor wrong.

Rule #4: Do not allow your imagination to be restricted by the current conditions of your life. Your imagination is unlimited, and we can easily get stuck. This means that in order to manifest, creating your desired life, you have to change what you believe to be true about yourself. "This is reality and just the way things are, so there is nothing I can do about it" are the type of thoughts that will taint and defile the great gift of "I am that I am" (meaning you are a mirror of God, made without error).

Creation originates in the world of spirit. By allowing your senses to have complete control over manifesting your reality, you are placing a barrier that will block your dreams and desires. There is no question that we all face difficult challenges in life, sometimes it seems like they just continue and there is no break. But that just proves the need to be more present than ever and consciously enjoy life. Challenges are the very ideas that evolve you; they help you create your reality. Growth is not possible if you don't change your thoughts, and applying the same idea as you did yesterday will keep you planted. If you feel stuck, listen and look for the signs that may be there to offer new ideas or a new direction. It may be a counselor of some sort, a teacher, a book, a movie, whatever the catalyst is, listen with great intent to make peace with your personal empowerment!

Much love and light!

*

The most interesting part of my day was that when I went back to find the book it was not there. After hours of searching I could not find it anywhere. Was it there for me to see that day as it would make such an impact on many. The idea that we are not a "survivor", we have survived and it is time to move forward is quite a challenge for many to hear, but I believe it is in this space that we truly begin to live.

CHAPTER 39
OFF THE MAT

JULY 10, 2013

It has been a very interesting week to say the least, with twists and turns that have dropped my jaw to the floor. Over the past two years I have really learned to quiet myself and listen to my inner heart, receiving guidance and direction that has made me feel alive. It is when I choose the voice of fear that I get slapped in the face by the universe ... it never fails.

One of the more interesting experiences is when guidance comes as the voice of a friend or teacher, especially when it comes continuously in the same words, as if it were a reminder. This past weekend was like a reoccurring theme being shared through a number of channels. It was clearly reminding me: when we invite friendships, relationships of any kind into our life, they should be filled with a connection of love. We are all different and definitely are all in different places in our evolution; this is sacred without judgment. If you don't honor this when you know it is the truth, inevitably you will suffer.

Coming back to Massachusetts after being in Chicago for five years was scary. It was not only scary because I was facing a very difficult life challenge; it brought back so many old lingering feelings of insecurity. I moved out to Chicago and unveiled into my true soul. I wrapped my life into all the beautiful things that are important to me, such as teaching yoga, supporting birthing moms in education, and as a doula. I just love this work and love how much I learn from each experience. However, the most important part of this move was sitting in the seat of my soul, a connection I never fully made.

Coming back to the place I grew up, I quickly realized the dynamics around me. There are very few yoga studios, and home birthing isn't as popular. The lesson as I saw it was learning to accept yourself fully without any security blankets to provide comfort. Know who you are and stand strong with your truth (evolution) without any distractions. With this came a lot of resistance, as old friends only knew me before I knew my true heart. Many of the relationships beautifully coasted together and were quite inspirational. Others crashed and burned because I didn't listen to my internal guidance. I tried to force relationships even when my gut knew the friendship was too different, and that caused even more hurt and suffering. However, with suffering comes great awareness that can be delivered honestly with love, which was another lesson in many books while on my journey of the Loveolution.

Last night my friend Cindy and I sat talking about the weekend. Even though it was filled with some difficulties, all either worked out or went the direction they needed to go. Not a moment later we heard Java Joe (my twelve-year-old lab) trying to get into the house. Cindy went to let her in and wham, Java had been sprayed by a skunk. We both jumped to the task without a moment to waste as I knew the faster we got her in the bath the easier it would be to get out the smell. Two hours later after many pictures, laughter, and a pound of sage, all was well. Immediately afterwards I got a thought to go look in my copy of *Animal Speaks* by Ted Andrews, which symbolizes animal totems that become present in your life. Similar the idea of a reflection, we have to stay connected to what shows up in our life. Animal Totems are a sign; similar to any other that will give you the guidance you need when life around you feels stressful. I was not too surprised by the message of the skunk.

It read, "The skunk is one of the most widely recognized mammals, but it is also one of the most misunderstood. People show great respect, and this is how the skunk teaches to give respect, expect respect, and demand respect. It helps you to recognize these qualities and to assert them with self-acceptance. The skunk moves along at its own speed and strong mind. Skunks are fearless but also very peaceful. Because they are peaceful by nature, they always give three warnings before spraying. Sometimes when a skunk shows up as a totem sign, it can teach us how to get positive attention without being arrogant or irritating. Sometimes it helps us deal with those relationships in our lives that are outrageously irritating.

"People with the skunk as a totem must learn to balance the ability to draw and repel people. Knowing there are times to embrace people and times to repel people is important to finding the proper balance to ensure prosperity and love. Skunks demand a new self-respect and self-esteem. It indicates lessons and times associated with increased spirituality."

We all need to look to the world around us for signs, messages, and guidance. This sign was a perfect message for me, along with continued wisdom from a friend. It was truly the perfect affirmation. I have embraced that we all need respect and this may require embracing a relationship or setting it free, but mostly it requires the wisdom to know the difference!

Learning all these lessons in such a short period of time has filled me with numerous emotions. I did not have a yoga community to connect with so I had to live my yoga, off the mat, which is really the greater lesson. Through many days of this journey I have been in awe of the lessons I have learned while truly living my yoga, the lessons that I have learned while being a student and teacher. As I wrote this book I spent a lot of time reflecting on the past year-and-a-half, which has taken me through the forests to the land where the grass grows, and back through the seas. I have been humbled and learned so much about myself that this project has served as my own private therapy. With each chapter a reflection of my life, emotions buried deep inside continually surfaced as I wrote about experiences. I realized that I am a much deeper person than I thought I was. I have experienced a rebirth, a new appreciation for life and feel ready to move forward to share.

There were days I wondered if I would ever be done sharing my story in a way that could make as much sense to someone else as it has for me. Many days and nights I questioned everything, taking giant leaps backward—or maybe they were leaps forward? Either way they were lessons in reconnecting to life after being in my bubble for so long. My gratitude and love repeats within me as I express my quest. With each breath I am grateful for the new invention of my life and all the learning, looking forward to the many lessons this journey will continue to introduce. I have felt that teeter between the spirit, mind, and body, grasping just how fine a line it really is.

Living whole has been a goal that I didn't know I had. It requires much attention and practice, but you release what is not serving you. You embrace all the beauty of oneness and love. I have done this over past months and am now putting oneness and love into action in a more natural way. I didn't fully understand how to move forward previously. This was a chapter that came right from my heart.

WHAT I HAVE LEARNED FROM LIVING MY YOGA "OFF THE MAT."

With a lesson this big there is some rite of passage where you get to share what you have learned with others—or maybe it is just that you want to see your progress.

It is nice to write in a journal, so you can see what you have learned and achieved over the landscape of a challenge in your life. When you take a deep breath and reach the bottom of that breath, pausing for a moment, you will feel a stillness that reflects a space. This space is called the doorway to your love window and where all our wisdom awaits. The following is the wisdom from my love window:

- I have learned that listening is critical to understanding and forgiving.
- The quiet and stillness of the mind comes with practice and patience. In addition, meditation is not the only way to find stillness and a quiet mind. There is something to be said for a moving meditation.
- I have learned that opinions, observations, and judgments are all very different. Opinions are just that and often become part of your own reflection. Observations are educational and from the heart teach a lesson. Judgments may be necessary in certain situations in order to make peace, learn a lesson, or to move forward, but if this is your greatest tool, you are a fool. **I have been a fool too.
- I believe everyone has the right to his or her own beliefs, which should be lovingly received. If you listen closely, you may realize that your beliefs are not too far apart.
- One of the greatest realizations in life is that we all are *love*. Great love! God is love, we are God; it is that simple. I believe from this journey we make it much more difficult then it has to be, but that that is part of the journey. Without this maybe we wouldn't evolve

- at all. With so many unknowns we must fall in the arms of faith and know a few certain the great truths- one being love.
- Love is the bottom line. All of the buzzing around you, all the temptations, and all fears can easily be squashed with love. Love is a temple climber, a rainy shower, and the best idea God ever had. It brings us all close and understanding of each other, sharing in each other's experiences without judgment or jumping to share yours. Love is a blessing and I am so thankful that I have that.
- Love is realizing that life goes on around you and that others need love too. It isn't a tit for tat but a delicate balance that keeps relationships healthy. Love is the oneness you feel in a hug.
- Love will lift the burden for another, even for just a moment.
- Love is forgiveness and kindness. Love is when you watch a child open the best present ever.
- Simply Love is all, and all is *Love*.

I am learning that in order to understand and feel true love, you must love everyone the same; this includes yourself. It is difficult to love those who have hurt others, committed crimes, stolen, or broken hearts, but we *must* love everyone the same. I am not there yet, but I hope that as the walls fall one at a time, I will be able to understand this and fully embrace it.

When I started my yoga teacher training, we all sat together to create "our mission statement," our vision for this class, a process that would teach us far into the future. We each took a few moments of connecting to breath and then our teacher, Wendy went around the table asking each of us what our personal intention was to unite us as one to create our goal of the training. A group of women who didn't know each other opened our hearts in love to set an intention together. It read as follows:

"Blue Sun Yoga teacher training group intention"
We unite as a group without judgment;
Inspire and learn from one another;
Combine our energy as a force for positive change;
Support one another in our individual growth;
Honor and respect each other;
Provide safety and support like that of a tribe;

Gain insight;
Practice harmony;
Fill everyone's sails with wind;
Share experiences and interpretations while being open to all ideas;
Practice patience, honesty, and be the best we can be;
Help one another in this learning process because we can rock!

Can you imagine, if we all contributed one positive thought from the heart, just how beautiful life would always be? May each group that comes together and each individual create his or her mission statement, sending out the call to the universe for guidance and light?

CHAPTER 40
BODY AS A TEMPLE

> The only time to look down on someone is when you're bending over to help.
> ~Amish Proverb

JULY 20, 2013

Last night I came across this Amish proverb, and it really spoke loudly to me as I was preparing to make my way to Dana-Farber today for a full panel of tests. This is always a difficult day filled with fear that dissipates into trust. Through much trust and listening to the wisdom that has been passed along, this proverb really melted my heart into a million pieces. I felt that these words didn't need anything to precede them as they speak right to the soul of the reader.

It is wisdom like this that makes a day like today bearable. Today was such a huge relief as I heard Dr. Sieffer ring out beautiful words of health! All my blood work looked amazing and I am great; he even said Tad looked great; overall just a great day. I didn't sleep last night and felt my heart beat out of my chest when I got to Dana-Farber, but then it all just melted away in minutes.

While Tad and I were waiting for the doctor to come to the room, I felt a moment where I was lost. A moment that took me through a flashback of fears and dashed dreams, a time where life paused. The "what if" that I work so hard to embrace and trust took right over. Thankfully Tad reeled me in and told me I was fine. How did he know?

However, while we were talking and I was backing away from the ledge, I looked into my large pocketbook to get something to distract me until the doctor got there. This morning at the early hour of four thirty I grabbed a couple of magazines off the table and stuffed them in my purse. Out the door we went as my dad gave me the good luck smile. It was a catalog called Sunset, which I had never heard of or seen, so where it came from is your best guess. I started combing through each page, looking at the jewelry, and as my mind continued in a fury of fear I turned the next page.

Tad just happened to look up as we both laid our eyes on the angel coin that has followed me, blessing me through this journey. Today was no different.

I have given the coin away, only for it to be given back to me by another. I have lost it, only to find it deep in my pillowcase. I have prayed with it, set intentions and buried it, and now see it in a magazine right when I needed the boost. Trusting these signs has been the door that has given me a great deal of peace. This peace has allowed me the space to truly learn the wisdom and lessons that comes from walking a path like this.

Walking down the hall after my appointment, I felt like I could fly and I was so grateful. However, in this environment you see those who are in an earlier phase of the journey and you just want to offer hugs. Although you can't hug a transplant patient, you can air hug, which can be a little awkward, so I just offer a loving smile that speaks a thousand words. It matters. It makes a difference. It can change a day. Whether you are leaving for deployment overseas, whether you are a transplant patient, or whether you are just crashing, we all need just the gesture that we are not being stared at or judged, but are loved.

Move outside your comfort zone by spreading love, a nice gesture to someone you don't know without an expectation of any kind in return. Here are a few ideas to get started.

1. Say thank you to any serviceman or servicewoman you see in uniform.
2. Hold the door for someone and start a small conversation.
3. Donating is a tricky part of giving, but you should give without notice. It is personal and if truly from your heart done privately.
4. Listen fully to the next conversation you have with a family member.
5. Apologize without excuses and just let it be.
6. Allow yourself to be taught, even if you are familiar with the topic, just listen; you may learn something new.

7. Do something that makes you feel uncomfortable.
8. Be yourself without any old expectations you may have had in the past.
9. Don't explain yourself when you turn down an invitation.
10. Love yourself, reach for the olive branch, and listen to the wisdom that comes with age.

It is the will of the human mind to keep a log of debts and credits, much like that of a banking system. This is a great example where we need to retrain the societal norms to move past this system, creating a heart balance. There is no question that if you keep withdrawing from the bank of life, you will run out of money … unless you keep putting money back into your account.

It is finding this balance that we all struggle with each day. It is the fear of lack, the fear that we will run out, the fear of being rejected or labeled. When you move past the worry and fear, you feel love. It is this space where we find a balance of giving without expectation of any kind. It is also the space where we receive without feeling we need to give back. It becomes the brilliant balance of giving and receiving.

CHAPTER 41
SHARING YOUR LOVEOLUTION

"THE LOVEOLUTION PROJECT"

Trusting in the voice of God, knowing internally that the source is what connects us all is part of our evolution.

"The body is the temple of God; in every body, God is installed whether the owner of the body recognizes it or not. It is God that inspires you to do good acts, that warns you against the bad. Listen to that internal voice, and you will not have suffering" (Sathya Sai Baba, Indian Spiritual Teacher).

The Loveolution is not yet a word in our dictionary, however, if broken down it means—any process of formation of growth and development.

Taking it one step further, the "Loveolution" is a process of creating oneness and the growth of loving. It takes a village ... a village to help us each personally evolve to one.

This Loveolution journey has not only helped me, but so many around me. It has encircled my life and touched the lives of many, taking on a life force of its own. I am setting it free as it has served its purpose for me. It is a beautiful, circular connection that brings us one step closer together.

If you feel that you have been through a journey that has changed your life and believe it would offer wisdom for others to continue to awaken please consider sharing your story at alwaysaloveolution@yahoo.com.

I look forward to reading your stories and sharing them with the world as there is always a Loveolution, and by sharing our tools and wisdom we continue to connect with a greater, deeper love.

As we come full circle, I want to thank you all for sharing this journey with me as I bared my heart and soul. I have learned a great deal from many around me, some that I have sought out, some that have simply appeared.

I believe that my vision boards (intention boards) were a big part of my healing, as I stayed focused, connected to my imaginative dreams. I opened up a large part of myself and now will reconnect to life in the most brilliant way.

WE HAVE A CHOICE!

We don't have to fight our way through anything, but if that is what we need, so be it. However, do it fully, leaving nothing behind. Create clear intentions, because what you intend to create begins to manifest itself in your experience.

Intentions allow us to feel the power of bringing conscious choice into everything we do. With vision and intention, "I have to" or "I wish for" turns directly into "I choose to" or "I am." Intentions help us leave a mark in life that is more effective and filled with integrity for life.

I like to use the words "mission statement," as this is ultimately what you are calling out to the universe. This is pure physics and has been proven time and time again. There are many ways that you can put your vision, mission statement, or intention into action, creating the very essence of your dream's desires.

Your intentions will begin to affect how you interpret your thoughts, blocking any thoughts that are not serving you. Intentions are created in the present moment through a practice of being. All your dreams and wishes you believe in are happening to you now. You envision yourself already having these "intentions," affirming them over and over again.

This is why the vision board is so important. When we can see daily what we are trying to create in our life, it becomes imprinted in our brain as it is called to action. It is similar to a goal, but the big difference is that a goal is something we try to achieve in the future. An intention is something we believe we already have achieved and are awaiting its presence in our life, as it will divinely be gently laid on the path of our journey.

Using a vision board is a way to view your imaginative dreams/intentions that you breathe in and out each day. Each morning you see, say, and seal these intentions to your heart. Making this tool more accessible was an idea I had while going through treatment. Create a site that would host your vision board, allowing you to view it in a moment's notice. Additionally, you can make changes to it when appropriate to your reality.

www.luvlution.com

Please visit this site to set up your free account. You will be able to create a beautiful vision board and your own personal mission statement. You can share this board with close friends, as with power they too will hold your intentions for you.

As you create your intentions you need to make way for new intentions. Remember that this is a sacred tool that will guide you with gifts for the greatest good of all. I believe ever so strongly that it was the intentions that I asked many to hold in their heart for me that created such a vast healing. This is what spiritual science shows us.

Remember; don't force yourself down a path because you feel it best. Listen to the signs, look for the opening, and move forward.

CHAPTER 42
THE MIRACLE

> Miracles are a retelling in small letters of the very same story, which is written across the whole world in letters too large for some of us to see.
> ~C. S. Lewis

When I first began writing *Always a Loveolution* and blogging at hollysloveolution.wordpress.com, I always wondered how this story would end. What wisdom would the last chapter reveal? What amazing lesson would have to unravel to meet the beautiful gift this book has shared? This was a journey so sweet it graciously guided me to each rock one breath at a time until I was ready for the next, allowing for just enough challenge to learn the lesson and just enough wisdom to share it.

So how does this sweet journey close it doors? I don't have the answer to this question. My thought is this book will do what it needs to do, taking on a journey of its own. I believe this book, for many years to come, will help others (including myself) evolve and realize that love and forgiveness are the only two facets of life that will break the chain of suffering. Realizing we do not have to suffer during life's greatest challenges, we can open our hearts to receive all the gifts the world has to offer.

This book is an experience that will forever evolve, each reader uncovering or drawn to parts that resonate on a deeper level. This will undoubtedly divinely release and reveal your true soul, your beautiful truth. There is no convenient time to be faced with any challenge, but the Loveolution offers a sense of preparedness.

This journey for me ends with a miracle that will continue to give. Through all of my vision boards, journaling, and affirmations, I thought maybe I used up all my miracles. I survived the Loveolution, I had Sawyer, and again I find myself asking for a miracle. Once again, it came by way of an immediate thought, which reminded me that there is no limitation on anything, God only deals with abundance; a lesson I quickly forgot.

When I was a child I had a spinal malformation called spondylolisthesis, a condition that required surgery to help me maintain an active, healthy lifestyle. I had surgery, and with the prayers of my fifth-grade comrades at a school dance and my family, I never suffered another moment. I played sports in high school and college, and I then became a yoga teacher. It wasn't until I was seven months into my pregnancy that my spine became another lesson. I was in so much pain; a battle between the ego and connection to God's soul.

I cried every day, struggling with doubt and fear as I watched my belly grow. It took over my every thought and handicapped a natural birth experience because of fear. After a very difficult delivery I thought my back issue would be a thing of the past. However, as the weeks passed the pain grew stronger, as did my mind and emotions. It is easy to say let it go, but physical pain is not something you can push aside—or is it? I know a number of experiences where people were in such shock they didn't feel pain, and I have seen several moms have a complete pain-free childbirth, truly amazing. However, in this moment I didn't know how to get out of my own way.

I did everything I knew possible. I went to acupuncture, I did yoga, I did acro-yoga, I bought an inversion table, and I took pain medication. After a full year of mind-numbing pain, in a moment when I just threw my hands in the air, I opted to have spinal surgery.

Unfortunately, I had yet to move past this huge block in my life. My spine continued to be a challenge in life, and I didn't know how to get through it. I begged God, I read every book on healing, books about chronic pain, but nothing seemed to help. Then one afternoon I got a phone call that changed it all. I had just been diagnosed with the Loveolution.

The brakes went on, and although I still had a significant amount of pain, my eye was on the greater challenge.

As I worked through all the lessons of the Loveolution, all the gifts and wisdom, I was so excited to move forward in life, sharing God's wisdom as I was guided. It was when I regained my strength that I realized my ego was going to put me to the test. The back pain was louder than ever. The pain no longer ebbed and flowed as it had the years prior, now it was constant. I was back to square one, but now I had a number of tools and wisdom to apply to it.

I began each day stating that I was healed, meditating on how it felt to have a fully mobile spine in my yoga practice. I created new vision boards to support the other work I was doing. I tried Ariel Yoga, which was simply amazing, the greatest traction I had ever experienced. I was giving it everything I had, and then I broke down. I again was lost.

I had a few leads, one being a doctor at New England Baptist; he was touted as one of the best in the country. However, he wanted me to get a full MRI with contrast before I could even get an appointment. In the meantime I was trying to meet with all kinds of different physicians moving across from allopathic to naturopathic, to hypnosis, to meditation; I again did it all. What was I missing was the last piece of the puzzle. A miracle!

I thought about this miracle as if it were a potential fantasy. I had experienced a few miracles, but the ego at its finest helped me question what this really was … it couldn't be a miracle.

I had an appointment to see a physiatrist, which is a physician who helps restore the physical anatomy after there has been any kind of serious injury including surgery. Sounded like a great fit, noninvasive, restorative, but after a two-hour drive I was six minutes late for the appointment and the doctor would not see me. He wouldn't even give me five minutes to identify if he could help me or not. The level of frustration I felt was far beyond any I have ever known. I was so angry when I got into the car, feeling so defeated. Can you believe I had the balls to yell at God? "You healed me from the Loveolution, and now I have to suffer with back pain every day?"

I drove home crying into the phone, telling Tad my sad story. He couldn't believe it and in the famous words of Tad, he said, "Holly, there has to be a reason behind this." I didn't want to hear it anymore. I was doing everything I could and continued to be kicked when I was down. I would not reschedule with this doctor because I found his behavior and choices to be so far away from where I aligned that I knew he couldn't help me.

After I centered and realized that my previous tantrum was a bad reaction, I knew in my heart there had to be a reason behind this diversion. Then … a single thought. I quickly reached for my phone and called Dr. Lims office. I shared my story with the kindly office manager, and sure enough there was a cancellation three months down the road. I felt a bit frustrated, but I took it.

The day of the appointment, Cindy accompanied me into the city watching the sunrise upon Boston Strong. We got there very early, but I didn't care, as I was so excited to get some answers.

After two hours of waiting, I was placed in a room, anxiously awaiting the doctor. When Dr. Lim came in, his kind eyes and heart mesmerized me. It totally took me by surprise, and I felt like God was holding my hand.

He was very empathetic to my situation and was impressed with my ability and love for yoga. He told me the previous surgery done in Chicago might have created more problems. He asked me where the pictures were from my MRI. He saw the report, but the CD that I handed his secretary just two hours ago was missing.

Taken by surprise, I jumped off the table, ran out into the reception area, and asked her if she had the CD I gave her. Thankfully Cindy saw me hand it to her, so I had "proof" that I was not crazy. No one could find the CD and I just stood there in utter shock. The whole point of this appointment was to see the new MRI film compared to my old films, and we had nothing. Again, I felt lost and questioned what I was missing.

We agreed that their office would call to get a new CD and then once he reviewed it, he would call me to discuss options. When he called the MRI center, they did not have my CD; it had somehow gotten erased. I was in such shock and in the moment was having a difficult time with being understanding.

They were extremely apologetic and scheduled another MRI a few weeks away. I guess one could say this is a lesson in divine timing or patience, but sometimes our human side wins the battle. I drove home in silence.

All this while Tad had to leave to go to Denver for work for a week, which turned into two months. The weekend he left, a skunk sprayed our dog, I had to bring one of my cats to be put to sleep, and God called home a friend. I was struggling to keep faith, but somehow I found what I call "a smidge."

I was feeling sorry for myself and again was unsure where to turn. I prayed all night and then I became extremely focused with my prayers. I asked for a miracle without guilt, with full faith and understanding that I am God's reflection.

While I was struggling with this situation I felt some level of guilt. This is why the ego is so difficult to soften, it finds every little loophole, which to create any emotion that will cause even the slightest suffering.

This week I had walked through Boston Children's Hospital to get to Brigham and Women's for my appointment. They are all connected like a city of hospitals; it is a Mecca of medicine and research; quite amazing. It was during my walk that I saw brilliance in children who faced very difficult circumstances and complete sorrow in the eyes of their parents. It was such awareness for me in that moment; no one can understand that unless he or she has walked the path.

Later that night while I prayed I was transported in time, visualizing the faces, and I felt extreme guilt. I had been given a gift and I wanted more, which was when I realized that again I was creating a boundary, a limitation to my experience that should deny me a miraculous healing. This was when I went down the rabbit hole.

As I got further into my meditation I brought myself to a beach, where I sat watching the waves. As each wave came upon the shore it brought the most beautiful arrangement of lights, and as it went back out to sea it stayed the same color. This confused me as I expected the wave to change color departing back to the vast ocean because it was taking with it all the things that were no longer serving me. However, as each wave rolled onto the shore, the colors just became more brilliant.

I slowly bent over to place my hands in the water, wondering if there would be any sensation from the color. When I stood up I saw a woman standing in front of me, reaching for my hand. She had very deep eyes that immediately spoke to me.

She walked me back up to the shore and guided me to a chair as she walked toward the other chair. It was like we were old friends sharing a glass on lemonade on a hot day. This is the beauty of meditation; it guides you and takes you wherever you need to be, if you truly accept. In one moment you can be in a field of tall grass and the next step you may be knee deep in a river so forceful that you need to find balance. This dreamlike state is just that and is one of those moments where you need to let go.

I remember this mediation quite vividly, excited to learn whom this woman was and what she had to say. However, that I may never know as she was there to give me a simple message. She peered into my eyes with such love and began to speak. She shared that I may not understand this today, but I will soon. She stated, "You have asked for a miracle. There are no such things as miracles because you are already aligned with the perfection of God." She stood up and walked into the ocean, and after a short walk she just blended into the beautiful ocean view.

I sat in silence, repeating the words over and over in my head. Then I smiled, realizing I have said this about every which way you can but was fooled by the word "miracle."

We as a society have labeled all the great things that happen, things we cannot quite make sense of or explain, as a miracle. However, a miracle is just your true greatness, your "real" soul reflection.

I have moments where I can explain this as if it was adding 2 + 2, and then it vanishes like the early morning dew, barely leaving a trace. It explains it all, through a feeling, without words, all wrapped into one. It is the most powerful piece of wisdom.

When I got up from my meditation I wrote down every detail that I could remember. When I read it over I went back to the boundary we create when we ask for a miracle. It is already given. We just have to figure out how to believe it.

Later in the week I had my appointment to get another MRI. I felt frustrated by the inconvenience but took a few moments of waiting to read. It is amazing when we feel alone in a sea of other waiting patients.

The MRI went as planned, and I was out the door in less than an hour. The doctor who reviewed the MRI ran into the parking lot just as I was starting my car. He asked if I was Holly Peckskamp. He asked if I would come back inside for a moment. Of course fear was making its way through every cell in my body; I felt numb.

He put two of the films on the white screen, and what I saw dropped me to the chair that thankfully was right behind me. Looking up at the screen was the most beautiful spine. I didn't feel any different, but my films showed a healthy spine. We looked at each other without words and just sat there. Finally I asked if this was a mistake, trying to make sense of any other possible outcome that could create this image. He was sure this was my film. He again went to go check and reprint the film for a third time.

I was still in the same chair looking at the film that showed no spinal fusion from when I was twelve, no hint of any surgery for that matter. I was healed, and for the first time in life my outside heart matched my inner soul.

The above story is my love window, my intention, and my dream! It is how I envision the final layer of my ego releasing. I don't know how this will move forward. I only have my faith. The final chapter showing the message that the door truly was never even there to close, which becomes the greatest lesson of all.

Each night as I lay my head down, I envision the above miracle. I see myself speaking at events sharing such a beautiful story. I see myself teaching beautiful yoga classes laced with love and peace, and attending to women who want a connected birth experience. These are my dreams, my intentions that were a rebirth from the Loveolution. As I know it will unfold in the greatest good, I continue to move from rock to rock, one divine step at a time.

Thank you, *Loveolution*!

RESOURCES AND TOOLS

1. Build an online vision board by visiting www.luvlution.com
2. To share your story, your Loveolution, please send to www.alwaysaloveolutioin@yahoo.com.
3. The Wellness Trek – How to get started by Patrick Hatwan
4. Eckhart Tolle the uncourse - www.eckharttolle.com/uncourse

RESOURCES

1. Law of Attraction, Jerry and Esther Hicks
2. The Spontaneous Healing of Belief, Gregg Braden
3. The Power of Intention, Dr. Wayne W. Dyer
4. Of Monkeys and Dragons, Michele Longo O'Donnell
5. Love, Medicine, and Miracles, Bernie S. Siegel, M.D.
6. The Light worker's Way, Doreen Virtue, Ph. D.
7. The Divine Matrix-Bridging Time, Space, Miracles, and Belief – Gregg Braden
8. God Never Blinks, Regina Brett
9. A Course in Miracles
10. Fierce Medicine, Ana T. Forrest
11. The Book of Awakening, Mark Nepo
12. Wherever You Go There You Are, Jon Kabat-Zinn
13. Science and Health, Mary Baker-Eddy
14. The Yoga of Jesus, Paramahansa Yogananda
15. The Four Agreements, Miguel Ruiz
16. Legacy of the Heart, Wayne Muller

17. Warrior of Light, Paulo Coelho
18. Meditation as Medicine, Dharma Singh Khalsa, M.D and Cameron Stauth
19. The Power of Now, Eckhart Tolle
20. Dying to be Me, Anita Moorjani
21. Law of Attraction, Magazine
22. Yoga Journal, Magazine
23. Above all Be Kind, Zoe Weil

THE WELLNESS TREK—GETTING A GOOD START

We all cherish myths. As Mark Twain once said, "It's much easier to fool the people than it is to convince them they've been fooled."

So, where do we start our journey? The trek is forever.

What if we don't know the first thing about what it means to be healthy? What it we don't know the first thing about what is required from us to promote our health?

We all know people who are sick. But remember that the absence of symptoms is not necessarily the presence of health. Most of us can be diagnosed with some sort of disease today. All of us should be aware that our health is our own personal responsibility.

Most of us can withstand tremendous hardships whether they're physical, emotional or spiritual, over long periods of time, under circumstances that do not look very good in the short term. The keys to surviving and remaining in good health throughout the challenge are that we get adequate oxygen, water, and nutrition that excretion is adequate, and we get good sleep. Couple those with a healthy spiritual connection, some exercise and a strong social network and things will generally turn out for the good.

Let's take a look at each of these in individual detail. Remember too, that the body is designed to function even under extreme stress. By design, the body's normal direction is toward balance, or homeostasis. The body will always struggle toward getting health stabilized. Provide our bodies with the simple essentials mentioned above and you can count on either improving bad health or maintaining what health you do have.

When we consider the world we live in today, it is patently obvious that things are not clean. The air is dirty. The water quality is not good. The foods we rely on are denatured, nutrient poor or they have been modified by agricultural technology.

The key to long-term health is to recognize that permanent neglect of any of these items will be detrimental to our health and vitality. When deficiencies happen, the consequence is degeneration. We will begin to see the physical and nervous system becoming upset and we will die from lack of rest and nourishment.

So, let's begin with some basic understanding of what we can all do in order to gain a strong sense of security that we're doing all we can, the best we can. The basics are quite simple and, when they are consistently applied, they are profoundly powerful.

Breathing is one of the body's ways of survival. It is often considered as the way in which oxygen is provided for our ability to survive. Try holding your breath for longer than 30 seconds. The obvious is that it becomes extremely difficult and most of us will gasp for another breath! WOW!! That's difficult and it sure isn't too much fun, unless you're a kid playing. But let's look at the deeper reality of breathing.

The overlooked aspect of what happens after oxygen is taken into the body via the lungs is that metabolism gets carried out. But, just like our cars, once the fuels are burned, there must be exhaust. So, breathing is associated with removal of those exhausts.

One measure of health is the number of breaths per minute. If we count the number of inhale/exhales per minute, most of us, if we're healthy will be in the range of 12 to 15 breaths per minute. Those who are chronically sick may have 20 to 30 breaths per minute.

Breathing is a primary path for excretion of toxins. It is not JUST for removal of carbon dioxide. So, let's consider what we can do to improve our health via breathing exercises.

A fun and exciting exercise is to consider this as one of our BEST routes to improving health. By retraining ourselves in the excretion of toxins, we not only deliver more oxygen and remove byproducts from metabolism, we also can support weight loss while we decrease the symptoms of bad health.

So a beginning is to count our numbers of breaths per minute. If we're shallow breathers, our goal is to decrease the count. It will require dedication and commitment too.

Inhale as deeply as you can and hold that for 5 seconds. Then, exhale, as fully and completely as you can. Do this for several breathing cycles. If you become dizzy, discontinue the exercise for a few minutes and begin again. Eventually, you will be able to do this for 15 or 20 minutes. Repeat this 4 or 5 times every day, and make it a regular part of every day. The results will amaze you!

<u>Drinking water</u> is perhaps the 2nd most important element for survival. When we are deficient adequate amounts of water in our bodies, the net result is dehydration. It is estimated that 90% of us are dehydrated. One of the symptoms of dehydration that is overlooked is that we "THINK" we're hungry, and so we eat. We snack and consume excessive amounts of liquids that are not supplying our bodies with adequate water. Remember that when we say water, we are not discussing just simple liquids. Sodas, energy drinks, sport drinks and various other drinks are not hydrating our bodies. In fact, the only way to properly supply our bodies with adequate liquid is by water. Pure water, clean water, water that is healthy is the only way to adequately hydrate, to supply our tissues with healthy liquid.

The tap water we have in our homes is not to be considered as appropriate. While the municipal water treatment facilities are mandated to deliver potable water, it is not safe water. So the need to do treatments beyond what the city water system supplies becomes crucial.

There are several options available for all of us. Remember that simply installing a faucet device may not provide proper filtering.

The suggestion would be that reverse osmosis systems or other filtering processes be considered.

Also consider locating spring water. The purest water on earth, at the moment, can be found in the icebergs around the north Atlantic. That ice is over 10,000 years old and has never been contaminated by industrial or human pollutants. It is not readily available, so the next best source would be deep spring water wells. Here we find the best waters for our basic needs. Locating them is as easy as using the internet and googling "deep spring wells".

For those families who cannot have a reverse osmosis unit in their homes or apartments, the next best step is to find a grocery store that has water machines and bottles that you can fill for purchase. Another alternative is to locate a water service company that sells and distributes drinking water. We can also rely on our own water wells if we're in rural areas but do have the water tested to see if there are agricultural pollutants that require removal.

Good nutrition is absolutely essential for all of us. Today, more than ever, nutrition that supplies appropriate support for health and vitality is going to be the key that supports a healthy and vigorous energy supply. Each of us requires protein, fats, carbohydrates and starches, but in varying amounts. Some people must consume more proteins that others while some require absolutely no carbohydrates at all. An example of a person that might not be able to survive with carbohydrates would be the Inuit Eskimo.

It needs to be stressed that the average person should consume 3 meals per day with light snacks.

It also should be stressed that grains are not healthy, even though we're inundated with the notion that grains supply vital nutrients and fiber. This is a fallacy and it needs to be understood that grains are unhealthy. The primary factor regarding the nature of grains is that the majority of them are genetically modified or hybridized. Our bodies DO NOT recognize those alterations and thus, they are toxic.

So, the question becomes; if grains are unhealthy, what is the alternative? Most diets for most people should consist of nuts, seeds, meats and fish, fats and oils and plenty of fruits and vegetables. The rule of thumb that fits most appropriately is that the diet should primarily be whole foods and plant based.

What does that mean? Whole foods are those that are not processed, meaning they do not come in a box, a bottle, a bag, a can or a jar. Processed foods are loaded with preservatives, food colors, white sugar (or high fructose corn syrup) and white flour, which are NOT the 4 basic food groups. And remember that USDA food pyramid is not a safe way to plan meals or menus.

Fats are an essential element for our bodies. Fats are one of the primary nutrients from which our bodies produce energy. So, LOOSE THE FEAR OF FAT!!

Dairy products are also a critical element of nutrients. Eggs are rich in sulfur which is crucial for all of us. When considering dairy, it is a good idea to consider "farm fresh", rather than what might be purchased in a grocery store.

Many people will not consider "farm fresh" as an acceptable source, but it is proven that the quality of and safety of "farm fresh" is higher than what can be purchased from a grocery store.

In the market place today, farmer's markets are a very solid and reliable source of foods that are "whole food-plant based". Do consider purchasing food for the table from farmer's markets. You will be richly rewarded.

Excretion was very briefly mentioned above in the breathing segment. Let's touch on this in more detail here. The body eliminates toxins in many ways.

Urination, defecation, sweating, tears, earwax, sebum and sputum are all pathways by which our bodies eliminate toxins and by-products of normal body functions. Keeping all of these functions working properly is not something that we pay direct attention to, but we do need to give some focus on what is going on with each one.

For example, if we do not sweat when we're exerting tremendous amounts of energy over long periods of time, while working or doing sports activities, etc, we should be concerned. Sweat is a process by which our bodies cool tissues. When this process is not working properly, we also are not eliminating by-products from the excessive metabolic waste products that are also naturally formed. Perhaps we're dehydrated and we should consider drinking more pure and clean water.

Urine should be something we check as well. If our urine is dark and smelly, it is an indicator that we're dehydrated. Consuming more water will naturally produce less smelly and more, clear discharge. We should also pay attention to excessive urination or lack of urine. In those cases, it is wise to consult a medical professional.

Defecation is something that most people pay little attention to. Our stools should be regular, meaning, for most people, at least one time and perhaps 2 times daily. The stools should be firm and floating, and not hard, stinking and sinking. These signs are indicators of our digestion, whether it is good or bad. When the stools are sinking and hard, it is a good indicator that there is a shortage of adequate fiber in the diet. It could also indicate a profound lack of adequate hydration. We must not drink liquids during our meals. Many people will consume several glasses of sodas, milk, coffee and/or teas with their meal. This is not a healthy thing. Liquids should be consumed 15 minutes prior to or following the meal so that digestive juices are not diluted. Digestion is best performed without excessive liquids. This then, leads to proper absorption processes in the intestines and then the colon functions properly.

Sleep is a crucial element of our lives. During sleep, there are many processes taking place that serve to bring us back to vitality each day. Each of us depend upon sleep as a vital part of our physical, emotional and spiritual health. Deprivation of sleep can produce enormous swings in emotions, as well as in our physical capacity to function on a daily basis.

On average, each person requires 6 to 8 hours of uninterrupted sleep each night. Our sleep should take place at night. If that is not possible because of our circumstances with work, etc, then the room should be darkened, so that no light is present.

Sleep that is interrupted with tossing and turning is termed disruptive sleep. If this is our normal night, then we should consider that we address issues of poor nutrition, lack of exercise or that dehydration issues be corrected.

Spiritual connections are valuable in many ways. The spirit of love, compassion, empathy, giving, etc., all impact our vitality and physical health. Our social interactions are impacted by how we view, ourselves, but our neighbors, family and everyone we come into contact with.

When we recover from our spiritual malady, we heal mentally and physically. This axiom is immutable. It works for each of us in varying degrees and application.

For some people, the issue of spirituality becomes disturbed and distorted by church, society, government and even family.

Finding the compass for caring and giving will serve each of us in ways that can never be measured diagnostically. No doctor or therapist is capable of a diagnosis of SPIRITUAL DEFICIENCY. Only by self-awareness and openness to the gift of love can we find our way to health, wellness and good vitality.

These are foundations for a strong and healthy YOU. They can all be a daily program of health and wellness. Each of us can apply them to any degree we wish and the only result will be improved health, in the physical, emotional and spiritual realm.

BLESSINGS.

ABOUT THE AUTHOR

Holly Ann Peckskamp is a mother, wife, student and teacher of yoga. After a successful basketball career Holly began looking for another form of exercise that would be kinder to her body. It would be a small studio in Boston, Ma where she met a passion that would forever change her life. After ten years of yoga practice, she trained to become a yoga teacher. The connection and philosophy of yoga became something she began applying off the mat to her daily life. In return she was given the gift of spiritual evolution.

Teaching many styles of yoga, she branched out and began teaching pre-natal classes. Seeing another opportunity to apply yoga to one of the most beautiful moments in life she became certified as a Doula. Continuing on the path for wellness and peace, she went through a yearlong training in Reiki Energy Healing and Meditation. It was during this time that her life changed in one single breath. This opened the door to her true spiritual evolution and gave birth to her book Always A Loveolution.

CPSIA information can be obtained at www.ICGtesting.com
Printed in the USA
BVOW07s2330260114

342961BV00002B/2/P